MARXIST
ANALYSIS
AND
CHRISTIAN
FAITH

René Coste

MARXIST ANALYSIS AND CHRISTIAN FAITH

Translated from the French by
Roger A. Couture, OMI, and John C. Cort

ORBIS BOOKS
Maryknoll, New York 10545

Originally published as *Analyse marxiste et foi chrétienne,* © 1976 by Les Éditions Ouvrières, Paris

English translation © 1985 by Orbis Books, Maryknoll, NY 10545
All rights reserved
Manufactured in the United States of America

Manuscript editor: William E. Jerman

Library of Congress Cataloging in Publication Data

Coste, René, 1922-
    Marxist analysis and Christian faith.

    Translation of: Analyse marxiste et foi chrétienne.
    Includes bibliographies and index.
    1. Communism and Christianity. 2. Communism and society.   I. Title.
HX536.C75713   1985   33 4'1   85-3119
ISBN 0-88344-342-2 (pbk.)

Contents

Translators' Preface

Few would deny that the most lively and controversial development in Christian theology at the present time is probably the confrontation with Marxism. Much of it comes under the heading of "liberation theology," whose most prominent exponents have been Latin Americans.

The origins of the discussion, however, go back to Europe, where Marxism itself originated. The writings of Althusser, Barth, Berdyaev, Bloch, Ellul, Garaudy, Girardi, Gramsci, Machovec, Metz, Moltmann, and many other Europeans have figured prominently in this discussion. To a considerable extent France has been the center of it, partly because Marxism has been a major factor in the labor and political movements of that country, partly because the French have always been good at *analyse* and *critique* and seem to enjoy the give-and-take.

Among the most competent and stimulating of the French theologians who have tackled the subject is certainly Professor René Coste. It was our opinion that no one has done a better job than he in analyzing Marxism and determining what in it is worthy of a Christian's approval and enthusiasm and what in it is not. We were therefore determined that he should be made available to American readers in English, and we thank Orbis Books for making this possible.

The reader will quickly notice that among his favorite words are "lucidity," "clarity," "coherence." These words are very important to the French academic mind; they are also important to the craft and science of theology, not to mention the craft and science of life.

As for the importance of Marxism, it is becoming evident, despite the slowness of America's reaction to it, that more and more Christians here as well as throughout the world are beginning to realize that the vitality and seriousness of their faith demand that they seek to answer the questions that it raises about that faith and its relation to the ultimate question that Jesus raised in the 25th chapter of the Gospel according to St. Matthew.

Acronyms

DDB   Desclée de Brouwer
MEGA Marx-Engels Historisch-Kritische Gesamtausgabe
NLB   New Left Books
PUF   Presses Universitaires de France
SCM   Student Christian Movement

Introduction

Starting Points of a Journey

"All Mistrust Must Be Abandoned . . ."

I should like to begin with the last paragraph of the famous Preface that Karl Marx wrote to his *Contribution to a Critique of Political Economy* (1859):

> This sketch of the course of my studies in the domain of political economy is intended merely to show that my views—no matter how they may be judged and how little they conform to the interested prejudices of the ruling classes—are the outcome of conscientious research carried out over many years. At the entrance to science, as at the entrance to hell, the injunction must be heeded:
>
> > *Qui si conviene lasciare ogni sospetto*
> > *Ogni viltà conviene che sia morta*
> > (Here all mistrust must be abandoned;
> > Let all cowardliness vanish here.)[1]

I propose a reading of this text on two levels: first, in relation to Karl Marx; second, in relation to the present inquiry.

In Relation to Karl Marx

The founders of Marxism are the primary object of this study. Of course I will not overlook the historical movement that they launched. On the contrary, I will keep it constantly before my eyes. We must attach a great deal of importance to contemporary Marxism because it is the Marxism of our own time and because it is the Marxism for which we bear responsibility before our contemporaries—and before God if we are Christians.

Special attention to the founding fathers seems justified for two reasons. Without full knowledge of their thought it is impossible to understand the historical movement that stems from them, a movement whose more conscientious contemporary protagonists are the first to insist that it requires thorough study. Also, I do not see how one could seriously call Marxism a doctrine if, on essential points, it strayed from the ideas of its founders.

Marx was himself the first to be convinced of the powerful originality of his thought. He was persuaded that the future was on its side and that it would revolutionize the world. He went so far as to believe that it was so precise, so rigorous, and so solidly based that any unprejudiced mind would have to yield to its logic.

He engaged in a major effort of pedagogy to make his thought accessible to the more militant workers. Instinctively he tended to believe that all those who did not submit to his ideas were revealing by that very fact that they were victims of "the selfish prejudices of the ruling classes," either as members of those classes—and thus consciously or unconsciously bent on falsifying the truth, so as to maintain their privileges—or as members of the exploited classes blinded by the ideology that those in power were only too successful in spreading among them.

On this point how could one deny that he was at least partially right? Though debatable on important points, his theory regarding *ideology* is illuminating. It is only too true that the ruling classes have a chronic tendency to elaborate ideologies that are to their own advantage, that they are assisted in this by intellectuals who have enlisted in their service, and that they themselves are often blinded by their own prejudices. How difficult it is for them, for example, to understand the psychology of workers and to discover their real needs. It is only too true that members of the working class, by some failure of self-consciousness, are vulnerable to ideologies that render them incapable of realizing that these very ideologies favor their own exploitation.

Beyond doubt, on these points Marx showed outstanding clairvoyance. All his life he wanted to be a revolutionary, and was it not a revolutionary's goal above all to confound the exploiting classes and to open the eyes of the exploited classes? He surely knew well that revolution normally involved recourse to violence and he accepted this eventuality without hesitation. But he thought that the principal weapon of the revolution was the manifestation of truth. That is why it was to be the great undertaking of his life. Few individuals in history have believed as strongly as he did in the power of thought or, even more precisely, the power of truth.

Does this mean that he himself was exempt not only from error but from prejudice as well? Prejudices he certainly possessed, not only in regard to religion and specifically to Christianity, but also in regard to the psychology of capitalists and even of the working class. And these prejudices have taken their toll and continue to take their toll in the historical movement that he launched. This advocate of truth must therefore himself submit to cross-examination by the truth.

He knew well that his theories would not be accepted by everyone. I have noted his explanation for this: ideological prejudices. He wanted his adversaries at least to acknowledge that his ideas were "the outcome of conscientious research carried on over many years." It was partly for his adversaries that he wrote that paragraph in his Preface—to let them know, to challenge them—and partly, perhaps even more, for those sympathizers who were shaken but not yet entirely convinced.

How could one deny that Marx engaged in lengthy, patient, and detailed research? All his life he was a slave to work, despite illness and prolonged misery. His intellectual curiosity was vast, his erudition impressive. And he was helped enormously by the complementary research of his friend Engels.

Can one as easily acknowledge the *conscientious character* of the research of Marxism's founders? An affirmative answer can be given but not without important reservations.

Note first that in spite of his great intellectual curiosity, Marx showed a total lack of interest in, and hence serious study of, something that must be recognized as a very important sector of human life: the religious sector, including Christianity. He was very young when he made up his mind on this subject, arriving at an assessment that we can describe as completely negative. Thereafter he never reassessed that judgment and it seems clear that he made no further study of the question. This did not prevent him from continuing to judge Christianity with the greatest severity.

"That there is not a word in this immense corpus that recognizes something of value in Christianity," Father Bigo has written, "shows that Marx never made the least effort, that he never even considered entering into a universe that remained entirely closed to him. Can a critique based on such peripheral knowledge carry any real weight?"[2]

Things were somewhat different with Engels, who had had a religious background and had studied Christianity with care in his youth. His knowledge of it, however, had been distorted in two ways: by the narrow, middle-class "orthodoxy" of the Protestant milieu in which he lived and by the one-dimensional, rationalist critique of the writings that had shaken the faith of his youth.[3]

Note also the "Manichaeism" that invades the psychological and moral judgments of Marx in the social field. The militant, revolutionary proletarian seems to him by definition endowed with remarkable clarity and the highest moral qualities. Capitalists, however, appear no less necessarily monsters of egotism, essentially motivated by the pursuit of maximum profit that makes them insensitive to human suffering and impels them to exploit to the utmost the employees of their enterprises.

My intention is not to make a case for capitalists. I wonder nevertheless if even in his day some of them were not motivated as much by ambition or the need to create something that would merit attention as they were by the pursuit of profit. One could retort of course that he was speaking as a sociologist and that he was describing social classes, not individuals. My response would be that sociology must take into consideration all the nuances of social reality.

Marx's phobias could drive him to the point of losing all critical judgment. His hostility toward Christianity was so strong that he did not hesitate to use the most outrageous gossip to discredit it. For example, he cited Daumer (in *Die Geheimnisse des christlichen Altertums,* Hamburg, 1847), who "proves," Marx maintained, "that Christians had really offered humans in sacrifice and eaten human flesh and drunk human blood in celebrating the eucharist."[4]

He himself did not believe it and he did not bother to conceal his own bad faith, at least not from his friend Engels. This is clear in his letter of May 3, 1854: "I have also sent to the *Tribune* a scandalous story on the 'Holy Sepulcher' and the 'protectorate' in Turkey; the supporting historical documentation will prevent our lads from seeing the malicious joke on Christianity that the article contains."[5] For him, then, against Christianity any means were legitimate.

In 1869 he wrote to Engels that "the priests, especially in Catholic districts, must be energetically attacked." The more they showed some social concern, the more he despised them. "These dogs," we read in the same letter [Bishop Ketteler of Mainz, and the priests meeting in Düsseldorf] "are flirting, where they find it suitable to do so, with the labor question."[6]

I must above all call attention to an objection raised in many quarters and taken up by Maurice Clavel with all the ferocity of which he is capable: "I intend to show that the mind of Karl Marx was set by the time he reached twenty-five and that he would spend the rest of his life searching for justifications, precedents, proofs, experiences, and 'scientific' experiments to support it."[7] Formulated so categorically, the objection goes too far. Yet I cannot deny that it contains a good deal of truth. Of course one could reply that Marx was a precocious genius, and the intuitions of youth can be legitimately exploited during an entire lifetime if they prove at once accurate and fruitful.

In Relation to the Present Inquiry

Do we seriously want to know the thought of the founders of Marxism, the colossal historical movement that they unleashed, as well as its doctrinal and practical dimensions at the present time? Immediately there opens before us an immense and very complex field.

Do we want to assess accurately its historical significance, its content of truth, and its value for civilization? One would then need to be competent in many fields of knowledge, notably sociology, political science, economics, and history, as well as philosophy.

Do we want to frame an objectively satisfying answer to the great question that I shall examine, expressed, for the moment, in summary form—namely, *how should an authentic Christian faith respond to Marxist analysis?* That will require all the competence described above, plus competence in theology as well.

The mass of information, the combination of intellectual competencies, and the breadth of horizon needed are such as not to be found in any one person alone. A collective effort of an interdisciplinary kind would be required. Let us at least be conscious of the complexity of the task. (I allow myself to speak also for you, the reader.) This realization will make us less sure of ourselves, less dogmatic, more open to dialogue and will give us in consequence a better chance to see clearly.

If possible, let us commit ourselves, as Marx did, to "thorough and conscientious research." Let us make every effort to avoid biases, to rid ourselves of them. These biases have many origins: our background (social, national, racial, religious), the intellectual and ethical training we have received, our personal relationships, our political preferences, our professions, our attractions or phobias, or simply our laziness and ignorance. We are continually challenged to make a major effort of self-criticism and insight into ourselves.

That is what I myself will try to do while recognizing my own limitations. The labels that have been applied to me vary according to the ideologies of my readers or hearers. I do not recognize myself under these labels because I maintain that my positions are not determined *a priori* and that I retain my freedom of inquiry and action. I have often proven to my own satisfaction the relevance of Nietzsche's observation: "From you they want a yes or no. Alas, do you want to place your chair between pro and con?"[8] Faced with complex realities, I see no other recourse than to try to grasp their nuances.

Let us note another Nietzsche aphorism that follows immediately upon the one just quoted: "Do not be jealous of these unconditional, insistent persons, you lover of truth! Never yet has truth hung on the arm of the unconditional." The discovery of truth is hardly compatible with a sectarian stance. I am looking for dialogue and am open to every suggestion and every criticism, whatever its source. I am grateful to those who help me to see more clearly.

In any case, Marx was right in quoting Dante and in applying to himself that famous couplet. He was not afraid to think for himself and to take positions that would provoke adversity. He was courageous. He was audacious. May his readers imitate him in that, even if the result should be that they come to disagree with him, and with others, profoundly.

Divided Loyalties

Let me say at once that in my opinion the basic requirements for a good society cannot be satisfied by the capitalist model, even under the more recent guise of neo-capitalism. Advanced industrial society in the liberal motif is still a society marked by capitalist domination.

Although reluctant to issue dogmatic and *a priori* condemnations, I am opposed to a society in which economic power is still essentially based on money—even if it is now increasingly indebted also to science—a society where social inequality remains substantial despite the progress made over the last century, where freedom is abused, whether by individuals in private or by those who wield various kinds of power in public and professional spheres. It seems to me that large sectors of advanced industrial society in the West have been sinking into a lamentable moral degradation.

Although not wanting to propose rigid formulas that might kill the spirit of initiative, create unbearable burdens, or provoke serious distortions, in view of the terrible complexity of contemporary problems and situations, I do support the goal of the greatest possible equality in the distribution of power and resources among all persons. I support the goal of a worldwide organization of collective life that would be at once harmonious and efficient. I am, therefore, against anarchy.

I speak of "goals" because history teaches us that concrete realizations are always imperfect when compared with the most noble and ennobling ideals. When it comes to structural changes in collective life, as in personal life, "the best is often the enemy of the good." Readers will understand that I do not invoke this proverb to justify either inaction or the proposal of reforms that are merely cosmetic!

For all these reasons, then, I situate myself in the socialist "utopia" that is at the base of Marxism—the utopia that is precisely the goal that I define as the best possible distribution of resources and power among all. By natural reason as much as by Christian conviction, however, I am fiercely opposed to the dictatorship, the totalitarianism, the omnipresent and omnipotent bureaucracy that characterize all the communist regimes that have existed up to this day.

Although I feel compelled to express serious objections to the scientific thought of Marx and radical differences with his philosophical ideas, I do feel a *profound admiration* for the power, the originality, and the fertility of his thought, even on points where I believe it necessary to oppose him. In almost all areas he forces us to rethink things in depth and reorientate ourselves.

Of course I do not share the boundless admiration for his doctrine shown by a Lenin, a Rosa Luxemburg, a Louis Althusser, a Roger Garaudy, or so many other Marxists. Otherwise I too would be a Marxist. But I react vigorously against those who, in my opinion, disparage him unjustly, especially if they have never made the effort to give him serious study. Hence I am not in agreement with the following judgments of Henri de Man: "It is rare that such a colossal scientific mountain has given birth to such a minuscule scientific mouse."[9] And: "Furthermore, Marx was a bookish type, a library rat, out of touch with the things of practical life and especially with working-class life."[10] I share the kind of admiration—expressed with his usual humor—of John Kenneth Galbraith in this regard: "I am a great admirer of Karl Marx but, unlike most of our contemporary Marxists, I do not think that what Marx wrote is valid either in its entirety or for all eternity."[11]

My admiration for the man is even greater. True, he had an overpowering, authoritarian personality, and he easily waged mortal combat with his friends—Engels being an outstanding exception—from the moment that their ideas differed from his, but he sacrificed his life for the revolutionary cause that he had made his own. What motivated him was his discovery of the tragic condition of the working class of his day. He wrote once to a friend:

As long as I was able to work, I had to make use of every moment to complete my book, to which I have sacrificed health, happiness, and family. I trust that this explanation needs no further postscript. . . . If one chose to be an ox, one could of course turn one's back on the sufferings of humankind and look after one's own skin. But I should have regarded myself as *impractical* if I had pegged out without completely finishing my book, at least in manuscript.[12]

How can we doubt the sincerity of those statements?

I greatly admire also a Rosa Luxemburg, an Antonio Gramsci, a Roger Garaudy. Garaudy demonstrated courage in questioning the Stalinist positions he had held earlier, acknowledging his errors, and accepting the isolation occasioned by the hostility of a party in which he had been one of the intellectual leaders and which no longer followed him in his "revisionism."

The other two have also—even more than Marx—sacrificed their lives for the revolutionary cause. They are, in a real sense, martyrs of Marxism. Even if, as happens here, I differ with them on essential points, it would be wrong not to admire that kind of witness.

Here, for example, is what Rosa Luxemburg wrote to her friend Walter Stoecker on March 11, 1913:

I assure you that I would not flee even if threatened with the gallows, and that for a very simple reason: I believe it is absolutely essential to convince our party of the idea that sacrifices are part and parcel of the customary responsibilities of a socialist.[13]

In 1916 she congratulated Karl Liebknecht for "having sacrificed himself for the proletariat, for international socialism." He proved, she added, "that in Germany also we know how to commit ourselves entirely to our socialist convictions."[14] In a letter to Sonia Liebknecht, after having written that "she felt more at home in the country, on the grass, surrounded by bumblebees, than in a party congress," she went on to say, "You know, however, that I hope to die at my post, on the barricades or in prison."[15] The manner of her death proved that she was true to that hope.

The Peruvian Marxist José Carlos Mariátegui (1894-1930)—little known in Europe—was also a person we can only admire.

Despite the reservations, especially of an ethical nature, that must be made in their regard, it can hardly be denied that Lenin, Mao Tse-tung, and Ho Chi-Minh were geniuses of action and giants of history. Despite the serious criticisms that certain communist regimes invite, especially by reason of their dictatorial and totalitarian character, they can point to important and impressive achievements. Why must one vilify or praise them simply because one's choice is for capitalism or communism?

Above all, I must acknowledge the generosity, courage, and unselfishness of so many militant Marxists. We can admire them without necessarily sharing all their convictions.

Confronted with Marxism then, I feel myself to be *divided*. For good reasons—of a scientific, philosophical, and theological nature—I cannot call myself a Marxist. And yet I recognize in Marxism important elements of truth as well as a historical movement whose powerful impact continues to produce its own consequences. At this time nothing challenges my mind so profoundly as this movement or forces me into as much ongoing debate.

To those who might be surprised by my receptive attitude I would reply with Karl Barth, "I can allow elements of Marxism to enter my head without for that reason becoming Marxist."[16] As for those who, on the other hand, might find that I am too critical, I would claim only the liberty of taking my own stand both as a human being and as a Christian.

First Steps in an Itinerary

My analysis of the present era and my attempt to work out theologically the responsibility of Christian faith have forced me to confront Marxism as a fact that is at once fascinating and irritating—in any case, a fact of such historical importance that one is compelled to look it squarely in the face and try to grasp its enormous dimensions. For some, Marxism is the new science, the new Promised Land, the new earthly paradise, replacing the Christian paradise in which many no longer believe, the new reality appearing so much closer to hand and so much more concrete! But others see themselves caught up in a terrible encounter with an enormous iceberg on some northern sea, so much the more frightening because what appears above the surface of the water is not the larger part. "Will we manage to avoid it?," some ask themselves in a kind of terror. "Will our small ship be shattered against this icy monster?"

For myself, Marxism has given me reason neither for fascination nor for terror. It has appeared only as an immense continent open for discovery, attractive to some and frightening to others, where some have claimed they found the key to the science of society, where others in its name reworked history, and where the changes so loudly trumpeted by propaganda seemed so often to be accompanied by terrible sufferings. Very quickly I came to realize that this exploration was essential and that it did challenge me profoundly, as a human being and as a Christian.

The communist party claims to be the party of the working class, its sole authentic defender. In France about a third of the workerforce votes communist, even if few workers are personally committed to Marxism. A worker's children cannot be insensitive to these facts. If they are also Christian, they must be concerned for another reason. Was not the gospel first proclaimed to the poor of Palestine? Did it not announce their "liberation"? Did it not invite us to a sharing in fellowship? Did it not propose to us the beatitude of poverty? In addition I was struck by the fact that a sizeable number of Christians, especially in the Mediterranean countries of Western Europe and in Latin America, were attracted to Marxism. For all these reasons I felt moved to study it with whatever resources of intelligence and faith I possessed.

As noted above, it is mainly among its founders that I have looked for an understanding of Marxism, following the example of its most respected living practitioners. I have given my reasons for this: on the one hand, the power and originality of their thought and, on the other, the decisive influence that that thought has had on the entire historical movement that claims its name, not to mention areas of thought beyond that movement. Naturally it is to Marx himself that I give preference, but the contribution of Engels is also very important.

The teachings of some of their followers, the political leaders in Marxist history, hardly provide the same interest. We are familiar with them, by reason of their impact on that history and the significance of their political power. Some of them have been great men of action and remarkably successful as teachers in selling Marxism to the masses (Mao Tse-tung comes to mind). However, if you search their writings for either depth or creativity of thought, the odds are that you will be disappointed and compelled to draw upon all your willpower to continue a tedious study. In my opinion Lenin and Mao are unspectacular as original thinkers and I cannot begin to understand Althusser's enthusiasm for Lenin's theoretical elaborations.

From the standpoint of ideas, Rosa Luxemburg is especially interesting, in my view, as a journalist, as a practitioner of the art of applying Marxist analysis to the events of which she wrote. Of all the historical leaders of the Marxist movement, however, it is the writings of Gramsci that I find the most stimulating. He too, a journalist of great talent, was unusually good at the application of Marxist analysis. As for the writings of Stalin (generally the product of pens other than his own) one really needed the gift of exceptional blindness or an extraordinary talent for flattery (helped perhaps by terror) to find in them the basis for praise, though many did so during his lifetime.

As to contemporary Marxist philosophers, it is particularly interesting to read Althusser and Garaudy as a kind of exercise in counterpoint. Each claims to show us the real face of Marxism and each, it must be acknowledged, advances impressive arguments for his own interpretation. Could it be that Marxism is, in reality, a veritable Janus?

In my opinion, the contrast between the views of these two famous philosophers reveals the ambiguity of Marxist thought in its very origins, which even the sophisticated labors of a Maximilien Rubel—to whom Marxist scholars owe so much[17]—have not been able to clarify. Althusser is impressive by reason of unusual success in reducing Marxism to precise conceptions, but does he not also dehumanize it? Does he not peel away whatever in Marxism is capable of attracting the most sympathy and arousing the greatest devotion?

Garaudy, by contrast, knows how to bring out what is peculiarly attractive to generous souls and, above all, to Christians. But is not his interpretation of Marx distorted by his current sensitivity to such values as subjectivity and liberty, not to mention his sympathies for Christianity? Nevertheless, despite whatever criticism one might level at the scientific character of his thought, he remains, by dint of his research and personal example, one of those who helps me the most in my own ongoing inquiry.

In addition to Garaudy I salute those other great names of the revisionist school of neo-Marxism: Adam Schaff and Leszek Kolakowski in Poland; Robert Havemann in East Germany; Ota Sik, Milan Machovec, and Vitezslav Gardavsky in Czechoslovakia; Lucio Lombardo-Radice, Cesare Luporini, Salvatore di Maraco, and Luciano Gruppi in Italy,[18] and others. Nor can we omit the names of the Austrians, Ernst Fischer and Franz Marek.

The Frankfurt School, so well known in Germany, is still unfamiliar to the French-speaking world (translations are just beginning), with the exception of Herbert Marcuse, as controversial as he is stimulating. Among contemporary German Marxists, Ernst Bloch has developed the most provocative ideas, especially for theologians capable of confronting them on their own terrain, as for example Jürgen Moltmann in his *Theology of Hope.*[19]

From the theological viewpoint it is a Protestant theologian and an Orthodox thinker who have been the most helpful in developing my own ideas about Marxism as seen in the light of the faith (the very axis of my inquiry): Karl Barth (1886–1968) and Nicholas Berdyaev (1874–1948).

Karl Barth has been most useful to me in thinking through the mission of the church in the political domain. It is the mission of a church wanting to remain absolutely faithful to its role of witness to the word of God and the salvation of humanity in Jesus Christ, and yet, because of that very mission, deeply involved in the problems of humanity, both from the standpoint of prophet and disinterested servant, seeking neither political power nor collusion with political power.[20]

Barth was a socialist. He was even a dues-paying member of social democratic parties at a time when they were still pretty strongly characterized by Marxism: the Swiss Social Democratic Party (SPS) in 1915 and the German Social Democratic Party (SPD) in 1932. He himself explained the meaning of that membership:

> Belonging to the SPD does not mean that I have committed myself to socialist ideology and the socialist worldview. As I understand the exclusive nature of Christian confession, I can seriously confess no ideology or worldview. . . . Socialism as an ideology and worldview I approach with neither fear nor love nor confidence. Membership in the SPD signifies for me simply a political decision. . . . My socialism is a purely private matter and it is precisely for that reason that I cannot renounce my party card.[21]

In short, in his case political militancy meant a comradeship in action and not in ideology. (Let us note in passing that this is exactly the position taken by certain Christians belonging to the French Communist Party and officially acknowledged by its leaders. The situation, however, was different: the social democratic parties to which Barth belonged predated the communist parties and were entirely independent of them.)

Though they are to be understood according to the precise meaning he gave above to his political membership, Barth did not hesitate to make some strong statements. Witness the following inscription written shortly before 1933 in a book he gave to his friend Fritz Lieb, a radical socialist: "To the representative of the Third International from a representative of the Second-and-a-Half International."[22] We shall deal later with his refusal to lump together Stalinist communism and Nazism, a refusal that scandalized many and aroused lively controversy beyond the Rhine.

Friedrich Marquardt notes that in Barth's lecture "Socialism and Christianity" of 1915, still unpublished, he declares more than once that "true Christians must become socialists if they want to take seriously the reform of Christianity, and true socialists must become Christians if they want to reform socialism."[23] In this we have a foretaste of the famous axiom of Ernst Bloch that we shall return to later: "Only an atheist can be a good Christian; only a Christian can be a good atheist."[24]

To understand Barth's socialism it would be necessary, however, to define it more precisely. It seems that he never brought himself to do this. For him, rather than a strict program, it stood for a kind of overall political orientation and ultimately some practical commitments of his own, for example, on the side of the workers in his parish of Safenwill when he was a young pastor. Also, his political and economic expertise was probably not very extensive. He was above all a theologian, one of the greatest, I think, in the history of Christianity (which obviously does not mean that a Catholic theologian can share all his ideas). As for the work of Marquardt, who claims to demonstrate the strength of Marxist influence on his theological thought, it is not sufficiently rigorous to be convincing.

Nicholas Berdyaev was born in Kiev, of noble parentage. An independent socialist, he tried at first to combine the thought of Marx with that of Kant. After 1901, following his preoccupation with the tragic element in life and in creative originality, especially under the influence of Nietzsche, he grew away from Marxism, retaining always, however, its demand for social justice.

Beginning in 1909, in Moscow, he took part in the theological renewal of the Orthodox Church. His nonconformism, however, quickly alienated him from the deeply conservative institution. In *The Meaning of the Creative Act* (1913) he described himself, at that time on the edge of the institutional church, as a prophet who had dedicated himself to the development of a Christian anthropology.

His reaction to the October Revolution was at first very negative. Soon, however, he accepted the revolutionary experience. He tried to promote within it freedom of thought and a renewed Christianity. He was imprisoned on two occasions. Vice-president of the Society of Writers, he founded in 1919 the Free Academy of Spiritual Culture. In 1920 he was named a professor at the University of Moscow. He was exiled in 1922 as "an enemy of communism'' with an absolute prohibition ever to return to his native land under pain of being shot to death.[25]

Berdyaev was very critical of Marxist theory and practice on essential points. At the same time he did not hesitate to acknowledge with generosity its more positive aspects. We shall have the occasion to study more closely these two inseparable sides to his evaluation of Marxism. For now let us note only his emphasis on the complexity of the relationship between Christianity and Marxism as well as his theory of history.[26] These are essential considerations for students of Berdyaev. The tragedy is that, from one side and the other, critics have too often simplified his thought and drawn negative conclusions.

As for Christian Marxists (some of whom call themselves simply "Christians for Socialism") it goes without saying that we must give them serious attention, although they are few in number. They have a real impact on public opinion, at least on the Christian side. This is not, by the way, an entirely new phenomenon. For quite some time Christians have thought that they could be at the same time Christians and Marxists, or Christians and communists. What characterizes the current phenomenon is, first, its extent and, second, the seriousness of its effort to provide an intellectual rationale.

On the subject of Christian Marxists I agree with the statement of the review *Lumière et vie*: "It is important that those who call themselves at once believers and Marxists should not be suspected *a priori* of being either false believers or pseudo Marxists."[27] It is, of course, unjust to condemn anyone *a priori*. Before making a judgment we must examine carefully the reality behind the label that these thinkers have chosen for themselves. For now, I will say only that the reality does raise some very serious objections, from both the Marxist and the Christian point of view.

NOTES

1. Karl Marx, *A Contribution to the Critique of Political Economy,* ed. Maurice Dobb (New York: International Publishers, 1970), p. 23. The verses quoted are from Dante's *Divine Comedy.*

2. Pierre Bigo, *Marxisme et humanisme,* 3rd ed. (Paris: PUF, 1961), p. 145.

3. The letters of the young Engels on this subject are extremely interesting: Marx-Engels, *Selected Correspondence* (London: Lawrence and Wishart, 1965).

4. Lecture of November 30, 1847, to the Cultural Association of Workers of London, in Marx-Engels, *Historisch-Kritische Gesamtausgabe* [MEGA] (Moscow: Marx-Lenin Institute, 1927–1932), I, 6, p. 640, cited in Charles Wackenheim, *La faillite de la religion d'après Karl Marx* (Paris: PUF, 1963), p. 301.

5. Marx-Engels, *Correspondance* (Paris: Editions sociales, 1974), Vol. 4, p. 118.

6. Letter to Engels of September 25, 1869, in MEGA, III, 4, p. 227, cited by Wackenheim, *La faillite,* p. 308; English trans. in Karl Marx, *On Religion,* ed. Saul K. Padover (New York: McGraw-Hill, 1974), p. 253.

7. *Qui est aliéné?* (Paris: Flammarion, 1970), p. 216.

8. *Thus Spoke Zarathustra*; cf. trans. by Walter Kaufmann in *The Portable Nietzsche* (New York: Viking, 1968), p. 164.

9. *Au-delà du marxisme* (Paris: Seuil, 1974), p. 328.

10. *Au-delà du marxisme,* p. 350.

11. Interview in *Le Monde,* November 5, 1974.

12. Letter to S. Meyer of April 30, 1867, quoted in Maximilien Rubel, *Karl Marx, Essai de biographie intellectuelle* (Paris: Marcel Rivière, 1971), p. 20; cf. trans. in *Letters to Americans, 1848–1895. A Selection* (New York: International Publishers, 1953), p. 73.

13. Quoted by Gilbert Badia, *Rosa Luxemburg* (Paris: Editions sociales, 1975), p. 772.

14. *Rosa Luxemburg,* p. 772.

15. *Rosa Luxemburg,* p. 694.

16. Quoted by Friedrich W. Marquardt, *Theologie und Sozialismus* (Munich: Kaiser, 1972), p. 313.

17. *Marx critique du marxisme* (Paris: Payot, 1974).

18. An excellent overview of the revisionist school of neo-Marxism is provided by Manfred Spieker, *Neomarxismus und Christentum* (Munich: Ferdinand Schöningh, 1974).

19. New York: Harper and Row, 1970.

20. René Coste, *La responsabilité politique de l'Eglise* (Paris: Editions ouvrières, 1973).

21. Quoted by Marquardt, *Theologie und Sozialismus,* p. 42.

22. *Theologie und Sozialismus,* p. 8.

23. *Theologie und Sozialismus,* pp. 22, 23.

24. Presented by way of preamble to his book *Atheism in Christianity* (New York: Herder and Herder, 1972), p. 9.

25. I warmly recommend Juan Luis Segundo's *Berdiaeff, Une réflexion chrétienne sur la personne* (Paris: Aubier, 1963).

26. *Christianisme, Marxisme* (Paris: Centurion, 1975), pp. 37, 38.

27. No. 117/118 (April-August 1974) on the subject "Christian Marxist," p. 199.

Chapter 1

The Two Worlds

Let me suggest an experiment: read in its entirety the famous Preface to the *Contribution to the Critique of Political Economy*, which is the most remarkable summary of Marxist analysis ever written by Marx himself, even though it cannot stand alone and was, in fact, decisively revised by *Capital*. Then open immediately the Gospel according to St. Matthew at the page on the beatitudes. Or else, if you are not easily discouraged, alternate the reading of Book I of *Capital* with that of the Fourth Gospel. Or, if you prefer, contrast Engels's *Dialectics of Nature* with the *Pensées* of Pascal.

The experience, which all can verify for themselves, is that of *two worlds*, at least in appearance totally different, where speakers do not have a common language, where even the same words do not have the same meaning, where writers pursue goals that are diametrically opposed, and they have a self-awareness that is entirely foreign to the others, to the point where they seem to belong to different species. It seems that their trajectories could never intersect.

At first sight, if you belong to one of these worlds, it does not seem possible to have the slightest relationship with any part of the other. Even from the intellectual standpoint alone, a considerable effort is needed to pass from one bias to the other.

Perhaps, however, the difference is not so total as it appears. Perhaps a few intersections are possible between the two worlds, intersections that will reveal persons with basically the same search for a better future, who refuse to accept certain evils and certain injustices. That, in fact, will be the working hypothesis of this inquiry.

Others go much further. They insist that they belong equally to both worlds. They call themselves *Christian Marxists* or *Marxist Christians*. Do they go too far in simplifying the problem?

We cannot forget that the founders of Marxism were not only atheists but fiercely anti-Christian and that the greatest leaders of the historical movement that they founded were, or are, just as anti-Christian as they were.

Nor can we forget the famous condemnation made by Pius XI: "Communism is intrinsically wrong, and no one who would save Christian civilization may collaborate with it in any undertaking whatsoever."[1] Christians cannot take such a warning lightly, even if they put it in its historical context and prefer to see things for themselves. Let us at least sketch in broad outline these two worlds: that of Marxist analysis and that of Christian faith. This will make it possible to spell out our itinerary.

What Is Marxist Analysis?

I do not intend to give a detailed account of Marxist analysis. The details can be found elsewhere by the interested reader. I limit myself to recalling the essential ideas and outlines, for frequently we see or retain only certain aspects of a complex reality, and we fail to see the forest for the trees. It is important moreover that I give my own interpretation, for even those proposed by Marxists are far from agreeing on every point.

Two preliminary questions need to be faced.

Which Marxism? Or, if you prefer, who is the real Marx? He whose entire life's work is considered without putting its parts into perspective, or merely the mature Marx? Or do we give preference to the young Marx, as do Garaudy and many Christians, or to the mature Marx, as does Althusser? The interpretations given by these two celebrated thinkers differ profoundly.

According to Althusser, the young Marx would be "no more than an avant-garde Feuerbachian applying an *ethical problematic to the understanding of human history.*"[2] He would have come into his own—a man of science in the full sense of the word—and would have created Marxism only after the "epistemological break" of 1845. One should then carefully avoid interpreting the works of his mature years in the light of the works of his youth. Only the reverse procedure would be legitimate—and then only in a critical way.

In my opinion, Althusser is right in an important respect, but the "break" is clearly not so decisive as he describes it. The mature Marx did not repudiate all the positions of his youth.

Which Marxisms? What are the theoretical constructs and the practical accomplishments realized by those who have made use of Marx to analyze and resolve problems that they had, or still have, to confront? We cannot ignore the fact that there are often profound differences even among "orthodox" Marxists and at the same time a no less profound kinship, at least on certain essential points, between neo-Marxists of the "revisionist" school and "orthodox" Marxists.

I have already noted that I will give preference to the original Marxism and have given my reasons for this, but on no account do I want to put the Marxist movement in a fixed mold. A historical movement cannot escape a state of continual evolution, especially if it is prolonged in time and extends over vast areas of humanity where it will have to face multifaceted combinations of circumstances.

This having been said, the next step is to define carefully the concepts we shall be using to study Marxist analysis.

First, what is *analysis*? As Father Cottier defines it, analysis is "a method of inquiry that consists in breaking down a complex reality into its simplest elements. This breaking down must also make it possible to classify those elements—that is, to determine their relative place and importance. Thus one will distinguish, thanks to the analysis, what is primary and secondary, essential and accidental, cause and effect, profound reality or mere appearance."[3] One could profitably turn here to the two stages of analysis sketched with penetration by Marx himself in the *General Introduction to the Critique of Political Economy.*[4] Analysis obviously moves toward *synthesis*. Therein only does it find completion.

An analysis that is at once political and theoretical includes the following procedures: (1) observation of reality by means of the various scientific disciplines, which means that this kind of analysis can only be multidisciplinary; (2) consideration of analyses made by others; (3) interpretation of reality in relation to our conceptions of the world and our proposals for social change; (4) development and examination of various hypotheses for action.

Politics is action. Political analysis is fully itself only if theory leads to action. A fifth procedure will then occur: the political decision, which will lead to a sixth and last: execution, which is to say, the constructive practice of history.

Most writers are content to say that Marxist analysis is a political analysis. That is too shortsighted a view of it. Let me introduce a new concept, that of *social analysis*. By this term I mean a fundamental analysis of the whole of human reality. Social analysis is divided into such categories as political analysis, economic analysis, sociological analysis, cultural analysis, religious analysis, historical analysis, anthropological analysis, and so forth.

Marxist analysis, which is meant to embrace all aspects of human reality, fits this concept exactly. It is fundamentally a *social analysis* in the sense we have just defined. Because it is intended for the benefit of the exploited, it must necessarily be a *social critique*, with the same conceptual breadth. Because it aims at changing the world on their behalf, to put an end to their exploitation, it must no less necessarily lead to a *social* and *revolutionary praxis*, which will in principle be total.

I agree entirely with the position of Rosa Luxemburg: "Marxism includes two essential elements: on the one hand analysis, critique, and on the other the active will of the working class that constitutes the revolutionary element. Whoever does only analysis or only critique does not represent Marxism, but a pathetic parody of that doctrine."[5]

We shall therefore understand by the concept of *Marxist analysis* in its full significance not only *social analysis* but also *social critique* and *social, revolutionary praxis*.

Precisely by reason of the breadth of its ambitions, Marxist analysis is a complex undertaking. I submit that it includes the following essential strata: a scientific stratum, a political stratum, an ethical stratum, and a philosophical stratum. All these strata interpenetrate and overlap one another. We are here using the metaphor of geological layers or strata, of which the most basic is the philosophical layer, provided that we do not forget that these layers act and react upon each other, as in the earth's crust.

It would be more accurate to use the concept of Marxist *systemic approach* in place of Marxist *analysis*. It corresponds well in fact, to a current definition of that approach—namely, "a global approach to the problems or systems studied [that] concentrates on the play of the interactions among their elements."[6] However, inasmuch as the term "Marxist analysis" is the most widely used, we shall retain it.

Scientific Stratum

The scientific stratum is naturally the most complex. For Marxists everything that makes up Marxist analysis in its core depends upon it. It is in their eyes the *fundamental science*, or as Althusser puts it, "the *theoretical domain of a fundamental investigation*, indispensable not only to the development of the science of society and of the various 'human sciences', but also to that of the natural sciences and philosophy."[7]

One may of course dispute such an assertion, but in any case let us not reproach Marxist analysis for its complexity: human reality is itself marked by a complexity whose extent we are beginning to discover more and more. We might even ask if the analysis is sufficiently complex, if it does not leave in the dark whole areas of reality, including perhaps certain of its most important dimensions.

The Marx of the mature years turned especially to *economic analysis*, which for him meant a critical analysis of the capitalism of his time. That was because of his conviction that production is in the end *the* determining factor of all human reality. (For Marx the infrastructure of society is the dialectic between the forces of production and the relations of production.) It is the factor that, in his opinion, determines all the others: superstructures or ideologies, politics, culture, religion, and the like. It is the materialist foundation of history, or historical materialism. A dialectical method is needed to interpret it.

Sociological analysis and *historical analysis* can be described together, for they are both centered on class struggle. The originality of Marx on this subject consists in the following: (1) his linking the development of social classes and the varieties of class struggle to the dialectic of the forces of production and the relations of production; (2) his affirmation that class struggle is the motor of history and is coextensive with all history, from the institution of private ownership of the means of production to the termination of that kind of private ownership; (3) his proposal of a revolutionary praxis of class struggle led by the proletariat, while giving it a utopia and a strategy; (4) his conviction that "all collisions in history have their origin . . . in the contradiction between productive forces and the form of intercourse."[8]

He believed that private ownership—the historical point of departure, to his mind, for class struggle—was the cause of all the evils of history. It was the true original sin, from the moment when it was first introduced into human life, but especially in the private ownership of the means of production in industrial society, which brings in its train the final paroxysm of the class struggle. Its disappearance and the substitution of collective ownership of the means of production become therefore the first revolutionary measures.

Although it may have contributed historically to the progress of humanity, for Marx capitalism means—and can only mean—exploitation of the proletariat. It accomplishes this by the extortion of surplus value (or surplus labor), leaving to the worker only a subsistence wage. No real improvement of working conditions can be expected under a capitalist regime.

Political analysis is built squarely on the preceding analyses and is concerned with unmasking the more clever games of the class struggle. The state is the tool of the dominant class. That is why, in Marx's view, it must disappear, and will naturally do so, in the classless society that he sees on the horizon. Bourgeois democracy is a delusion, the mask worn by the bourgeoisie to ensure its continued exploitation of the workers.

The principal characteristic of the Marxist *analysis of culture* consists in showing that the dominant class seeks to impose its ideology on the whole of society—including the classes it exploits—and that it is successful in so doing to a significant degree. This ideology is obviously dictated by its class interests.

The principal development of the Marxist analysis of culture has come from the introduction of the concept of *the state's ideological apparatus* by Gramsci, later picked up by the Althusser school. It extends to all the systems—religious, the different churches; educational, both public and private schools; political; juridical; trade union; familial; and so forth—that function in the service of the dominant ideology.

The Marxist *analysis of religion* sees it as at once the sign and the cause of a basic alienation. The disappearance of religion is indispensable for the liberation of humanity. The atheism of the founders of Marxism is fundamental and essential in their eyes.

The core of Marxist *anthropological analysis*, its theory on the human personality, was formulated in Thesis 6 on Feuerbach: "The human essence is no abstraction inherent in each single individual. In its reality it is the ensemble of the social relations."[9] This definition is, in the words of Lucien Sève, "the riddle of philosophical anthropology solved, the *foundation of a scientific anthropology*, and *the cornerstone of every scientific conception of man*."[10]

Political Stratum

The political stage is clearly essential to Marxism, in the sense of will, theory, and praxis aimed at a profound transformation of the world by the proclamation and preparation of social revolution in the strongest sense of the term.

Its point of departure lies in the conviction that capitalism is burdened by such radical contradictions that it runs inevitably toward its own ruin. This will lead to the capture of power by the proletariat and the advent of the socialist state.

Along with this thesis, continually restated, the theory envisions the establishment of a revolutionary movement under the control of the proletariat constituting itself as a political party. From the time of Lenin, it becomes a disciplined elite charged with involving the entire proletariat, of which it claims to be the infallible guide. Its strength comes from its conviction that nothing can stop the march of capitalism toward its final collapse. For Marx and Engels the historic role of the proletariat lies in its mission to liberate humanity.

The goal is the realization of a classless society, seen as a free, worldwide association of workers, which will necessarily be a society of abundance. Then, we are assured, will follow perfect fulfillment of all.

To reach that goal, according to the founders of Marxism, it will be necessary to pass through a stage known as the *dictatorship of the proletariat* by reason of the opposition that the bourgeoisie must inevitably foment when faced with dispossession of its power and its privileges. The founders were persuaded that this phase, though hard on the opposition, would be brief.

Ethical Stratum

Although Marx was reluctant to theorize about questions of morality and although the Marxist ethic poses serious problems, the ethical stage is essential to Marxism and to an explanation of its impact. Marxism proposes an end to the exploitation of the mass of humanity. Can one speak of exploitation and oppression without reference, at least implicitly, to an ethic?

Philosophical Stratum

More fundamentally still, revolutionary Marxism is a *conception of the world*, a philosophy, that the founding fathers believed to be a component that was not only integrated with but, in their eyes, inseparable from their analyses and their revolutionary action, "the only solid ground in the world," the only "possible philosophy," as Althusser assures us.

It was Gramsci who contributed the most toward defining Marxism as a conception of the world, a *Weltanschauung*, a concept to which he attributed the most basic, the broadest significance as an original and universal way of understanding society and the universe, and of orienting human activity. Hence the remark of Bigo that Marxism is, in fact, an "overall view of existence."[11]

Marxist theoreticians usually pose the equation: *Marxist philosophy = dialectical materialism*. Insofar as it is a complete philosophy it comprises:

a. Philosophical materialism (or one might say metaphysical or ontological materialism), which refuses to recognize the possibility of a life of the spirit that would be independent of matter, from which follows the necessary denial of the existence of God.

b. Epistemological materialism.

c. Historical materialism.

"We Communists," insisted Marchais in 1970, "adhere to a philosophy that is materialist and dialectical."[12] He was just as insistent in his spectacular *Appeal of the Communists to the Christians of France* (June 10, 1976):

> No tactical consideration will ever lead us to obscure that which differentiates this philosophy from others, to look for philosophical agreements that are impossible and illusory. Communist theory is founded on scientific materialism.

Later he stated that his party, "in a positive, constructive spirit," would commit itself to "the promulgation of our conception of the world—that is to say, of dialectical materialism."

We shall have occasion to discuss further many of these points in the course of our study. In any case our plan leads us to examine Marxist analysis in all its fullness and complexity, not limiting ourselves to certain individuals who claim allegiance to that analysis but actually retain only a few elements of it.

What Is Christian Faith?

I shall use at the start a word heavy with meaning for so many generations of Christians over the course of the centuries, a word that is rich with all the density of their lives, with their doubts and their courage, with their joy and their temptations and their sins, ultimately with the persecutions that they had to face, perhaps even with their martyrdom. That word is *credo*.

Those who pronounce it in sincerity bear witness that, for them, reality is not merely the universe revealed to them by their senses, their reason, and the science of their time. They bear witness that they believe the universe to have other, more profound dimensions that have been revealed to them by the intervention of the word of God. That word was not *owed* to them, and they were incapable of discerning it by themselves. It comes to them from beyond the horizon of humanity, even though, in their eyes, it concerns that humanity in its entirety. They bear witness that the result for them is a *fundamental and decisive conception of the world* that is not simply one more among all the conceptions of the world that reason can fabricate, but is the light that illuminates all of them. They bear witness that their reason yields freely to that word, and that they have complete confidence in the one who pronounces it and in whom they see their final fulfillment.

Gerhard Ebeling points out that faith, in its Christian acceptation, is not part of the universal religious experience. It is a specific concept of *biblical* revelation. It originates in the Old Testament and acquires its full significance only in the New. We can therefore say with him that in the strictest sense

"Christian faith is not a special faith, but simply faith." And we can conclude with him that "the word 'faith' can be widely used in an absolute sense, without any explanatory addition."[13]

Although using Ebeling's concept as our point of departure and keeping it within the framework of our inquiry, I shall, as he himself suggests, subject it to "critical reflection." What we want is to rediscover and to think through "the nature of Christian faith" for our time. We must strive to understand it "in critical distinction from everything that is unessential and much that is wrong, which has got confused with Christian faith."[14] My expectation is that our confrontation with Marxism will encourage and assist us in this endeavor.

Note from the start that I regard the content of the two great Christian creeds—the Apostles' Creed and the Nicene Creed—as forming the foundation and the essence of the faith.[15]

I agree with Wolfhart Pannenberg that "today's widespread lack of comprehension of the creedal formulae is a call, not for their abolition, but for their explanation."[16] I also agree when he expresses the hope that Christian communities "will once again see the point of repeating the creed in Sunday services," and I agree for the same reason that he invokes: "It is joined together with the whole of Christendom, beyond the barriers of time, in the basic substance of its faith."[17]

In this perspective the axis of the confession of Christian faith is surely Jesus Christ, and not only the one God, as in Judaism and Islam. I shall make mine the formulation of Joseph Ratzinger that is at once so simple and so full: "I believe in you, Jesus of Nazareth, as the meaning (*logos*) of the world and of my life."[18]

I commit myself totally to Jesus Christ in my search for meaning. I am convinced that this meaning exists and that it is precisely he who gives it, that he gives it to the universe, to human history, and to my own life. He is, in my belief, a man who lived in a particular time and a particular place: Jesus of Nazareth. It is on him that I base my life, at least if I wish to be consistent with the confession of faith that I profess.

Thus I commit myself to a man, but at the same time more than a man. Otherwise I could not "believe in" him, according to the authentic meaning of this fundamental concept of Christianity. "Why should we go on believing in Jesus if in him we only have to do with a man like other men?"[19] The author of the Second Letter of Clement expresses it with a striking insight: "Brothers, we must think of Jesus as God, as him who judges the living and the dead. We must not think little of our salvation, for by thinking little of him we also think little of our hope."[20]

Certain current interpretations on this subject, wherein faith has not known how to resist being undermined by the human sciences—including, in many cases, by Marxist analysis—have led directly to such an impoverishment of faith. It is true that the faith of a contemporary adult should include the courage to confront this challenge, simply that it might in fact become

adult and capable of responding to the demands of our time. But the courage
and clarity of consistency are also required. If Jesus Christ is not more than
man, if he is not also God, then I can certainly admire him, be inspired by his
spirit and example, but I cannot "believe in" him in the true sense of the
term—that is, I cannot see in him "the meaning of the world and of my life."

Let me add that the *historical dimension* is part and parcel of the essence of
Christian faith. Jesus Christ is recorded in history and his resurrection was
experienced as a historical fact by a certain number of men and women who
were the beneficiaries of his appearances on earth. And there are two other
reasons. The Christian faith is bound, by the events that gave it birth, to the
history and the hopes of the Jewish people. And, according to the will of
Jesus Christ as the apostolic church understood it, Christian faith can be
lived authentically only in a full integration with the community of those who
believe in him. One can of course legitimately adopt a critical attitude toward
the church. This may even be a duty that springs from an honest awareness of
the demands of the gospel. But one can never knowingly cut oneself off from
the church and still remain a Christian: the church is the *irrevocable locus of
the faith.*

What I have just written implies a two-fold position. First, that the essence
of Christian faith can be expressed with clarity even in the fragmented culture
that is currently ours in the West, and it is possible, even in the context of that
culture, to accept without reservation the original formulations of the apostolic church. This might be called "historical identity and continuity." Second, that it is with a deliberate act of commitment to the fullness of the
Christian faith that I undertake this confrontation with Marxism. Even if it is
not obvious, that faith is already present in everything I have said.

A Multi-faceted Confrontation

Of course an intellectual exercise that consists in first defining the essence
of Marxist analysis and then the essence of Christian faith can be only a
preliminary step. At that level one runs the risk of only comparing two abstract schemas. It has the advantage, however, of presenting in all their stark
clarity the truly fundamental problems. An encounter between Marxism and
Christianity that seeks more than indifference, a series of anathemas, an ambiguous dialogue, or an unthinking commitment to one or the other, has to be
a formidable confrontation.

It is important that Christians realize from the beginning that their faith
has been, for all practical purposes, totally dismissed by the founders of
Marxism as having no value—totally, it seems, by Marx; almost totally by
Engels. It is true that they inherited this rejection in large part from Feuerbach and the bourgeois philosophy of the eighteenth century. On this point
the great historical leaders have shared, or share, the convictions of the
founding fathers.

A thinker of the caliber of Althusser sees in the faith—even under its most modern form following the *aggiornamento* of Vatican II—an ideology only in the negative sense of the word—namely, an intellectual exercise that is incapable of grasping reality and is inspired by interests that are foreign to the genuine pursuit of truth.

Let us not pretend otherwise: the great majority of consistent Marxists share the same point of view, as do of course many non-Marxists. To them the theologian appears as a sort of clown whose routine one knows in advance, aware that it has no relation to reality, no matter how much effort may have gone into freshening up the language and adapting it to the latest advances of modernity. All this only provokes a smile. In short, no one can take it seriously.

It is true that other Marxists, at least among neo-Marxists of the "revisionist" school, express a positive attitude and even some sympathy in regard to Christianity, interest themselves in the Bible and even in theology, seek dialogue with Christians, think even that Christians can become Marxists without abandoning the essence of their faith. However, when one takes a closer look at what they are about, can one honestly say that they no longer look upon Christianity as an ideology whose objective content would inevitably be destroyed by a commitment to the science of Marxism? Here again do we not see the same attitude among a number of non-Marxist nonbelievers?

On this level, which touches on the essence of faith, we find ourselves in a cultural context far vaster than Marxism. Here we encounter currents of thought that emanate from Nietzsche and Freud, and whole blocks of structuralism and linguistics, as well as the pragmatic materialism of an advanced industrial society of the liberal type—in short, the cultural context of "the death of God."

As Nietzsche put it, "The most important of more recent events—that 'God is dead,' that the belief in the Christian God has become unworthy of belief—already begins to cast its first shadows over Europe."[21] The remark was astute, even though the spread of atheism has been far from general and has, in fact, been subject to surprising setbacks. Marx deliberately intended to situate himself *beyond* the death of God—much too quickly, it seems, inasmuch as his disciples, more than a hundred years later, continue to meet on their road a Christianity that refuses to die.

Perhaps those who question the essence of the Christian faith have little knowledge of it. The hypothesis is worth considering. Doubtless Christians are responsible for this to a considerable extent by reason of the caricature they have given of that faith in their thought and in their behavior. We must admit it: their faith may have been only a "false faith."

Our approach will be that formulated by Karl Barth: "Is there no truth at all in the East's counteraccusation? We shall not dismiss it merely by reproaching those in the East for their false belief. We are being asked about our own faith."[22]

Our goal is not at this point a dialogue with flesh-and-blood Marxists. It is even more fundamental. It is to be open—at the deepest level of our faith—to the shock of Marxist analysis, and then to try to reformulate it in the light of the full truth, *at* the level of thought as well as that of action.

Our faith dare not be like a weathervane, for then how could there be any consistency to our thought? Neither can it be a ghetto faith, impregnable to the various shocks and influences of the outside world. On the contrary it must be a responsible faith in the very heart of the world where the impact of Marxism is substantial and materialism assaults us from every side.

Was that not in fact the situation confronted by the young Thérèse de Lisieux in her convent, closed to the great cultural currents of the nineteenth century, in a milieu that was at once pietistic and traditional? She wrote one day, "Thoughts assail me such as the worst materialists might have." In our time can faith become adult without having experienced such a confrontation? Has a faith exposed in depth to the tensions of its time ever been a comfortable faith?

The condition of the believer, especially in a time of negation and confusion such as ours, is like that evoked by the opening scene of Paul Claudel's *Soulier de satin* ("The Satin Slipper"): the Jesuit priest bound to the mast of a frail boat that is battered by the fury of the sea. He lives within himself the fate of his brother Rodrigue, the unbeliever who has turned away from God. This poetic evocation contains a striking insight. If one has not experienced such tensions in one's own interior life, how can one bear a witness to Jesus Christ that can be perceived by those who experience negation and confusion?

It is therefore from within the faith that the *confrontation* I am proposing will unfold, under a threefold structuring:

1. *Marxism questions and challenges the faith.* This challenge is one of the most formidable that has ever confronted the faith over the course of the centuries. At least in its original and dominant form, it claims not only to have unmasked and diminished the faith, but also to have demonstrated that it is totally invalid and pernicious. Instead of turning against this challenge and refusing to meet it, we shall open ourselves to it, welcome it, expose ourselves to its radical critique. That does not mean that we shall allow ourselves to be swept away by the fury of the storm.

The indictment, seen from the viewpoint of our faith, will be interpreted as an invitation from the Lord of history delivered through those very events that seek to deny the Lord. It will be taken as a challenge to become aware of our deficiencies of thought and action, and to make the changes that will enable us to live a life of more authentic faith. And it will be welcomed as an invitation that will inspire us to live our faith in a more creative way.

2. *In its turn faith critiques Marxism.* I use the term "critique" here in the sense of sifting or screening. If faith founders, if the believer becomes purely and simply Marxist, then the confrontation is ended. But we are concerned with a faith that intends to survive as faith and to give proof of its clarity and coherence. *A faith critiqued will become a faith that critiques,*

formulating its own objections and laying bare the weaknesses of a system of thought and action that can no more claim infallibility than can any other human system.

3. *We must then reformulate the faith for our time.* The first two levels of the structure are those of direct confrontation. After that it is possible to begin an independent, original process: an attempt to develop a new theory and a new praxis of the faith for our time.

Confrontation with Marxism can lead not only to a more responsible faith but also to a better understanding of the essence of faith in Jesus Christ, in the sense intended by Karl Barth when he wrote: "The reading of all kinds of literature that belongs typically to *the world* is strongly recommended to those who wish to understand the Epistle to the Romans."[23]

NOTES

1. Encyclical *Divini Redemptoris* (March 19, 1937), no. 58, English trans. in *The Church and the Reconstruction of the Modern World: The Social Encyclicals of Pius XI*, ed. Terence C. McLaughlin (Garden City, N.Y.: Doubleday-Image, 1957), p. 390.

2. *For Marx*, trans. Ben Brewster (London: Penguin, 1969), p. 46.

3. "Valeur de l'analyse marxiste," in *Nova et vetera* 46 (1971), p. 173.

4. In Karl Marx, *Grundrisse. Foundations of the Critique of Political Economy*, trans. Martin Nicolaus (New York: Vintage, 1973), pp. 100-102. The following comment by Lenin is interesting: "The spirit of Marxism requires that each thesis be analyzed: (a) from an historical perspective; (b) in relation to other theses; (c) by taking into consideration the concrete experience of history" (*Collected Works*, Russian ed., Vol. 35, p. 20, quoted by Constantine Gouliane, *Hegel ou la philosophie de la crise* [Paris: Payot, 1970], p. 25).

5. Address of May 25, 1907, to the Congress of the Russian Social-Democratic Workers Party meeting in London, quoted by Gilbert Badia, *Rosa Luxemburg* (Paris: Editions sociales, 1975), p. 66.

6. Joel de Rosnay, *Le macroscope. Vers une vision globale* (Paris: Seuil, 1975), p.17.

7. *For Marx*, p. 26.

8. Marx-Engels, *The German Ideology,* in *Collected Works,* Vol. 5 (New York: International Publishers, 1976), p. 74.

9. Cf. Marx-Engels, *German Ideology,* p. 4.

10. *Man in Marxist Theory and the Psychology of Personality*, trans. John Mc-Greal (Atlantic Highlands, N.J.: Humanities Press, 1978), p. 50.

11. *The Church and the Third World Revolution*, trans. Jeanne Marie Lyons (Maryknoll, N.Y.: Orbis, 1977), p. 153.

12. Interview in *La Croix* (November 19, 1970).

13. *The Nature of Faith*, trans. Ronald Gregor Smith (Philadelphia: Muhlenberg, 1962), pp. 20–21.

14. Ibid., p. 18.

15. For this reason I consider it non-Christian to maintain, as Wolfhart Pannen-

berg does, that in the virgin birth of Jesus Christ we are dealing with a legend. Even if he writes that it "can be asserted in this case with complete certainty," in my opinion his argument is not convincing: see his *The Apostles' Creed in the Light of Today's Questions*, trans. Margaret Kohn (London: SCM, 1972), p.73. For even graver reasons, I am constrained to express fundamental reservations regarding Hans Küng's *On Being a Christian* (Garden City, N.Y.: Doubleday, 1976).

16. *The Apostles' Creed*, p. 14.

17. *The Apostles' Creed*, p. 14.

18. *Introduction to Christianity*, trans. J.R. Foster (New York: Seabury, 1979), p. 49.

19. Pannenberg, *The Apostles' Creed*, p. 16.

20. *2 Clement*, I, 1f, quoted in Ratzinger, *Introduction to Christianity*, p. 250.

21. *Joyful Wisdom*, trans. Thomas Common (New York: Frederick Ungar, 1960), p. 275.

22. *The Church between East and West*, trans. Stanley Godman, in Karl Barth, *Against the Stream. Shorter Post-War Writings 1946–52* (London: SCM, 1954), p.141.

23. *L'Epître aux Romains* (Geneva: Labor et Fides, 1972), p. 405. Eng. trans., *Epistle to the Romans* (New York: Oxford University Press, 1968).

Chapter 2

The Fundamental Debate

It is the significance of Marxism that it belongs to those realities of our time which we cannot ignore without penalty in determining our own position. It is neither possible to make up one's mind about it without at the same time making up one's mind about the leading motifs of modern intellectual life, nor can we take up our own position in this realm without facing up to Marxism.[1]

Helmut Gollwitzer, in writing the two sentences above, put his finger on a very important truth. *Marxism, by what it affirms and what it denies, compels us to ask ourselves the fundamental questions of life.*

By its pretensions, by its accomplishments both negative and positive, by the hopes and the passionate commitments it inspires, and by the ferocious opposition it provokes, Marxism has such an impact on our contemporary reality that it is not possible to understand it without having devoted serious study to the subject. In one way or another you are led to take sides and to locate yourself in relation to it, because you are compelled to locate yourself somewhere and to define yourself for yourself and for others in relation to the time we live in. How can you do this seriously without looking Marxism straight in the face?

Let us take note also with Gollwitzer that communism, "as the most massive antireligious force," has "the openly avowed goal of making Christianity an affair of the past."[2] It is true that not all Marxists are ferociously anti-Christian and some of them are even anxious to dialogue with Christians. Nor should we forget the "Christian Marxists" or "Marxist Christians." The collective movement that is communism remains no less profoundly marked by its original anti-Christian dynamic.

Although the famous reproach against Christianity that it is "Platonism for the people" comes from Nietzsche,[3] there is no question that many Marxists would gladly accept it for their own. Does not Platonism evoke for them the quintessence of idealism, ineffectiveness, and illusion? It is true that Glucksmann could write ironically of Leninism that it is also "Platonism for the people,"[4] but in another sense: as an indictment for having established

27

the totalitarian utopia for the famous philosopher. It is therefore also from the perspective of our faith that we are called to this face-to-face encounter. Christians who cannot accept it seriously will be incapable of dealing with the most basic problems that confront the faith and its promulgation in our time, especially in the context of industrial society.

Two Worldviews

I have already quoted a sentence of Georges Marchais dating from 1970. I am going to repeat it and add the two sentences that follow:

> We communists owe allegiance to a materialist and dialectic phil-osophy.We do not wish to create any illusions on this point: between Marxism and Christianity there is no possibility of theoretical agree-ment, no possibility of an ideological convergence. Communist workers have their worldview, Catholic workers have theirs.[5]

This statement is the more significant because it occurred in the context of a dialogue in which its author was clearly trying to overcome certain prejudices and win converts. The fact that he may not be an intellectual in no way dimin-ishes that significance. Quite the contrary: it is all the more revealing of the ideology taught in the party schools. Let us not forget either that, although he was then only an assistant secretary general, he spoke as a responsible official of one of the most important communist parties in a noncommunist country.

It is not by accident that official communist doctrine presents communism not only as a revolutionary program of action, but also as a *specific world-view*. There can be no doubt on this point. In the Soviet Union the official philosophy—the only one tolerated—consistently makes ironclad statements on this subject:

> Dialectical materialism is the theoretical foundation of the practical activity of our party. The party of Lenin and Stalin resolved, and re-solves, all the problems of program, strategy, and tactics in complete agreement with the doctrine of dialectical and historical materialism. The politics of our party rests on the foundation, as hard as granite, of a dialectical and materialist vision of the world.[6]

We are already acquainted with Althusser's exclusive admiration of Marx-ist philosophy; he regards it as the only "philosophy possible." Let me add that, for him, "Marxist philosophy, founded by Marx in the very act of founding his theory of history, still has largely to be constituted,"[7] and that it is fundamentally linked to scientific Marxist analysis. In fact, speaking of Marx's writings, he concludes:

> These works carry with them not only the Marxist theory of history, contained in the theory of the capitalist mode of production and in all

the fruits of revolutionary action, but also Marx's *philosophical* theory, in which they are thoroughly steeped, though sometimes unwittingly, even in the inevitable approximations of its practical expression.[8]

This remark is of the greatest importance, explicating the complementarity of philosophical and scientific analysis. Philosophy (worldview) and scientific analysis are in organic relationship with each other in Marxist analysis, in constant interaction. The first conditions the second, and is conditioned by it. This does not mean that there is no distinction between them, but rather that the distinction is difficult and cannot be made without taking into account their dialectical relationship.

We know also with what insistence Gramsci attempted to define Marxism as a worldview that was at once fundamental and all-inclusive. In his view it was also the only one acceptable, at least for the present period of history. "On the intellectual plane," he wrote, "Marx opens the curtain on an age that will probably last for centuries—that is, until the disappearance of political society and the arrival of 'regulated' society. It is only then that his worldview will be surpassed, the concept of necessity surpassed by the concept of liberty."[9]

Sartre uses the same language: "I consider Marxism the one philosophy of our time which we cannot go beyond."[10] A little later he adds, "What has made the force and richness of Marxism is the fact that it has been the most radical attempt to clarify the historical process in its totality."[11]

Analysis will highlight the fundamental concepts. Thus the Soviet *Short Philosophical Dictionary* lists these basic categories of dialectical materialism: matter, movement, time, space, quality, quantity, reciprocal relation, contradiction, causality, necessity, form and content, essence and phenomenon, possibility and reality, and so forth. For historical materialism it lists: the mode of production, socio-economic formation, the forces of production, the relations of production, base and superstructure, class, revolution, and so forth.[12]

Althusser goes to the heart of the matter when he credits Marx with the "formation of a theory of history and politics based on radically new concepts: the concepts of social formation, productive forces, relations of production, superstructure, ideologies, ultimate determination by the economy, specific determination of the other levels."[13]

I have already noted that Marxist materialism is not only epistemological and historical but also fundamentally metaphysical (or ontological, or philosophical). Of the two founding fathers it is especially Engels who formulated it under its metaphysical aspect in his *Dialectics of Nature*. He writes there that the human spirit is "the highest product of organic matter."[14] He speaks there in striking language of the march of the universe toward its inevitable end.[15] He assures us that there is nothing eternal but matter, which is eternally changing and remains eternally the same.[16] He speaks ironically of "those numerous natural scientists who are inflexible materialists within their science, but outside it are not merely idealists, but even pious and indeed orthodox Christians."[17] He goes so far as to deify matter.[18] Marx agreed with him.

With Lenin the theory became a "dogma": "Marxism . . . is dialectical materialism, which has fully taken over the historical traditions of eighteenth-century materialism in France and of Feuerbach in Germany—a materialism that is absolutely atheistic and positively hostile to all religion."[19]

Metaphysical materialism necessarily includes atheism. Thus *Marxism claims to supply ultimate answers to ultimate questions*. For Marx no consistent revolutionary, no one familiar with scientific praxis and free from archaic prejudices, can think otherwise.

Perhaps it is not necessary to go so far, but this is Jacques Maritain's interpretation of the communist conception of the world, which he set down some time ago in *Integral Humanism*:

> Communism as it exists . . . is a complete system of doctrine and life claiming to reveal to human beings the meaning of their existence, answering all the fundamental questions posed by life, and manifesting an unparalleled power of totalitarian envelopment. It is a religion, and a most imperious religion, certain that it is called to replace all other religions, an atheistic religion for which dialectic materialism is dogma and of which communism as a regime of life is the ethical and social expression. Thus atheism is not demanded as a necessary *consequence* of the social system . . . ; on the contrary, it is presupposed as the *principle* of this system. . . . And that is why communist thought holds so ardently to it, as to the principle that stabilizes its practical conclusions and without which they would lose their necessity and their value.[20]

The first and third sentences of this interpretation can be fully verified in the founding fathers, and the whole of it in Soviet and Chinese leaders, as well as in those who rally to either of them.

Certain "Marxisms," it is true, reject metaphysical materialism and atheism, or claim that they are not essential to Marxism, even if they have historically been a part of it. What is certain is that Marx and Engels themselves looked upon them as essential aspects of their doctrine and as self-evident characteristics of the revolutionary movement that they were founding.

Neo-Marxists of the revisionist type, while personally remaining materialists and atheists and continuing, in fact, to espouse materialism and atheism—Roger Garaudy, Leszek Kolakowski, Ernst Fischer, and others—are inclined on the whole to look upon Marxism no longer as "a worldview" but more modestly as "a method"—"a method of thought," according to Kolakowski, "a scientific method of analysis of society," according to Fischer. This is the distinction on which the majority of Christians who adhere to Marxism rely in order to justify their position.

On this subject I first pose the following question: is not the Marxist method profoundly permeated by its founders' conception of the world, and is it possible to prescind, to abstract, from it? I note further that neither the founders of Marxism nor "orthodox" Marxist theoreticians have ever recognized this dichotomy.

Such a worldview, at least in its basic metaphysical principles, is thus radically anti-Christian. It is necessary only to examine them in order to realize this immediately. (This statement in no way prejudices, directly, other aspects of Marxist analysis.)

In calling this worldview "anti-Christian" I am speaking of its objective content; I am not judging its intention. Karl Barth, on the contrary, writes from a judgmental standpoint in the following remark: "It [communism] is not anti-Christian. It is coldly non-Christian. It does not seem to have encountered the gospel as yet."[21]

This statement would probably be regarded as inaccurate by a significant number of Marxists. It *is* accurate for those among them who share fully the mentality of the founders. At least in appearance they were strangers to Christianity, almost as if it had never existed. (Were they as untouched by it as they thought? That is another matter.)

Let us note in passing that the founders were not the only ones to be strangers to Christianity; many who hold the liberal ideology are just as much so as they were. Metaphysical materialism and atheism are far from being peculiar to Marxism. On this point Marx and Engels have remained the heirs of the bourgeoisie.

By this last statement I mean to raise a very important question. Liberal ideology, it is true, does not of itself require such fundamental options. It can accommodate itself very easily to belief in God. But is that not because such a belief is not really authentic and has no real impact on the life of society? Is it not a fact that practical materialism, which so profoundly characterizes advanced industrial society of the western variety, is also, on the level of faith, a form of poison—a poison that is the more dangerous because it poisons without your being aware that you are being poisoned?

Is it not the pernicious influence of this practical materialism—often reinforced by the theoretical materialism of numerous philosophical schools—that explains, in the final analysis, the serious crises that the churches are presently facing throughout the West? Wishing to be open to the world, have they not permitted themselves to be secularized by the world in a negative way? Taking our cue from the perceptive remarks of Gollwitzer, could we not say that "the easygoing tolerance with which middle-class atheism treats religion" means that it does not really take it seriously, whereas "in Marxism, as in atheism, Christian faith has again an opponent that takes itself—and therefore also takes the faith—seriously?"[22] (This last statement suggests a subtle qualification of the text of Karl Barth quoted three paragraphs above. Clearly it is not always possible to hold a consistent discussion on Marxism.)

Which Christianity?

Let us acknowledge that the radical indictment of Christianity implicit in the Marxist conception of the world has its share of truth when it comes to the historical behavior of Christians in the course of the centuries.

Although in its metaphysical dimensions it goes beyond the legitimate reach of the indictment it issues, materialism sees itself as a radical reaction against all "spiritualisms," all "idealisms," that do not take seriously the concrete conditions of human life, that even ignore them by reason of indifference or contempt, that play into the hands of the dominant class, that are determined that reality shall not be unmasked. This is a salutary reaction. There is no doubt that many currents of thought and much Christian behavior deserve to be indicted on this score.

We have been concerned about God, but have we also been concerned about humanity? Have we not too often forgotten that concrete service to human beings is a test of the authenticity of our love for God, as we are reminded by the First Epistle of St. John? "They who have no love for the brothers and sisters they have seen cannot love the God they have not seen" (4:20). Is it not true that the theology, preaching, and even the official teaching of the church during the nineteenth century, with some notable exceptions, reveal a serious ignorance of the exploitation in which workers were victimized during the growth of early capitalism? What was heard most of the time was indeed "idealistic" or "spiritualistic," in the pejorative sense of those terms. Heaven made one forget earth. The earth was abandoned—and no questions asked—to those who knew only too well how to exploit it in their own interests. Or else, because the true texture of reality had not been analyzed, only palliatives were proposed, when what was needed was to attack the root causes of injustice.

Should we then be surprised when those who were conscious of the deficiencies of this "angelism" became disgusted with it and were moved to attack it violently? As lived by Christians it revealed itself in the end to be a radical failure to take seriously the action of God in history, the mystery of the incarnation, and the fundamental demands of the gospel.

Which God?

Pursuing this same line, what is the precise meaning of the negation of God that we find in Marxist philosophy? What god does it reject? The tyrant god? The Santa Claus god? The god of Aristotle, safely enshrined in the sky? The god who justifies conservatism, supreme defender of ownership? The god of resignation? The stopgap god who compensates for all the lacunae in human knowledge? Or, on the contrary, the God of the Bible? The God who is infinitely above us—the "Wholly Other"—but who is at the same time infinitely close to us in Jesus Christ? The God who is infinitely powerful but also disarmed before the freedom of humanity, a freedom God has willed? The God of promise who does something altogether unique? The God who has been and is involved in human history? The God who calls for justice, for a concrete commitment to the service of others? The God who, through the prophets and Jesus Christ, has not ceased to denounce injustice, indifference, and egotism, and who has been the friend and defender of the poor?

On all the evidence, it is not the biblical God whom Marx, and his posterity after him, reject. Because Marx either did not know or did not know how to discover God. Because he could not imagine that God could be *that kind* of God. The god whom he in fact rejected was one of those varieties listed above—caricatures of the biblical God, the true God. For Marx, if the caricature-god were real, then that god could only crush humanity, take away its independence, freedom, autonomy. And these were the values that Marx believed in above all else. Hence the need for him to suppress God in order to save humanity.

Obviously our answer might be that Marx could and should have pursued the subject further and discovered, at least intellectually, the God of the Bible. He concluded much too quickly that the problem was resolved in a negation. The objection is worth considering. But are not Christians in good part responsible for his error? Have not caricatures of the biblical God frequently been the actual content of their faith? At least, did not their behavior lead one to suppose that to be the case? For example, was not the interpretation of Romans 13:1-7 ("Let every person be subject to the governing authorities") formulated most often within the context of a reactionary ideology in which God was made the guarantor of conservatism and exploitation?

It is true that in the course of the centuries saints, theologians, and reformers of the church have themselves denounced vigorously all the caricatures of God that have spread throughout the Christian world. The Marxist challenge has had a beneficial impact inasmuch as it has compelled us to emphasize images that have some social significance. The question of God does indeed have a political dimension.

Which Worldview?

As to the concept of "worldview," I think it is useful to apply it to the definition of the most fundamental and objective content of the Christian faith, because it permits us to understand better its specific character and decisive importance: faith in the Holy Spirit, creator of the universe; faith in the One God; faith in the God who is the lord of history and who, throughout it, orients humanity toward an absolute Future, in the God who in Jesus Christ became one of us, in the God who is Father, Son, and Holy Spirit.

That faith—and all the other elements of the Judeo-Christian revelation—is truly a conception of the world, a conception that is clearly theological and not philosophical, although it implies and demands a philosophy. What characterizes it—especially if we compare it with Marxism—is first the fact that, although it is fundamental, it is not "integral" or "total." It respects fully the freedom of rational and scientific research. It does not directly propose a specific social program, because for that it relies on the free responsibility of men and women. Also, by its very nature it cannot legitimately be imposed by force. The historical facts that contravene this statement are condemned by the very principles of Christianity. The commitment of faith must be and continue to be free.

By contrast the Marxist conception of the world, especially in the context of Marxism-Leninism, has been an "integral" or "total" conception. It touches directly on every aspect of life in society and does not hesitate to resort to every kind of pressure available to the power of the state.

So it is that faith is moved, in its turn, radically to challenge Marxism and, at the same time, to become more truly and actively aware of its own world-view.

We are confronted with the most fundamental problems of being and of the origin of the universe and the absolute. Marxism affirms with the greatest vigor the unity of being when it advances the principle that everything is matter and that spirit can only be a manifestation derived from it. Therefore, if it persists in this viewpoint, will it not arrive necessarily at the "deification" of matter suggested by Engels? In this way, without wanting to, does it not establish the principle of an Absolute? The basic difference between biblical monotheism and Marxist metaphysical materialism is therefore that, for the Bible, the Absolute is spirit, transcendence; for Marxism it is matter that has become the Absolute. Where then lies the greater discernment and coherence in the perception of reality?

Besides, is not Marxism itself, in all its revolutionary dynamic, which makes up its *raison d'être*, in contradiction with its own metaphysical materialism? As Bartoli points out, "The Marxist faith in an economic system that will serve everyone, the anger of Marx at economists who will not understand that the relationships they write about have nothing human about them, his faith in humanity—these are all irreconcilable with a consistent materialism."[23] If we are talking about pure materialism, then those who hold power are right and can abuse it as they wish, to satisfy their own interests and ambitions, or to abandon themselves to sadistic instincts, as long as they can do so with impunity, whether they be capitalist employers or political dictators. To what can one appeal against them if not to a superior power that has no other justification but itself?

An "integral" conception of the world, such as the Marxist, carries with it the terrible, almost inevitable, risk of dictatorship and totalitarianism. Berdyaev noted this with penetration in *The Origin of Russian Communism.* First in the case of Lenin:

Lenin was a revolutionary to the marrow precisely because through his whole life he defended an integral totalitarian outlook of life and permitted no infringement of it whatever. From this arose a thing which is difficult to understand at first glance—the passion, the fury, with which he fought against the smallest declension from what he saw as orthodox Marxism.[24]

Would it not be here, in the final analysis, that we find the explanation of the fact that all communist regimes to date have been of the dictatorial, and even totalitarian, type?

Marxists want us to take seriously the practical importance of their world-view. We do so by calling their attention to a consequence of that view that is too easy to justify by the backward state of Russia at the time of the October Revolution, by the pathological character of Stalin, or the necessities of the struggle against capitalism, whether internal or external.

Stung by the radical challenge of Marxism, it is essential then that Christians return to the biblical God, to a more authentic faith in God than they have generally demonstrated in the past. Let them discover that the option for God is at the same time an option for the promotion and liberation of humanity, liberation from all exploitation and all injustice, but also the more radical liberation from all sin! The God who created the world is spirit, transcendence, intelligence. Faith in that creation is an option for spirit, transcendence, and intelligence as opposed to simple matter, and therefore for what is highest in the scale of being and in the life of each person in particular and humanity in general.

(This does not mean that matter is devalued in Christian faith. It is assumed by the spirit in the unity of a human being called to resurrection. It is good in itself according to the narrative of creation. Food has always been considered a gift of God. Material elements—water, bread, and wine—have become the material foundation of the sacramental structure of the New Covenant.)

This God is a personal God. Faith in God is therefore an option for the human person, for all human persons, to help them free themselves, to help them become aware of their weaknesses, their sin, their crimes, to call them to conversion.

The creator God is creative transcendence, creative freedom. To believe in God is, therefore, to opt for liberation of the exploited and oppressed, for the pursuit of freedom, for a freedom that is appropriated in a responsible and socially conscious manner, for the dynamism of commitment and of action.

This God is also love. To believe in God is therefore to opt for a concrete love of our neighbors, for disinterested service in their behalf.

The God of promise is the God who ceaselessly calls us to face the future and thereby deters us from enclosing ourselves in a bygone past. Marxism wants to destroy God in the heart of humanity. Paradoxically, when Christians frankly accept a face-to-face encounter with Marxism, God can lead them to a deeper discovery of God in God's truth and therefore to a faith that is more alive and more authentic.

Marxism denies the Absolute. But perhaps it is unconsciously searching for

it. At least that seems to be the case with certain Marxists, as with other men
and women. "But their desperate search poses a terribly pressing question:
among laypersons and priests today, how many would be able to point out to
these anxious searchers the road that leads to an encounter with the Absolute?"[25]

Truth and Action

The problem of relating "truth" and "action" is as fundamental in Marxism as it is in Christianity, though obviously in a very different way. An
exploration of the point of contact between these two approaches is, however, of the greatest interest and reveals some surprising parallels.

In Marxism we must first examine the problem of "theory" and "practice." The conceptualization of this problem outlined by Althusser is particularly stimulating.

According to him—the same holds true in Marxist analysis—it is the concept of "practice" that comes first. By this concept he understands "any
process of *transformation* of a determinate given raw material into a determinate *product* . . . using determinate means."[26] (If this definition is taken literally, the concept, in his opinion, can be applied to all activity.)

He distinguishes several categories of "practice": "social practice," the
complex unity of practices existing in a particular society; "the practice of
transformation of a given nature . . . into useful products" (let us call it
"economic practice"); "political practice"; "ideological practice"; "theoretical practice". He adds that the latter includes "scientific theoretical practice" and "prescientific theoretical practice, that is 'ideological' theoretical
practice."[27] Thus practice embraces theory itself.

As for the concept of theory—again according to Althusser—it takes on
different meanings, which he attempts to distinguish by the way he writes the
word—namely, theory, "theory," and Theory. Written with a lowercase t,
theory refers to every theoretical practice of a scientific character. Written
with a lowercase t and in quotation marks, "theory" refers to the theoretical
system of a particular science—for example, the theory of universal attrac-
tion. Written with an uppercase t, Theory refers to the theory of practice in
general—namely, "the materialistic *dialectic* that is none other than dialectical materialism."[28]

Theory and Practice

If there is one principle on which Marxist theoreticians are all in agreement, it is clearly that of the *interdependence of theory and practice*, of their
mutual fertilization. As practice stimulates and fertilizes theory, so the latter
does in turn to practice. Marx wrote once to Ludwig Kugelmann in regard to
his own relentless theoretical labor: "I consider that this work which I am

doing is much more important for the working class than anything that I, personally, could do at a congress of any kind."[29]

Lenin said, "Without theory there can be no revolutionary practice." He also said, "You develop theory so that you may not be out of step with life." For his part Mao Tse-tung declared, "Without a correct political viewpoint you are without a soul." In 1942 he insisted that the students of the Party School deepen their study of historical reality and of Chinese revolutionary practice in the light of Marxist theory.[30] "Deviations attributable . . . to a theoretical deficiency are always costly, and may be *very* costly," notes Althusser.[31]

Where then is "truth"? Of what does it consist? How does one discover it and who is capable of discovering it? All of these questions are in the end inseparable, in the Marxist point of view. It excludes absolutely all transcendence and all abstraction that is not rooted in history.

The following lines from *The Communist Manifesto* resemble a triumphal declaration of war: "There are eternal truths such as freedom, justice, and so forth, that are common to all states of society. But communism abolishes eternal truths, it abolishes all religion and all morality, instead of constituting them on a new basis; it therefore acts in contradiction to all past historical experience."[32] Juvenile language? Without a doubt. It nonetheless represents a continuing conviction of Marxism that it constitutes a "cultural revolution" that is radical in its introduction of historicity into every question of truth and morality. What then does it propose?

Its response is basically formulated in the *Theses on Feuerbach* and, first, in Thesis 2: "The question whether objective truth can be attributed to human thinking is not a question of theory but it is a *practical* question. Humankind must prove the truth—that is, the reality and power, the this-worldliness of its thinking in practice. The dispute over the reality or non-reality of thinking which is isolated from practice is a purely *scholastic* question."[33] It is therefore history—or, to use other words: efficiency, success—that substantiates truth and, in the last analysis, produces it. I am not indulging in abusive simplification. Mao Tse-tung said it straight out: "What succeeds is correct, what fails is false."[34]

Therefore truth is determined by its impact on history, by its effective power to transform the world, by its influence on the future: "The philosophers have only *interpreted* the world in various ways; the point is to *change* it."[35] Henceforth truth is concerned with "makeableness" *(Machbarkeit),* comments Ratzinger with insight. It directs attention to "the future of what humankind itself can create."[36] The interpretation of the famous axiom of Gramsci, "to tell the truth is revolutionary,"[37] should therefore be dialectical: a statement (of supposed truth) may or may not lead to a revolution; it is only the success of that revolution that can generate and substantiate its truth.

Let us note, however, that in the Marxist perspective it is not a question of just any transformation of the world. Although it cannot escape all contradiction with all general principles, truth, in the Marxist perspective, can be only: (1) A class truth, that of the class of the oppressed and exploited who have become conscious of their lot and are determined to change it, therefore of the revolutionary class (the proletariat, according to literal Marxist "orthodoxy") to which one may bind oneself by adopting its interests or by helping it to perceive those interests; (2) a truth that is explained and conceptualized according to Marxist analysis (the only one that is fully scientific).

From there it is but an easy step to believe that "truth," substantiated by the success of revolutionary practice, is *the* truth, that Marxist science enjoys an impregnable certitude for thought and action, and that it therefore constitutes the criterion of all truth. Even very serious scholars have not hesitated to take this step. Thus Gramsci assures us that Marxism is "the surest interpretation of nature and of history" and that it provides "an infallible method, an instrument of the most perfect precision to explore the future, to foresee events affecting the masses, to direct them and thereby to control them."[38]

Official Soviet philosophy presents many Marxist theses as absolute truth, as, for example, a certain Rutkevich in his work, "Praxis, Foundation of Knowledge and Criterion of Truth" (Moscow, 1952):

> All the fundamental theses of Marxism-Leninism and an immense number of its particular theses concerning philosophy, economic science, socialist theory, and the class struggle are absolutely true. That matter is the primary element and conscience a derivative element, that the collapse of capitalism is inevitable, that the socialist order will succeed capitalism as inevitably as day succeeds night, that the socialist economic system opens an unlimited scope to the development of productive forces, and so forth—these are absolute truths, proven by praxis to the point that nothing in the future can ever again put them in question.[39]

In 1936 the following response was given in a police investigation: "The *pravda* (a word having a positive meaning of "truth") is what I have read today in the editorial of *Pravda* (the newspaper) and everything that is not contained therein is not objectively true. As for your miserable *istina* (a word meaning "abstract truth") statements, they do not even count."[40]

Obviously not all Marxists agree with such ridiculous language. But do they not often give the impression of regarding themselves as the sole custodians of truth and does that not explain the difficulty of achieving a true dialogue with them, even with those who consider themselves Christians? Is not Marx himself largely responsible for this? "If a truth is *crystal* clear," he wrote, "it is because it *seems* crystal clear to the masses; if history's *attitude* to truths *depends* on the *opinion* of the masses, the opinion of the masses is absolute, infallible, it is *law* for history, and history proves only what the masses do *not* consider as crystal clear, what therefore needs proof. It is the masses, therefore, that prescribe history's 'task' and 'occupation.' "[41]

Does not such assurance pose a problem that is extremely serious, especially when we consider the sinister reality that it has too often served to conceal? Apart from faith in the word of God, can human thought legitimately claim such certainty, especially in the realm of philosophy and political action? This pretension is sharply challenged by leftist thinkers today. Consider the biting irony of Maurice Clavel: "Thus Marxism was destined from the beginning to enjoy a total, unheard-of success in this world, conferring upon the ignorant the certainty of knowing everything, to idiots the illusion of thought, to the poor the easiest of faiths, to the state apparatus the absolute mastery of souls."[42] For him "the terrible crimes of Marxism, everywhere in that world where it holds power, are not the work of any Marxist in particular and still less the work of saboteurs, traitors, deviations, or deviations from deviations, but of the doctrine itself."[43] His indictment strikes at the heart of Marxism: these crimes are in no way an accident of history (attributable to a person, according to the theory of Khrushchev, or to a bureaucracy, according to many others) but the very logic of the system. "The forty million dead—not to speak of the tortured—in the Gulag are, and are alone, in the logic of Marxism, the sole check on the system in the end inasmuch as the leaders fear that they may themselves become its victims."[44]

The accusations of André Glucksmann are similar. "To the question, 'Who is right, the one who has the power or the one who is under it?,' Marxism answers every time, 'The one who has the power.' "[45] No less sharply he describes "the science of governments that dominate the people by all the means that Marxism reveals to them."[46] These charges must of course be proven, but in any case it would be a serious mistake for Marxists to sidestep them.

Our discussion of "truth and action" leads to the problem of the *verification of Marxism in those regimes that claim loyalty to it.* For some these regimes reflect its true reality, either as verification of its correctness, or as witness to its radical deficiencies. For others these regimes represent its betrayal. That is the opinion of a certain number of Marxists outside the official parties. And these Marxists are the first to find fault with, for example, the U.S.S.R. in the name of what they believe to be the true Marxism.

The unfortunate part is that *the thought of Marx, in its richness, is at once complex and ambiguous.* Text in hand, one can draw from it, in practice, the most contradictory conclusions: as much in favor of liberty (of anarchy and rejection of the state) as of dictatorship and totalitarianism. As far as I am concerned, I do not think that Lenin substantially betrayed it. But just the same the question remains: was this great visionary (and I intend no sarcasm) sufficiently aware of the practical consequences and implications of his revolutionary objectives? The question, however decisive, will always remain unanswered.

An Absolute Reference Point

My critique of the problem I have outlined has only begun. I will return to it in relation to faith. But let me first acknowledge the extraordinary power it has to challenge us, so that I may have the right to challenge it in turn on that same plane of faith.

Has not the historical behavior of Christians, in fact, frequently been at odds with the profession of faith that they make? Faced with the misery of the masses or of individuals, have they not too often been content with pious sentiments or empty words? How often have they closed their eyes so as not to see the misery, how many times have they passed by with indifference, as if these unfortunate ones were not their brothers and sisters? Worse yet, how many among them have themselves been exploiters or oppressors, whether by ignorance, or by opportunistic or even sadistic intent? Let us not overridicule the tableau of history, but still let us look reality in the face. Too often the practice of Christians has been very different from the truth of the gospel, especially because the gospel calls so earnestly for a life that is consistent with its message. The result has been that they bore a counterwitness, for the truth of the gospel can be discovered, or even fully understood, only in a life that is consistent with it.

We are back again with the problem of "theory and practice." "Theory," from the viewpoint of faith, is the theology that is founded on the word of God in Jesus Christ. "Practice," from the same point of view, is the life of Christian communities and individuals. It also embraces "pastoral care," or the activity of their leaders.

Dichotomy is common. On the one hand we see isolated theologians without real contacts either with "pastoral care" or with Christian communities, except perhaps with some intellectual circles. On the other hand there are pastors without any deep theological training, and Christians to whom they offer banalities as intellectual nourishment for their faith, or even an ideology falsely related to the gospel.

This dichotomy is regrettable, both for theology, which runs the risk of becoming rigid and losing itself in byzantine quarrels instead of confronting real problems and thus becomes incapable of responding to real needs, and also for the "practice" of Christians and of pastors, who are thereby deprived of intellectual tools essential to think through their faith and their pastoral activity. When will we understand that the interaction of theology and a lived faith is more necessary than ever before?

As for the excessive self-assurance of Marxists—whether irritating or laughable—it can itself provoke a beneficial awareness. Whatever it is about it that annoys us or moves us to irony, have we not ourselves too often been guilty of the same thing? *L'Univers,* for example, saw Gallicanism in "any failure to regard as law even the secret desires of the pope, or the intentions of those who were more or less close to him." Even the great Cardinal Mercier, in the pastoral letter that he dedicated to the election of Pius XI, saluted the papacy as "the accepted and cherished supremacy of one conscience over all consciences, of one will over all wills."[47] The following rule is contained in the *Spiritual Exercises* of St. Ignatius Loyola: "If we wish to be sure that we are right in all things, we should always be ready to accept this principle: I will believe that the white that I see is black, if the hierarchical church so defines it."[48]

One could multiply examples from the past. As for the present, are we not only too often aware of the peremptory affirmations, or condemnations, made by Christians? Do they not reveal an enormous naivety?

The Marxist question compels especially Christians to discover the twofold character, inseparable and dialectic, of their faith: as truth (hence as thought, as theology) and as practice concretized in life.

The objective content of the faith is meant to be pondered. We forget too easily that Jesus Christ said of himself: "I am the way, and *the truth,* and the life" (John 14:6) and that the word of God is spoken to us in order to be understood. The biblical texts that underline its objective and compelling content of truth are numerous. Believers are asked to use all the powers of their intelligence to explore endlessly the depths of the word that has been addressed to them.

True, faith cannot be reduced to purely rational knowledge and it is impossible to enclose it in a system of thought that would reject all transcendence, all intervention of God in history, all communication from God to humanity. Nonetheless it does present a body of thought that one may formulate in specific concepts, that gives a coherent response to the ultimate questions posed by human intelligence, and opens to that intelligence broader perspectives of meaning.

To insist on this content of thought does not mean that we intellectualize the faith or deny its eminently existential character. "Christian belief is not an idea, but life; it is not mind existing for itself, but incarnation, mind in the body of history and its 'We.' It is not the mysticism of the self-identification of the mind with God, but obedience and service."[49] It is faith in, commitment to, and communion with God and with others *in* God. It is an integral orientation of life, but one that respects the liberty of each and the specific demands of rational inquiry. It is a new way of living, in the light of the gospel. When it is true to that gospel it is a formidable dynamism that can transform humanity and the world, and in no way can it be characterized as conservatism or something purely private. As Tertullian remarked, "Christ called himself truth, not custom."[50]

In the face of our laziness, our cowardice, our egotism, our peculiarly human behavior that is all too trivial in its conformity to our prejudices of class or race or nation or culture, we are called to conversion—conversion to an authentic practice of the gospel spirit. But such a conversion requires in turn an active perception of our faith that is at the same time illuminated by that faith. The Christian faith is authentic only when it becomes a dialectic of truth and practice, of thought and action.

It is entirely legitimate to speak here of the primacy of practice, but only on condition that we see clearly that practice must be consistent with the word of God, whether consciously or unconsciously. Such is the meaning that underlies the famous saying of Jesus: "Those who do evil hate the light, and do not come to the light, lest their deeds be exposed. But those who do what is true come to the light, that it may be clearly seen that their deeds have been wrought in God" (John 3:20–21).

Acceptance of the Marxist challenge only makes it easier for us to raise a radical objection. Marxism sees itself as the fundamental truth, even for the ultimate questions, at least for the present period of history. A Christian could never accept this, because acceptance would necessitate a denial of the very essence of Christian faith. For the Christian there is, and can only be, *one absolute reference point*: God in Jesus Christ, who alone can give the ultimate, and certain, answers to the ultimate questions and reveal their definitive meaning. This absolute truth cannot be absorbed in its entirety by the human believer. We can only open ourselves to it; its discovery will never be better than highly imperfect. Our attitude must be one of modesty and openness to dialogue, of "poverty" in the gospel meaning of the word.

As regards a knowledge of humanity and of history or the problems of the organization of society, the Christian must grope, like everyone else, with the best tools available at the time. Logically, faith will lead to the understanding that no science, including Marxist science, is infallible. Faith thus makes possible a greater realism and lucidity.

The Christian will also be glad to see that neo-Marxists of the revisionist school have themselves questioned this pretension to infallibility (even if their conception of truth is itself debatable)—for example, when Garaudy speaks in this regard of "universal relativity." (From the standpoint of reason as well as faith certain truths must be recognized as sure and permanent, as *true* for all, and not as simply relative to a given culture or a particular history.) Although wishing to be resolutely Marxist they refuse to look upon Marxism as the key to all truth. They believe that there is valid knowledge outside it.

Lombardo-Radice admits that in applying Marxism to your thinking you arrive at the conclusion that it too has its obvious gaps as well as some clearly one-sided aspects, and that it needs to be completed and developed by the use of complementary truths, however one-sided these may be in their turn. For Adam Schaff the political position of the thinker is in no way decisive for the truth or falsity of his opinions. Although the tendency of neo-Marxists is to limit the principle of pluralism to the domain of socialism, it is no less true that their way of seeing things poses a radical challenge to the original and traditional idea of Marxism as a worldview. When Garaudy maintains that the need of our time is the capacity not for dialectic but for synthesis, we are far from traditional Marxist doctrine. It is understandable why he is treated as a "heretic" by official communism.

Dialectical Critique

In examining the question of "theory and practice" in Marxism we end by focusing on *the problem of the truth of Marxism itself,* its truth as an analysis of human reality, its truth also as a revolutionary blueprint. This is an extremely difficult problem. It is impossible to give it a simple solution that would be acceptable to everyone, for two reasons. First, because Marxism is itself an extremely complex and often contradictory reality, at least when we look at it in the totality of its history. Second, because it would be necessary to agree on criteria of evaluation, which are themselves relative to the particular options of each analyst.

As Berdyaev wrote, "In communism there is a great untruth . . . but it also contains much truth, and even many truths."[51] He continues, "In communism there are many truths . . . and only one untruth; but that untruth is so enormous that it outweighs all the truths and spoils them."[52] That "one untruth" that has for him such a decisive importance is atheistic materialism. "Its spirit," he notes, "is the negation of spirit, the negation of the spiritual principle in humankind; its untruth is its rejection of God. . . . Communism is inhuman, for denial of God leads to denial of humankind."[53] A little later he adds, "Such is the final result of the denial of God, of his image . . . in humankind. . . . All the negative aspects of communism follow from that."[54]

From the viewpoint of Christian faith one must obviously reject as false and an objective lie *everything that, in a conception of the world, proceeds from metaphysical materialism and atheism.* The objection on this point is basic and we must carefully point out all the consequences that follow from it in other areas of theory and practice. Our basic position—the only one consistent with faith in Jesus Christ—in no way necessitates the conclusion that one must reject Marxism in its entirety. This would be an injustice to it and a foreclosure on the truth.

The only correct attitude is to be, like Berdyaev, careful to look for every element of truth in Marxism. As Soloviev puts it, "To overcome the lie of socialism, one must have grasped the truth of socialism." We must therefore also reject a simplistic anticommunism as well as a complacent admiration, for these are emotional responses, in no way scientific. We must *screen* Marxism as objectively as possible while being careful to understand it in all its complexity.

In that way we will find in it *important elements of truth,* passing over other elements that we will deal with later.

The Marxist critique of bourgeois and capitalist society, of its contradictions and weaknesses, is of course far from totally convincing. The picture that it paints is too black. It is Manichean: the bourgeoisie appears to be the incarnation of evil, a class that is, and can only be, exploitive and oppressive, whereas the proletariat is manifestly idealized to the point of becoming a class incapable of sin or stupidity. Although Marx insists that he wants only to attack structures and not individuals, the capitalist whose portrait he draws is motivated only by the worst intentions. The Marxist critique of money and profit is clearly too condensed. The famous theory of surplus value, on which hinges the Marxist critique of capitalism, cannot itself escape serious objections, for, as Clavel has shown with some insight, it "forgets or ignores the industrial character of production that it pretends to explain."[55]

Nevertheless the Marxist critique of bourgeois, capitalist society contains much truth. It highlights the class struggles that undergird capitalist society, something that no analysis had done so clearly before. It denounces the extreme social inequalities, the tragic condition of the working class in the first phase of capitalist industrialization. It questions the exclusive legitimation of power in the industrial enterprise in terms of the ownership of capital. It exposes the masks and subterfuges of liberal ideology: its polarization around money and profit, its extreme individualism, its concern for the interests of the ownership classes, so quick to hide behind the mystique of human rights, freedom, or some preestablished harmony. Even if it has been extremist or simplistic, it—more than any other—has had the merit of revealing deep wellsprings of socio-economic reality and of provoking a challenge to them that has been historically productive. Berdyaev was not wrong in describing as "brilliant" the "Marxist critique of capitalism."[56]

We shall have occasion to show that Marxism has not understood the profound reality of "the Christian phenomenon" and that, in consequence, the radical critique that it claims to have founded is off the mark. It is nonetheless true that in denouncing the hypocrisy or social ineffectiveness of Christian groups holding the levers of power, the historical collusion of the churches *with* power on too many occasions, their conservatism, their ideological support of the dominant classes, the irrelevance of theological and pastoral discourse in social matters, Marxism strips away the mask of a reality of which the churches were unconscious or that they consciously concealed.

In the same way it is true that class struggle has had, and has, an impact on the reality that is the churches. Here again it is Marxist analysis that makes us aware of this. In other words one might say that it helps us to perceive more clearly the "negative secularization" of the church. In this way it drives us back, indirectly, to the gospel, which is the first to challenge it radically. Seen, and critiqued, in the eyes of faith, Marxism can even serve as a source of revelation in regard to the judgment of the word of God.

The *Marxist revolutionary vision* unquestionably possesses a positive content that deserves to be considered with the greatest attention.

The idea of a *planned economy* (at the national level and even at the world level), although it is not of Marxist origin, has certainly received, thanks to Marxism, its first important articulation in modern times and its first real applications. This is an idea of the greatest importance for the future of humankind. The more the world becomes one, and the more the means of communication grow complex, and society itself becomes more diversified, still more imperative does concrete organization become.

This is not to advocate a rigid centralization on the Soviet model. By its excesses it leads to political sclerosis and the negation of individual and group initiative. Only planning that gives full play to freedom is beneficial. That is precisely what we have learned from the serious deficiencies of Soviet planning as well as from an analysis of its frightening negative results. Economic planning, fortunately, is not necessarily the straitjacket invented by Stalin. Without Marxist theory and practice, however debatable, we would certainly not have seen so clearly the vital importance and the necessary modalities of balanced economic planning. Those who hold to liberal ideology still seem reluctant to admit this.

The drive to transform society into a *society of workers* can lead to the inhuman excesses of a "Gulag Archipelago," as in the time of Stalin, or to contempt for those who cannot, or will not, engage in economically productive labor: the handicapped, cloistered nuns, and others. It can also become the mystifying ideology of the dictatorship of the proletariat—that is, of productive (especially manual) workers—while a bureaucracy decrees itself total power. But this evolution is not inevitable. It can, on the contrary, lead to a rediscovery and realization, on a sounder basis, of the value of manual labor and of workers in general, as well as of the fundamental legitimation of power on the strength of labor and no longer on that of money. From the standpoint of our faith even more than of reason, such a goal embodies an eminent value for civilization.

We can say as much for other components of Marxist ideology, such as: the goal of putting an end to the exploitation of subordinate classes by privileged classes (those that direct and control) or of dominated peoples by dominating peoples; the goal of transforming unequal societies composed of antagonistic classes into societies characterized by a clear social equality, at least in tendency; the goal of breaking down national egotisms and developing a society, and an organization, that would be worldwide; the goal, finally, of radically transforming the existent social order so as to create a society that would be more just and more egalitarian.

Here again the very serious deficiencies of communist regimes should not blind us to the high human value of such goals, nor lead us to think that their realization, or at least their approximation, is impossible. It is unfortunate that the deficiencies lead many into social conservatism. The analysis of deficiencies, on the contrary, should be read as an indication of roads to avoid and as a stimulant to the creative imagination.

What is at the heart of Marxism, what explains its powerful impact on the masses, as well as the prodigious devotion that it has inspired in men and women who have sacrificed their lives to it, is *the socialist idea, the socialist utopia*—that is, the vision of a society that is more just, more companionable, more united, made real by an equitable sharing of resources and power among all. Up to the present only patriotism and religion, and perhaps the revolutionary ideology of the struggle for "human rights" at the end of the eighteenth century, have demonstrated as great a power to mobilize persons. The great works of civilization, the great processes of social transformation, presuppose *great ideals that are capable of mobilizing energy*, that appeal to what is best in persons and not merely to their own egotistical interests. The merit of Marxism is that it understood this remarkably well, despite its metaphysical materialism and, in theory, its original amoralism (subsequently abandoned, at least by the historical leaders). From this point of view it teaches a highly important lesson to advanced industrial society of the liberal persuasion.

That it presents itself as the *only* scientific socialism is a pretension that one need not ratify. That the achievements clearly associated with it are everywhere questioned because of their dictatorial and totalitarian quality is a fact that compels serious reflection. But it is essential to realize that socialism is not inevitably "the fantastic younger brother of almost decrepit despotism," as Nietzsche believed.[57] Certainly it has been, and is, that. (The foresight of Nietzsche and of Dostoevski on this point were prodigious.) But it can also be something else.

A priori, nothing about it makes it incompatible with freedom, provided one does not try to impose an official ideology that pretends to answer all the ultimate questions, and provided further that one assumes political and economic structures that are not totalitarian. If these conditions apply—that is, if socialism foreswears presenting itself as the Absolute—if additionally it is applied in a competent and realistic way, then, by reason of its own goals of justice, solidarity, equality, and fellowship, it is entirely consistent with the fundamental goals of the Christian faith for the life in society. Moreover, it seems obvious that a world such as ours—more and more unified—has an urgent need for putting that solidarity into genuine practice.

Perhaps the word "socialism" is too charged with a negative history for too many of our contemporaries and harbors for them too many ambiguities. The *word* is not important. What is decisive is the growth of awareness in the direction just indicated and the implementation of such awareness in the change of appropriate structures. Such is the meaning of the following position of Berdyaev: "For me the social system most consistent with Christian conscience is that I would call personalist socialism or social personalism, which I would oppose to Marxism."[58]

A page that we are going to read from Karl Barth dates from 1949, the period of Stalinism at its peak and shortly after the fall of Nazism. Barth's refusal to put Hitler and Stalin on the same footing brought him much reproach. However, he did not ignore Stalin's crimes, less well known then than now. His basic stance stemmed from the fact that Nazism seemed to him a totally negative reality—a work of death in every sense of the word. Whereas, despite the crimes and inhumanity of Stalinism, there was, at bottom, something positive and constructive in communism. What he wanted especially to bring out was communism's enormous power to challenge liberal industrial society. By its very existence it unmasks the fundamental weakness of that society: not knowing how to resolve, either for itself or for the world, the *social question* in the strongest meaning of that phrase—that is, an equitable share of participation by all levels of the population in economic growth and a balanced introduction of all underdeveloped countries in the dynamic of industrialization. Despite the real progress achieved within advanced industrial society itself, this question remains, and it remains particularly acute

in the relationships between that society and the underdeveloped countries.
Here is the page from Karl Barth:

> It is pertinent not to omit to discriminate in our view of contemporary
> communism between its totalitarian atrocities as such and the positive
> intention behind them. And if one tries to do that, one cannot say of
> communism what one was forced to say of Nazism ten years ago—that
> what it means and intends is pure unreason, the product of madness and
> crime. It would be quite absurd to mention in the same breath the phi-
> losophy of Marxism and the "ideology" of the Third Reich, to mention
> a man of the stature of Joseph Stalin in the same breath as such charla-
> tans as Hitler, Göring. . . . What has been tackled in Soviet Russia—al-
> beit with very dirty and bloody hands and in a way that rightly shocks
> us—is, after all, a constructive idea, the solution of a problem which is a
> serious and burning problem for us as well, and which we with our clean
> hands have not yet tackled anything like energetically enough: the so-
> cial problem.
> Our western "no" to the solution of this question in Russia could
> only be a Christian "no" if we had a better conscience with regard to
> what we mean and intend with our western freedom, if we, too, were
> attempting a more humane but no less energetic solution to this prob-
> lem. As long as one cannot say that of the West. . . , as long as there is
> still a "freedom" in the West to organize economic crises, a "freedom"
> to dump our corn into the sea here while people are starving there, so
> long as these things can happen, we Christians, at any rate, must refuse
> to hurl an absolute "no" at the East.[59]

Marxism as Science

A critique of Marxism must deal with the basic problem of its *scientific
character*. We have noted that it is not simply a scientific process, although it
makes such a claim, because, as we have demonstrated, in its complexity
there are also political, ethical, and basically philosophical elements as well.
Its scientific character, however, is very important and can in no way be
denied, even if we are forced to challenge many of its aspects.

At this level what we must say, from the viewpoint of the Christian faith, is
that we fully recognize the reality and the role of a scientific procedure, provided that it is truly such and in the measure that it is such, and provided
further that *it then compares the scientific critique employed by Marxism
with other scientific approaches*. I will offer here only a few remarks of a
rational kind that the faith requires in order to situate itself.

It is probably Althusser and his school who have highlighted with the most
force and insight, and in a style that is much more serious than Soviet Marxism-Leninism, the novelty and importance of Marxist science. It will be
enough to quote the following aphorisms of Althusser: "The theoretical rev-

olution that Thesis 11 [on Feuerbach] announces is therefore in reality the foundation of a new science. . . . Marx opened up a new, third continent to scientific knowledge, the continent of history. . . . [The new science] is materialist . . . like all science. . . . Materialism is then quite simply the rigorous attitude of the scientist before the reality of his object. . . . Historical materialism means therefore the science of history.''[60] We could say a great deal about these aphorisms. Do they qualify without question as scientific? Are they not impregnated with a whole philosophy? Let it pass for now.

I readily acknowledge that the scientific rigor of Marx went far and remains exemplary. Engels emphasized it: ''the unparalleled conscientiousness and strict self-criticism which he practiced in his endeavor to fully elaborate his great economic discoveries before he published them.''[61]

This does not mean that his method was purely scientific, or that Marxist science is free from error, even when practiced by its brilliant founder in person. Its errors of prediction are countless. How many times was he not convinced that the hour of revolution had sounded! Up to the present, history has not confirmed his essential ''scientific'' prediction—which constitutes the very axis of that science—that the socialist revolution would burst forth at the most advanced point of industrial society.

Of course we should refrain from sarcasm, as Althusser notes, and here he gives evidence of a certain modesty: ''That is why communists know that they can be mistaken. But what distinguishes communists is that they possess objective criteria.''[62] Agreed, we might say. But are they the only ones?

This highly touted science is furthermore not free from truisms. For example, this sentence of Althusser, which expresses at once an aphorism of Mao and his admiration for him: ''For, as Mao puts it in a phrase as clear as the dawn, 'Nothing in this world develops absolutely evenly.' ''[63] Is it necessary to be a genius to formulate such a sentence? It is true that Althusser sees here a kind of inspired quotation in support of what he calls ''the law of the unequal development of contradictions.'' I respond: must one be a great sociologist to recognize that?

This excessive and frequently flaunted assurance among Marxists—which reminds one of that to which theologians are too often prone—gives them a dogmatic attitude that can weaken their own analyses and make them less apt for dialogue. Maurice Clavel writes:

> I think I can explain the character of Marxist dialecticians. Others search; they *know*. Anxious idealists gladly convert so that they might find in this universal science and its precise and infallible predictions an increase of strength and reassurance. Soon they too will *know*. Then *events* will be at fault. And the poor will be quieter, if we just tell them that we know.[64]

By its very pretensions Marxist science confers upon its adherents a strong feeling of security. That contributes to its success with many adherents who need such a security blanket—as happens in Christianity of the "integrist" type. Great moral strength is needed to confront risk, groping, uncertainty.

Let me say that, in general, if the tool forged by Marx continues to have so much success with many followers, it is not primarily because of its scientific rigor, but because of its *power of emotional suggestion*. What primarily attracts persons to Marxism is that, by its social critique, it supplies an answer to profound dissatisfactions and all too real frustrations that are caused by the evils of current social systems. Also, by its revolutionary proposals and the very excess of its conviction, it gives birth to hope.

What I have just stated is not in itself a criticism. Certainly I shall have to criticize the Marxist social critique, and question certain important aspects of its revolutionary plan. But here, if I were to formulate a criticism, it would be against those social systems that have given birth to such frustrations and created such despair.

The following confession of José Mariátegui on his own journey will help us to see that certain commitments to Marxism can be a personal act of great seriousness: "On my journey I encountered a faith. That is all. But I encountered it because my soul had set out early on the search for God. I have the soul of a fighter. . . . My sincerity is the only thing that I have never renounced."[65]

I shall add a few other observations.

Perhaps the cacophony that one hears in discussions on the scientific character of Marxism comes from the fact that Marx's concept of "science"—which his disciples have inherited—is much wider than in most contemporary interpretations by non-Marxists. The following remarks of Georges Cottier on this subject are pertinent:

One finds . . . in Marx the desire to do scientific work by virtue of a faith in the power of reason. More precisely, science for him means at the same time science in the modern sense and *Wissenschaft*, or exhaustive knowledge of all that is, which is the totality of history, inherited from Hegel. This *Wissenschaft* is the hallmark of the philosopher or sage, and it is from this, from its ambitions, that the link with messianism appears. Philosophy, become "historical materialism," is gnosis, knowledge of the supreme destinies of history.[66]

A properly scientific critique of Marxism must distinguish with care the different levels of Marxist "science": science in the strict sense of the word, philosophy, and the revolutionary prospectus, which is at the same time of the political and the ethical order.

In this sense we can state with André Malraux that "no science can answer the question: what are you doing on earth?"[67] The categories that can claim to do this are of a different order: myth, philosophy, theology. . . . To the extent that Marxism claims to answer the ultimate questions, it is, as we have seen, far from science and, at this level, takes on other forms.

In the same way we must take note that every analysis of society, including the scientific, whether it be simply interpretive, critical, or revolutionary, is ultimately characterized by a worldview, a philosophy, an ethic (eventually a theology). The ultimate criteria of such an analysis can only be *metascientific*. This is not a weakness but an opportunity, for it represents a break with all determinism and provides for human freedom, carrying forward human existence and its future.

What is important is the quality of the criteria chosen and the lucidity with which the analyst makes use of those criteria. If the analyst is Christian, it is precisely at this level that the faith will come into play, if the analyst chooses to be consistent with it. Some metascientific criteria will be of the rational order, others of the order of faith. It is the same with Marxism, understandably enough, except that many Marxists, following the founding fathers, are unwilling to admit it by reason of their exaggerated conception of science.

That is why, on this point, the lucidity of a Mariátegui was particularly important when, though proposing to do scientific work, he did not hesitate to declare: "Once more I repeat that I am not an impartial and objective critic. My judgments are nourished by my ideals, my feelings, my passions. I have a definite, driving ambition: that of contributing to the creation of a Peruvian socialism."[68]

Let us be well aware, finally, that *no science is infallible*, the humanistic sciences even less than others. Marxism has the right to claim a scientific character, but such a claim cannot block the road to criticism in its regard, whether it be scientific, philosophical, or theological. On each of these three levels it must furnish the proof of its truth.

Marxism as Critique

Thus the critical method we propose in regard to Marxism could be called "*dialectical*," according to the following schema:

1. Submission of diverse analyses and social programs to Marxist critique, and especially submission of "our" analyses and "our" programs.

2. Critique of Marxist analysis from the viewpoint of other analyses and other social programs, and especially from the viewpoint of "our" analyses and "our" programs.

3. On the basis of this confrontation, elaboration of new analyses and new social programs for the present period of history.

Phase one of this schema is that of the acceptance of the *challenge* of Marxist analysis.

Phase two could be called: *the critique critiqued*.

Phase three affirms at once the freedom of analysts—their declaration of independence—and their intention to confront the problems of the present moment of history with the best methods available, of which some could be post-Marxist. *A priori*, at least, the possibility must be considered. We cannot forget, in fact, that Marxism forged its basic tools in the nineteenth century, faced with a historical situation that is not ours and in a cultural context that is not ours. Perhaps these tools are still valid. In any case it must be verified.

Faith will intervene at every level, on the plane of metascientific criteria, as we explained in our description of the functioning of the analysis of societies.

In this process Marxism is clearly no longer the absolute reference point. In the eyes of faith only the word of God can be that: still more concretely, the word of God in Jesus Christ. In the eyes of reason itself everything that elaborates human thought belongs to the same order of the contingent, the relative, the provisional. Every theory must prove its own validity and none can embrace the whole of reality without error. This insistence on the relativity of Marxism, as I propose it, and its exposure to a rigorous critique do not prevent me from taking it very seriously: I accept the necessity of modifying my own analyses and my own social projections in the light of any truth revealed by Marxism.

Jacques Ellul, an expert on Marxism, has described Marx, Nietzsche, and Freud considered together as "the three geniuses, humanity's great malefactors."[69] In my opinion such a censure is not owed to them but to some of their readers and disciples. If their readers are lacking in maturity and turn to them as if to oracles, if their disciples become Stalins or Hitlers or advocate pansexualism, then in fact their influence does reveal itself as profoundly harmful. If, on the contrary, *we* give proof of maturity and study their works in depth, the devastating critique to which they expose us can prove beneficial. Such is the case with Marxism, without which we would be less well equipped to analyze contemporary reality and to foresee and prepare for the future of humankind, and this despite the very serious objections we may have against it.

Certainly we cannot forget the inadequacies of the Marxist critique of capitalist society. It takes insufficient account of the fact that it is first of all an industrial society; as a result it overlooks the inherent logic of socialist industrialization. It does not pay sufficient attention to the specificity of the scientific and technological phenomenon. Its analysis of the social role of the mass media, of the democratization of the whole ensemble of cultural problems, is too limited and therefore partial, even if it does have its own merits. Its insufficient attention to the problems of bureaucracy has had catastrophic consequences in communist regimes, especially those of the Soviet type.

The Marxist distinction between infrastructure and superstructure is open to question. According to the theory, science belongs to the superstructure. But, by reason of its now decisive role in the economy, does it not become an essential element of the infrastructure, and even the most important, owing to its impact on technology in the advanced industrial society of today and the postindustrial society of tomorrow?

It remains nonetheless true that "the idea of understanding societies, and more especially modern industrial society, on the basis of its economic organization is an excellent method of analysis. The mistake of materialism is to apply this method in a dogmatic way."[70] An economist of the caliber of Jean Marchal could write that many of the contributions of Marx are "irreplaceable contributions that one day will have to be incorporated into science."[71] Let us acknowledge these contributions, but reject at the same time everything in Marxism that is one-sided—for example, its critique of capitalist society.

> Thus, without really contradicting each other humanism, liberalism, and Marxism have, in successive stages, contributed to our cultural heritage and shaped our ethic. Their obvious current failures, the complexity of the social critique that stems from them, the impossible project of explaining everything with one economic theory—all these do not oblige us to attribute all the evils of this world to one single cause—for example, capitalism. There were atrocities before it; there are today, apart from it, many more atrocities than the organization of the relationships of production alone is sufficient to explain.[72]

Our critique is therefore *a critique by* yes *and* no, *a dialectical critique.* Christians, in the prophetic tradition, moved by their faith both to an acceptance of all that is true and a rejection of all that is false, should be the first to understand and practice such a style of criticism.

This critique, as I conceive it, is perfectly in line with a famous paragraph of the encyclical *Pacem in Terris* (No. 159) on the distinction between false philosophical theories and the historical movements that grow out of them. John XXIII writes:

> It is, therefore, especially to the point to make a clear distinction between false philosophical teachings regarding the nature, origin, and destiny of the universe and of humankind, and movements that have a direct bearing either on economic and social questions, or cultural matters, or on the organization of the state, even if these movements owe their origin and inspiration to false tenets.

I have carefully distinguished the different levels and articulations of Marxist analysis, while emphasizing that the worldview that inspires it has a profound impact upon it. I have noted my opposition, on grounds of both reason and faith, to certain essential aspects of that philosophy. I shall return to them.

"Although the teaching," continues the pope, "once it has been clearly set forth, is no longer subject to change, the movements, precisely because they take place in the midst of changing conditions, are readily susceptible to change." I agree completely on the flexible quality of historical movements. It seems to me, on the other hand, that the teachings are not necessarily so immutable. Of course Marxism, taken as the original teaching of the founding fathers, has been fixed by their deaths. Of course it has deeply influenced the historical movement that came from it, and the most insightful of contemporary Marxist theoreticians strongly urge a return to the sources. And of course, too, Soviet Marxism-Leninism remains terribly frozen.

Nevertheless, derivative Marxist theories are far from being in agreement on all points even among officially "orthodox" Marxists. Divergences are still more pronounced if the positions of neo-Marxists of the "revisionist" school are taken into account. The history and the personality of each theoretician have their own impact on their work. And it can be expected that the future will see an even greater flexibility. It is therefore essential that we pay attention to all the signs of evolution.

"Besides," John XXIII concludes, "who can deny that those movements, insofar as they conform to the dictates of right reason and are interpreters of the lawful aspirations of the human person, contain elements that are positive and deserving of approval?" This is clearly my attitude as well, an attitude imposed by faith itself, which is so respectful of every sound achievement of reason.

The famous mandate of St. Paul was given for our general instruction: "Test everything; hold fast what is good, abstain from every form of evil" (1 Thess. 5:21–22). The criteria to which he himself had recourse were of the order of faith, centered on the supreme Reference Point. But he did not hesitate to make use also of criteria that were of the order of reason.

Post-Marxist Faith

My procedure up to now—that of avoiding an *a priori* rejection of Marxism and of agreeing wholeheartedly, though with a critical discernment, both with its contributions to the corpus of human truth and with its challenge— brings me back in line with Karl Barth's remark vis-à-vis Marxist criticism of the church and the Christian faith: "We shall not dismiss it merely by reproaching those in the East for their false belief. We are being asked about our own faith."[73]

We have seen it before and shall see it again: the faith has been radically questioned, both on the level of its effectiveness and its fundamental truth. We have been forced to respond to some ultimate questions in its regard. Will it survive or will it not survive? If it survives, will it not be forced to accept some profound changes? But if so, will it remain an authentically Christian faith?

Karl Barth follows the remark just quoted with some radical questions of his own:

Whence has the East derived its godlessness if not from the West, from our philosophy? Is its cold non-Christianity something so completely different from the wisdom that is allowed to swagger about even here in the West in every street and in every newspaper and (naturally, toned down a little) even in our churches to a very large extent?[74]

We dare not forget that Marxist metaphysical materialism and atheism depend essentially, directly or indirectly, notably by way of Feuerbach, on the materialist philosophers of the eighteenth century, who drew on the liberal ideology. The two important points—that Marxism sees its materialism and its atheism as dialectical, and that it situates them at the heart of its historical materialism—are not decisive here, whatever Marxists may say about it. There is no question that in our time metaphysical materialism and atheism are widespread throughout advanced industrial society and especially—though less so than in the nineteenth century—in the higher circles of philosophy and science. In any case *practical* materialism is even more widespread, as we have noted, even among those who intellectually believe in God and in Jesus Christ.

Both types of advanced industrial society that we are familiar with at the present time are profoundly marked by materialism and atheism. The basic difference on this point, and a very important one, is that they are imposed in one society as the official ideology and not in the other.

Karl Barth continues: "Whence does it draw its sustenance, this non-Christianity, if not from the offense that has been given to it by the fragility of Orthodox, of Roman, and of Protestant Christianity?"[75] Such a bald statement needs qualification: contemporary non-Christianity is not simply the result of the deficiencies of Christianity. It has many other causes, notably the dynamic peculiar to industrialization, urbanization, and various ideologies.

The Marxist analysis that emphasizes this cause and looks to it for the progressive death of Christianity is correct for what concerns the primary importance of this factor of non-Christianity (and not simply dechristianization). As for the deficiencies of the churches and individual Christians, they are not universal. The inconsistency of thought and will on the part of many, as well as their cowardice or lack of daring are, however, all too frequent.

What are we looking for? A faith without defects but turned in upon itself and therefore without missionary thrust? A faith looking only to its own security? A frightened faith? A faith bent by every wave of change? An incoherent faith? Its surrender perhaps or slow agony? Or, on the contrary, a faith that is open, audacious, coherent, lucid, and courageous? In a word, an adult faith? That was the fundamental dilemma of the faith in the Roman Empire of the first centuries, just as it is now in the terrible darkness of contemporary neo-paganism.

Post-Marxist faith—the title of a book by Father González Ruiz[76]—is the object of our present investigation. And our overall procedure leads us to this perspective.

In this area the most original and daring efforts seem to be those found in works on liberation theology and works by Christians for Socialism—especially, on the theoretical level, the writings of Gustavo Gutiérrez,[77] Hugo Assmann,[78] and Giulio Girardi.[79] For some of these efforts it would be more exact to say "belief in the wake of Marx," astonishing though that may seem at first sight when one thinks of the radical anti-Christianity of the founder of Marxism.

It is true that the modern theory of democracy and the doctrine of human rights were born in a climate of frank opposition to the official churches. Nonetheless, this origination, which could appear suspect in the eyes of the faith, did not prevent the churches—though only after a very long time— from recognizing their essential truth and even their profound agreement with Christianity. In my opinion the problem is different in the case of Marxism, for three reasons. First, because Marxism is tied to a name, to someone who claimed to have developed an integral and indivisible theory, whereas the theories of democracy and human rights are not bound directly to any name. Second, because the Marxist worldview marks profoundly, as we have already noted, both Marxist science and practice. Third, because, among the promoters of democracy and human rights some were openly Christian and their doctrine revealed an obvious Christian heritage. The comparison therefore is far from convincing. The possibilities of agreement between Christian faith and the more or less extensive use of Marxist analysis must be examined for their own sake.

Girardi's "Christian Faith and Historical Materialism"

I shall directly consider here only the current phase of Father Girardi's effort, most especially in his article, "Christian Faith and Historical Materialism,"[80] which I have chosen because it seems to me the most representative of his present line of inquiry.

His position is that of a Christian who has made a revolutionary option and is trying to analyze his faith scientifically. For him such an option in our day, if it is to be valid, can only be the Marxist option. And the only analysis that appears to him fully scientific is Marxist analysis. His objective is to confront in all its fullness and sharpness the problem of the relationship between revolutionary truth and Christian truth.

By reason of his fundamental Marxist option he adopts historical materialism as the grid upon which he analyzes the Christian fact. This leads him to propose the *essential theses* of what he calls a *materialist analysis of Christianity:*

1. *Christianity is a human fact.* It is human beings who have religious experiences, for which they say they find the ultimate cause in a suprahuman reality. We should study them with the following analytical rule: "Before we look for whatever is inexplicable, irreducible, or mysterious in such experiences, we must separate out whatever in them is explainable and reducible" (p. 267).

2. *Christianity is a historical phenomenon.* When you are concerned, as a Marxist, to uncover the historical substructure of ideologies, you will find, on the one hand, that "dominant Christianity tends to think of itself as a system of supratemporal truths" and, on the other, that the Christian reality

is profoundly affected by the different social systems in which it has existed (p. 267).

3. *Christianity is a class phenomenon.* From all the evidence it would be going too far to try to explain the entire history of the church in terms of class struggle. But an analysis in terms of class struggle will reveal that, since Constantine, that history has been marked by a continuing alliance with power (which, in a hostile society, is always that of the dominant class) and that "under different forms this alliance thereafter marks the entire thought and action of the church, and especially all interpretation of the Bible, which henceforth will be read in such a way as not to question power but to justify it" (p. 268). For this reason the church today is strongly influenced by bourgeois culture, and the different movements for church renewal from the Reformation to Vatican II pursue before all else the requirements of adaptation to a society of the liberal type.

4. *Christianity is a structural phenomenon.* If the theory of ideologies is applied to Christianity, it will appear as "a superstructure"—that is, a phenomenon whose "derivation and foundation, whose explanation and meaning, reside elsewhere: in the economic substructure and the struggles that tear it apart, and in the collective unconscious" (p. 270).

Such an analysis of Christianity raises serious problems. Girardi locates them in two areas:

1. *Contradictions between historical materialism and Christianity.* From the Marxist viewpoint one will raise basic questions on commitment to the church, on its mission of truth, on its holiness, on its unity, on the presence of God in its midst, on its future. The questions are posed bluntly: "What is from now on the sense of this commitment and this fidelity to a community that one must regard as a political enemy? . . . Finally, what is the future of a religion that is part of the illusions of a particular epoch?" (p. 273).

2. *The "cleavage" between historical materialism and Christianity.* Apparently, Girardi notes, between Christianity and revolutionary commitment there lies an unbridgeable abyss. To wish to be at the same time Marxist and Christian involves "the inner rending of the human personality" (p. 279).

> In the course of this experience many Christians reach the conclusion that they must choose between Christian truth and revolutionary truth. But a growing number of Christians refuse to choose. They are determined to pursue revolutionary truth to the very end, and they believe that they encounter there, in unsuspected ways, the most profound demands of Christian truth [p. 280].

This is precisely the position of Marxist Christians and of Girardi himself. (But note that Girardi does not say "Marxist and Christian"; he says "revolutionary and Christian." I want to call attention to the content of the word that he prefers to use.)

A solution must be found. Girardi formulates his solution in five theses, on which he comments at some length.

1. *Historical materialism represents, in relation to ideological and utopian thought, an epistemological and analytical scission, but this scission finds its true meaning only in relation to the revolutionary scission.* The argument is therefore first of all revolutionary. It is a question, we are told, of placing oneself "in the position of the proletariat, and in a general way, of the popular classes struggling for their liberation and for the transformation of society" (p. 283).

2. *The revolutionary character of the science of history compels that science to establish a dialectical relationship with a renewed ideological and utopian thought.* "In this way militants have the feeling of making a more profound decision for the poor by joining the class struggle; they choose to be more deeply faithful to the demands of love by seeking those scientific and political instruments that will provide them with historical impact; they will choose freedom by fighting to create the economic and political conditions *for* freedom" (p. 286).

3. *Christian revolutionary discourse follows from a dialectical relationship between the religious and the profane, in which the dominant role belongs to the profane, and in the last analysis to the economic; it therefore becomes a question of a Christian "materialist" discourse* (p. 288). Let us note immediately that this is the crux of the theory elaborated by Girardi; from the objective viewpoint of the faith, it also makes it the most questionable.

Christianity has now been subordinated to the Marxist interpretation by way of historical materialism. Does it not therefore become an ideology no different from the others? Does it not exclude completely the intervention of God in its foundation? Taken to their logical conclusions, many of the author's statements would lead in this direction, which cannot be what he intends, because he is sincerely Christian. The reinterpretation of Christianity that they involve destroys its objective meaning. It is a "modernism" or a "Bultmannism" of a new kind.

Far from showing us an agreement between them, Girardi has only rendered more acute the cleavage between the Marxist worldview and the essence of Christian faith. The objective result thus goes counter to his intentions. But let us return to the presentation of this thought.

4. *Historical materialism transforms and radicalizes the critique of Christianity, while still permitting one to accept the critical demands of the prophetic tradition* (p. 299). In the paragraph bearing this title, Girardi develops some observations that are very penetrating; authentic Christian thought is clearly evident. For example, "This confidence in the church, despite the contradictions of its witness, reveals the test to which the faith of the militant is constantly subjected" (p. 302). How could anyone disagree? But are we not by the very statement at the very opposite pole from historical materialism?

5. *Reflection on the basis of historical materialism can become a major locus for Christian creativity* (p. 302). This major locus of Christian creativity, upon which will be developed a kind of theology that is qualitatively different, according to Girardi, is "the fertilization that occurs between Christian truth and revolutionary truth" (p. 305), arising from the fact that the thinker is at the same time both Marxist and Christian. He asks us to distinguish carefully between "a theology that dialogues with Marxism and a theology that incorporates it" (p. 306). The difference is, in fact, radical. But I must ask if theology can really incorporate Marxism without destroying it. Or will it not rather be Marxism that destroys theology, at least for someone who wants to explain Christianity in the final analysis by economics?

This long article merits an exhaustive study, individuating and examining all its statements. It is quite impossible to accept or reject them purely and simply, by reason of the nearly continuous interweaving of the true and the false that the critic is compelled to disentangle. On the other hand, Girardi's inquiry is unquestionably original and provocative, even if we are inclined to diagnose contradiction at the very point he claims to find coherence. My response to it is the problematic that I am developing throughout this book.

I do not fault Girardi for applying Marxist analysis to the study of the Christian reality, but rather for granting to that analysis a kind of exclusive right of domain, exempt from all criticism. I fault him, in his theory and not his intention, for stripping from the word of God its status as the absolute reference point. In his text it is reason, as it functions in Marxist analysis, that has the last word; faith takes second place. How can it still be the true faith? I do not question the "subjective" faith lived by the author but rather its objective formulation. His mistake is not in wanting to be revolutionary and in trying to elaborate a theology based on revolutionary praxis, but rather, for lack of the critical spirit, in conceding to historical materialism and other fundamental concepts of Marxism more truth than they in fact contain.

"Post-Christian"?

My inquiry therefore will not center on Girardi's concept of post-Marxist faith, though I want to remain open to every element of truth in Marxism. Before defining post-Marxist faith, I want to point out that it would be inaccurate to say purely and simply that it is *post-Christian*. It *would* certainly be that if we looked only at the European sociological Christianity of the nineteenth century—at least that of the bourgeoisie and the petty bourgeoisie— which Marx critiques so sharply for its meanness, its hypocrisy, its narrowness of mind and heart. But it is in no way post-Christian if we are speaking of an authentically gospel Christianity. Marx never encountered it in living Christian communities or could not see it, blinded as he was by his philosophical prejudices, which not only belittled the faith but denied *a priori* any intervention by God in history.

I shall have occasion to note that the explanations of the birth and development of the religious phenomenon—especially of Christianity—that historical materialism has offered are singularly simplistic and inadequate in relation to the reality that they propose to analyze. Marxism—like Maurrasism—by reason of its exclusive polarization on social structures, has proven incapable of understanding the profound realities of religious experience, even when it has given some attention to them. The most significant example of this myopia is doubtless that of Gramsci, some of whose observations on popular Catholicism are nevertheless very interesting, as one may learn from reading his "Notes on Machiavelli."[81]

Marxism could be said to be post-Christian only if it has assimilated and assumed Christianity, even if it then rejected it dialectically, somewhat as, according to its theory, socialism would arise from the ashes of capitalism. However, it was born and developed on another terrain.

In the light of these remarks a *post-Marxist faith* is a faith that is no stranger to Marxism but, on the contrary, welcomes its challenge and resists it vigorously, is even revitalized by it and rendered more ready for its mission of accepting the historical realities of our time, of witnessing here and now to Jesus Christ, and thus cooperating in the conversion of the world. In this way Marxism is accepted and assumed with all its truth deliberately recognized, but its errors and its limitations also perceived and analyzed. It does not escape its own critique.

Faith that has been personalized must find its own way. It is renewed in its internal dynamic and in the dynamic that drives it outward toward evangelization. It becomes, through the free responsibility of Christians, constructive, dedicated to the creation of a dynamic program that will transform the world in the light of the gospel: not simply an auxiliary for the construction of socialism or an advanced liberal society, but an *independent and original dynamic.*

Such a faith is not self-propelled. It will never know the warm security of the ghetto. It may have to face the test of doubt, or at least of all kinds of misunderstanding and opposition, as well as the torments and uncertainties of action. But in what epoch of history has an open and missionary faith ever been easy?

Our inquiry, which takes Marxism seriously, leads us deliberately to see in it a *stimulating challenge to our faith.* This is a positive consequence of what Berdyaev was referring to when he wrote: "Communism ought to have a special significance for Christians, for it is a reminder and denouncement of an unfulfilled duty, of the fact that the Christian ideal has not been achieved."[82]

By the radical negation of which it is the object, faith is stimulated to rethink itself in depth, to prove its own validity, and to redefine with precision what constitutes its own essence. By the accusations that indict Christians—often justly—because of the contradiction between the ideal that they profess and their behavior, it is stimulated to refashion itself as a movement of thought and daily action, as theory and practice, both being indispensable

to its authenticity. By those other accusations that reproach it for its historical ineffectiveness—also richly deserved—it is stimulated to discover better,
to formulate better, and to realize better the impact it must have on human
reality—*must* have, because the gospel indisputably aims at the transformation of human relations by a conversion of hearts.

At this level of historical impact—where faith discovers, both for its own
sake and as a goad to return to its own origins, the formidable challenge to
transform the world (contained in Thesis 11 on Feuerbach)—it will stand
revealed, as we shall see below, as the giver of ultimate meaning to history,
the messenger of essential hope, the herald of human dignity in its fullness. It
will give prophetic witness to love—if we humanize it—as the most indispensable force of history. It will be welcomed as the harbinger of the light and of
the sovereign energy of the Holy Spirit. *This* is the gift of New Testament
faith, understood correctly as personal commitment, as responsible and creative thought and action in the warp and woof of our time.

Understood and lived in this way, faith is courageous, daring, confident,
and creative, convinced of its validity and its real potential. The person who
lives it does not hesitate to identify with the confident assertion of St. Paul:
"I am not ashamed of the gospel: it is the power of God for salvation to
everyone who has faith" (Rom. 1:16). As Karl Barth put it so well: "Believers
discover in the message of salvation the power of God for deliverance, the
first rays of eternal salvation, and the courage to take their place as sentinels."[83]

NOTES

1. Helmut Gollwitzer, *The Christian Faith and the Marxist Criticism of Religion*,
trans. David Cairns (New York: Scribner's, 1970), p. 6.

2. *Christian Faith,* p. 7.

3. Preface to *Beyond Good and Evil* (1885), trans. Marianne Cowen (Chicago:
Regnery, 1949), p. 2.

4. *La cuisinière et le mangeur d'hommes* (Paris: Seuil, 1975), p. 175.

5. Interview in *La Croix* (November 19, 1970). It will be noted, as reflected in a
quotation cited earlier (p. 20), that he repeated this unyielding statement in his *Appel des
communistes aux chrétiens de France* of June 10, 1976.

6. M.A. Leonov, *Précis de matérialisme dialectique* (1948), quoted by Gustave
Wetter, *Le matérialisme dialectique* (Paris-Bruges: DDB, 1962), p. 283.

7. *For Marx*, trans. Ben Brewster (London: Penguin, 1969), pp. 30-31.

8. *Reading Capital*, trans. Ben Brewster (London: NLB, 1970), p. 32.

9. *Il materialismo storico e la filosofia di Benedetto Croce* (Turin: Einaudi, 1972),
p. 75.

10. *The Problem of Method*, trans. Hazel Barnes (London: Methuen, 1963), p.
xxxiv.

11. *Problem of Method*, p. 29.

12. Quoted by Gustave Wetter, *Le matérialisme dialectique*, p. 389.

13. *For Marx*, p. 227.

14. Moscow: Foreign Languages Publishing House, 1954, p. 32.

15. *Dialectics of Nature*, p. 49.

16. *Dialectics of Nature*, p. 54.

17. *Dialectics of Nature*, p. 267.

18. *Dialectics of Nature*, p. 54.

19. *The Attitude of the Workers' Party to Religion*, in V.I. Lenin, *Collected Works*, Vol. 15 (London: Lawrence Wishart, 1963), p. 402.

20. Cf. trans. by Joseph W. Evans (New York: Scribner's, 1968), pp. 36-37.

21. *The Church between East and West*, trans. Stanley Godman, in Karl Barth, *Against the Stream* (London: SCM, 1954), p. 140.

22. *The Christian Faith*, p. 5.

23. *La doctrine économique et sociale de Karl Marx* (Paris: Seuil, 1950), p. 35.

24. Trans. R. M. French (London: Bles, 1948), p. 118.

25. Joseph Folliet, "L'expérience de l'absolu," in *La Croix* (November 9, 1972).

26. *For Marx*, p. 166.

27. *For Marx*, p. 167.

28. *For Marx*, p. 168.

29. Letter of August 23, 1866: quoted by Etienne Balibar, *Cinq études du matérialisme historique* (Paris: Maspero, 1974), p. 28; English trans. in Karl Marx, *On the First International*, ed. Saul K. Padover (New York: McGraw-Hill, 1973), p. 420.

30. *On the Correct Handling of Contradictions among the People* (February 27, 1957), quoted in *Mao Tsé-Toung* (collective work) (Paris: L'Herne, 1972), p. 112; English trans. in *Selected Works of Mao Tse-tung*, Vol. 5 (Peking: Foreign Languages Press, 1977), pp. 384-421.

31. *For Marx*, p. 169.

32. In *Marx-Engels Reader*, 2nd ed. (New York: Norton, 1978), p. 489.

33. Cf. *The German Ideology*, in *Collected Works*, Vol. 5 (New York: International Publishers, 1976), p. 3.

34. *Where Do Correct Ideas Come From?*, quoted by C. Cochini, "La pensée de Mao Tsé-toung," in the collective work *Mao Tsé-toung* (Paris: L'Herne, 1972), p. 129; English trans. in *Selected Readings from the Works of Mao Tse-tung* (Peking: Foreign Languages Press, 1967), pp. 405-6.

35. Thesis 11 on Feuerbach: *The German Ideology*, p. 5.

36. Cf. *Introduction to Christianity*, trans. J. R. Foster (New York: Seabury, 1979), p. 36.

37. *Il materialismo storico e la filosofia di Benedetto Croce*, p. xvii.

38. *La costruzione del partito communista (1923-1926)* (Turin: Einaudi, 1971), p. 13.

39. Quoted by Gustave Wetter, *Le matérialisme dialectique*, p. 547.

40. Quoted by André Glucksmann, *La cuisinière et le mangeur d'hommes*, p. 169.

41. *The Holy Family*, quoted by Maximilien Rubel, *Karl Marx. Essai de biographie intellectuelle* (Paris: Rivière, 1971), p. 141; cf. trans. in *The Holy Family or Critique of Critical Critique* (Moscow: Foreign Languages Publishing House, 1956), pp. 107-8.

42. *Ce que je crois* (Paris: Grasset, 1975), p. 95.

43. *Ce que je crois*, p. 99.

44. *La cuisinière et le mangeur d'hommes*, p. 100.

45. *La cuisinière*, p. 64.

46. *La cuisinière*, p. 68.

47. See my *Théologie de la liberté religieuse* (Gembloux: Duculot, 1969), p. 471.

48. English trans. by Anthony Mottola (Garden City, N.Y.: Doubleday-Image, 1964), pp. 140-41.

49. Ratzinger, *Introduction to Christianity*, p. 64.

50. *De virginibus velandis*, I, 1, in *Corpus christianorum*, Vol. 2, p. 1209, quoted by Ratzinger, *Introduction to Christianity*, p. 97.

51. *The Russian Revolution*, trans. Donald Atwater (London: Sheed and Ward, 1931), p. 54.

52. *The Russian Revolution*, p. 54.

53. *The Russian Revolution*, p. 81.

54. *The Russian Revolution*, p. 83.

55. *Ce que je crois*, p. 312. This author develops his thesis extensively in his earlier work *Qui est aliéné?* (Paris: Flammarion, 1970).

56. *Christianisme, Marxisme* (Paris: Centurion, 1975), p. 41.

57. *Human, All-Too-Human*, Part I, No. 473, quoted by Glucksmann, *La cuisinière et le mangeur d'hommes*, pp. 93-94; English trans. by Helen Zimmern (London: Allen and Unwin, 1909), p. 343.

58. *Christianisme et réalité sociale* (Paris: Ed. "Je sers," 1934), p. 8.

59. *The Church between East and West,* pp. 139-40.

60. *Lénine et la philosophie* (Paris: Maspero, 1969), pp. 22-26.

61. 1885 Preface to Book II of *Capital*, in Karl Marx, *Capital* (Chicago: Charles H. Kerr, 1925), p. 8.

62. Quoted by Saul Karsz, *Théorie et politique: Louis Althusser* (Paris: Fayard, 1974), p. 315.

63. *For Marx*, p. 201.

64. *Qui est aliéné?*, p. 42.

65. Quoted by Y. Moretic, *José Carlos Mariátegui* (Santiago: Ediciones de la Universidad técnica del Estado, 1970), p. 103.

66. "Marxisme et messianisme," in *Nova et vetera* 49 (1974), p. 55.

67. Television program *Le peuple de la nuit* (April 29, 1975).

68. Quoted by Moretic, *José Carlos Mariátegui*, p. 115.

69. *Hope in Time of Abandonment*, trans. C. Edward Hopkin (New York: Seabury, 1973), p. 52.

70. Henri Niel, *Karl Marx* (Paris: DDB, 1971), p. 169.

71. Preface to first edition of Pierre Bigo, *Marxisme et humanisme*, 3rd ed. (Paris: PUF, 1961), p. vii.

72. Jacques Attali and Marc Guillaume, *L'anti-économique* (Paris: PUF, 1974), p. 227.

73. *The Church between East and West*, p. 141.

74. *The Church between East and West*, p. 141.

75. *The Church between East and West*, p. 141.

76. *Croire après Marx* (Paris: Cerf, 1971).

77. *A Theology of Liberation*, trans. Caridad Inda and John Eagleson (Maryknoll, N.Y.: Orbis, 1973).

78. *A Theology for a Nomad Church*, trans. Paul Burns (Maryknoll, N.Y.: Orbis, 1976).

79. The most important publications of Giulio Girardi in the present phase of his work are: *La nuova scelta fondamentale dei cristiani* and *I cristiani di oggi di fronte al marxismo*, in Convegno Nazionale Bologna (September 1973), *Cristiani per il so-*

ialismo (Milan-Rome: Sapere edizioni, 1974), pp. 154-201 and 202-37; "Foi chrétienne et matérialisme historique," in *Parole et société* (1974), pp. 263-306; "Vers de nouveaux rapports entre marxisme et christianisme," in *Lumière et vie*, No. 117/118 (April-August 1974), pp. 156-86; "Vérité et libération," in *Etudes théologiques et religieuses* (1974), pp. 271-97; *Chrétiens pour le socialisme* (Paris: Cerf, 1976).

80. In *Parole et société* (1974), pp. 263-306.

81. *Note sul Machiavelli, sulla politia e sullo Stato moderno* (Turin: Einaudi, 1966).

82. *The Russian Revolution*, p. 54.

83. *L'Epître aux Romains* (Geneva: Labor et Fides, 1972), p. 45.

Chapter 3

World History and the Coming of the Kingdom of God

Marx was still very young when he decided on his life's work, even though it took some time to work out its final formulation. This is how he expressed it in 1844, in his *Contribution to the Critique of Hegel's Philosophy of Right*:

> It is the task of history . . . once the other-world of truth has vanished, to establish the truth of this world. It is above all the task of philosophy, which is in the service of history, to unmask human self-alienation in its secular forms, once its sacred form has been unmasked. Thus, the critique of heaven is transformed into the critique of the earth, the critique of religion into the critique of law, the critique of theology into the critique of politics.[1]

It was therefore to the elaboration of a *science of history* that the young thinker wanted to make his contribution, although the form of his ambition then took on a highly philosophical coloration. In that respect he was very much of his own time. The science of history was then in full flower; it fascinated the most brilliant minds.

Marx's contribution would reveal a powerful originality. Of that he was perfectly aware, perhaps to an extreme: the founders of Marxism would claim nothing less than the delivery of the ultimate explanation of the unfolding of history in its entirety. I shall examine this claim in the section of this chapter entitled "*The* Explanation or *An* Explanation?" (p. 65).

Let us note immediately: the originality of the Marxist contribution to the science of history is not purely scientific. In fact, Marx's contribution was not simply in coming to a better *understanding* of reality. In that, however, he did distinguish himself from most of the intellectuals of his time. What he ultimately envisioned was the founding of *a revolutionary science*, capable of becoming the driving force of a social critique of capitalist society and of the development of a new, radically different, social practice. Drawing inspiration from a number of unrealistic social utopias, he was to propose a utopia that was powerful in its ability to mobilize energy and on behalf of which he tried, all his life, to show that it was entirely realistic. I shall examine this effort in the section of this chapter entitled "The Utopia of the Classless Society and the Absolute Future of the Kingdom of God" (p. 86).

The author of this revolutionary science is radically opposed to all transcendence. That is why he ferociously rejects all religion—Christianity, above all—but also because he sees in it an incorrigible conservatism. That is, evidently, a philosophical position. The more mature Marx will claim to have given up philosophy. In fact the philosophical approach will remain constantly entwined at the very heart of his scientific work. I shall therefore devote a section of this chapter to the problem of the religious positions of Marxism: "Opium or Dynamite?" (p. 74).

The Explanation or *An* Explanation?

If there is one claim of Marxism's founders that their disciples recognize it is surely the claim that, by their new conception of history, they succeeded in throwing light on its entire course and even in providing a single explanation of it: *the* explanation—historical materialism. Althusser writes: "It is because Marx's theory is true that it has been possible to apply it with success; it is not because it has been applied with success that it is true."[2]

(This is almost the language of religious believers, let us note in passing. Marxists frequently express themselves in religious language. How could it be otherwise, given the depth that Marxism reaches?)

In *For Marx*, Althusser's formulation, admittedly, is more sober; he speaks simply of "the Marxist science of the development of social formations (historical materialism)."[3] In Soviet usage, this term includes all the sciences of society, encompassing at once ethics, aesthetics, the philosophy of history and of law.

To understand exactly what is involved, we must return to the founding fathers. Agreement is fairly general on their basic texts. I shall give special attention to the one that is almost unanimously regarded as the most important: the two famous pages from the *Contribution to the Critique of Political Economy*, which one might describe as a *synthetic exposition of Marxist analysis by Marx himself*. Inasmuch as the first four sentences are by far the most important, I quote them in their entirety:

> In the social production of their existence, persons inevitably enter into definite relationships, which are independent of their will—namely, relationships of production appropriate to a given stage in the development of their material forces of production. The totality of these relationships of production constitutes the economic structure of society, the real foundation, on which arises a legal and political superstructure and to which correspond definite forms of social consciousness. The mode of production of material life conditions the general process of social, political, and intellectual life. It is not the consciousness of per-

sons that determines their existence, but their social existence that determines their consciousness.[4]

This is a dynamic conception of social life and of history. "Persons" are put forward as the producers of their own history. Persons? That is not quite accurate, according to the most precise thought of Marx. For him, more accurately, it is through their social relationships that they make history, through their existence as masses, the structures that they conceal, their antagonistic structural relationships. It is not the human person that is under consideration here, it is society: more precisely still, a specific concrete society, with all its contradictions.

It is, in fact, "social production" that Marx is writing about here. The theoretical goal of Marxist analysis is to explain the origin of social existence and its evolution. (Let us never forget that his practical goal is revolutionary.) It is a question of finding, if possible, the main thread—or axis—of this evolution. Marx believed that he discovered it in the "production of material life" understood in its broadest meaning: economic production at every stage of history. He frequently repeats in his writings: we must keep our feet on the ground; without material existence—without food, clothing, shelter, and, at our stage of industrial society, without machines—human existence is impossible.

As Engels was to write a little later, "The materialist conception of history starts from the proposition that production, and, next to production, the exchange of things produced, is the basis of all social structure."[5] In proclaiming itself so insistently materialist the Marxist conception of history, in the style of a confession of faith, means to insist that human history is rooted entirely in matter and that it remains permanently bound to it in an impenetrable dependence, even through all the spiritual phenomena that germinate from it. Later they will call this conception *historical materialism*. Here is a first approximation of its meaning: *an attempt to explain all historical evolution by the economic factor.*

This is, I emphasize, only a first approximation. Marx will give more precision to his thought by way of a whole rigorous *conceptual edifice*, at least in appearance. Thus we have structure and superstructures, forces of production and relationships of production, mode of production and social formation.

Structure, as he explains it, is an elliptical form whose conceptual meaning is "the economic structure of society" seen as "the real foundation" of the entire edifice; as I said just above, economic life in its totality. It is often called "the infrastructure." We could as easily speak of "basic structure."

The *superstructures* include the whole juridical, political, and ideological edifice, or culture in the broadest sense of the term: philosophy, religions, and so forth. Althusser notes that "except in his *Early Works . . . Marx never included scientific knowledge in it.*"[6]

The *forces of production* comprise the agents of production, their work tools or machines, and the work itself that they perform. The *relationships of production* are the relationships that the agents of production have with each other, notably under the aspect of command and execution. The structure, or economic life, is the dialectic that goes on between the forces of production and the relationships of production. The *mode of production*, on the other hand, is the abstract logic of a system—for example, that of the capitalist system, founded on the absolute power of those who possess industrial and financial capital, with its obvious repercussions on the political and ideological plane.

As for *social formation*, it is a concept signifying the concrete, and complex, reality of a specific historical society in which several abstract modes of production interact, together with all their peculiarities and the multiple causes of those peculiarities. Examples of such societies would be England at the time of Marx or France in the second third of the twentieth century.

The major theoretical problem of Marxist analysis is to determine the ways in which the basic structure influences the superstructures, or economic life influences the other aspects of social life. Only a narrow mind would be tempted to try to explain everything, for example, on the basis of the water mill, the steam engine, or computers. Despite their eagerness to find a single explanation, the founders of Marxism were very careful not to fall into such a simplistic approach.

Of the two it is Engels who was the better able to nuance their common thought on this subject, notably in his letter of January 25, 1894, to Hans Starkenburg:

> We regard economic conditions as the factor that ultimately determines historical development. . . . Here, however, two points must not be overlooked: political, juridical, philosophical, religious, literary, artistic, and other development is based on economic development. But all these react upon one another and also upon the economic base. It is not that the economic position is the *cause and alone active*, everything else being a passive effect. There is, rather, interaction on the basis of economic necessity, which ultimately always asserts itself. . . . So it is not . . . that the economic position produces an automatic effect. Persons make their history themselves, but only in given surroundings that condition it and on the basis of actual relationships already existing. Among these relationships, the economic—however much they may be influenced by political and ideological relationships—are still ultimately the decisive ones, forming the clue line that runs through them and alone leads to understanding.[7]

We can readily acknowledge that the introduction of this concept of *ultimate determination*, as well as the explanation of the reciprocal play of the superstructures, provide a real flexibility to Marxist analysis. But does it not, we might object, considerably blunt the point, or, to put it another way, does it not still grant too much to the economic factor?

Let us say then, by way of a second approximation, that historical materialism is the *socio-economic theory of history*—that is, the theory that the technico-economic factor determines in the last analysis the evolution of societies and of all humanity.

Let me emphasize again that the best Marxist analysis tries to avoid simplistic interpretations of this theory, as indicated by the following, most welcome remarks of Althusser:

> The economic dialectic is never active *in the pure state*; in History, these instances—the superstructures, and the like—are never seen to step respectfully aside when their work is done or evanesce as pure phenomena, to make way for his majesty Economy as he strides along the royal road of Dialectic, when the Time comes. From the first moment to the last, the lonely hour of the "last instance" never comes.[8]

I shall soon discuss this theory in its entirety. At this point let us acknowledge that it is powerful and impressive in its attempt to give a single explanation of the totality of historical evolution. There is no shortage of arguments in its favor, especially in a society of the industrial type where the technico-economic factor is clearly of primary importance.

Let us also acknowledge that the perspective it opens up constitutes a radical change in regard to earlier questions. According to this view it is no longer politics that holds the center of the stage, nor is it war, nor culture, nor religion, but the economy—that is, the production of goods and services by the work of men and women. Without a doubt it teaches us *to read history in a different way* and to discover there forces and influences beneath the surface to which we had formerly given too little attention.

Christian and Marxist Deficiencies

I shall at once go even further in accepting the Marxist conception of history and acknowledge that it contains an *important element of truth*. Let us take industrial society as an example, the one precisely that early Marxism analyzed first of all, at least in its original phase. It is obvious to all that the geographic and human landscape was radically changed by the technological inventions that succeeded one another since the end of the eighteenth century: the steam engine, loom, railroad, electricity, and so forth. The conditions and methods of work for most of the population were completely transformed and enormous urban concentrations were the result.

In the same way modes of thought and culture were affected by the changes in the economic apparatus. New social relationships emerged together with tensions that were often extreme between the two major axes: the holders of industrial and financial capital on the one hand and those who performed only the labor of execution on the other—the bourgeoisie and the working class. A complete reorientation of history resulted in which technology, social conflicts, and changes in ways of thinking continued to interact with cultural modifications and the events that they brought with them.

We could make similar statements about more distant epochs or other kinds of society still in existence, although the observation might be less obvious. Thus the characteristics of an agrarian economy with weak technology might explain by and large the economic modalities of medieval Europe, but there are other historical elements, in themselves foreign to the economy, that explain feudal institutions.

However that may be, it is with good reason that the interpretation of history in terms of technology and the dialectic of forces of production with relationships of production has won acceptance in the science of history, though not exclusively. Earlier interpretations that were centered on the action of great leaders, wars, the evolution of ideas, religious and artistic phenomena, were clearly inadequate. They overlooked essential causalities. This decisive change in historical method seems to be largely due to the influence of Marxist analysis.

From the viewpoint of Christian faith, let us acknowledge the all too frequent deficiency of Christian communities and theologians in the analysis of historical reality. Taken altogether, the churches in nineteenth-century Europe were not aware of the extent of the change in society resulting from industrialization, because they were too exclusively bound to the old rural aristocracy, the petty bourgeoisie of the liberal professions, and the peasantry. The industrial and financial bourgeoisie (the new leading and dominating class) as well as the working class (the new dominated class) were born and developed outside their influence and without contact with them, except for some isolated exceptions.

The churches recognized often enough, for example, the misery of workers but did not know how to distinguish its true causes: the insufficiency of wages in relation to productivity, the general harshness of working conditions, the excessive length of the workday, the terrible timidity of social legislation, and especially the unbridled monopolization of economic power by the holders of capital. Church representatives talked about charity—most often only in terms of almsgiving—when they should have been talking about justice.

Theology defended the dominant conception of ownership with as much fervor as did the ideologues of the bourgeoisie. If it balked at other human rights, it had only tenderness for the right of ownership. "Ownership, because everyone disposes only of what is their own." The quotation is of course from *Capital*.[9] But what theologian had read that work when it first appeared? Irony aside, if *Capital* was quoted in any theological work of that period, it was doubtless in a tract on ownership.

There was no bad will involved. Nor was there any conscious collusion with the upper classes of society. It was quite simply ignorance of reality, because theologians did not understand that a serious theology—and therefore a meaningful statement from the church—concerning political, economic, and social questions, required a serious study of the corresponding human sciences. And by reason of this ignorance they were not aware that consciously or unconsciously they were victims of the prejudices of the ruling classes and were promoting under the guise of faith what was an ideology of class.

The theology of the incarnation was confined to the mystery of the incarnate word. Theologians did not see that the divine example called for an "incarnation" of the churches and of Christians, in terms of a profound opening to the world, sharing in fellowship the hopes and sufferings of the poor and exploited, and struggling for a more just society.

All too often, moreover, the concept of "the world" was interpreted only in a negative sense, as the empire of evil. Preachers condemned it vehemently from the lofty eminence of the pulpit. They forgot that they had a mission to cooperate in its salvation.

Even an encyclical as innovative as *Rerum Novarum* in the area of the social teaching of the church, despite its great merits and the scandal that it caused in conservative circles, remained rather timid in its analyses. How much more vigorous its diagnosis would have been if it had been drafted by someone who, in all critical independence, knew how to assimilate the Marxist method!

On the other hand, although historical materialism contains an important and indisputable element of truth, it also calls for critique. Economic life is more influenced by cultural factors than even an Althusser is willing to admit. Even when it operates on matter, human work is first of all thought and decision. Manual skill itself is the product of an entire human being—mind and body—and not simply that of a biological organism. Did not Marx himself strongly emphasize that it is the intervention of psychogenetic factors that makes the radical difference between human work and even the most intelligent of animal activities? He explains:

> What distinguishes the worst of architects from the best of bees is this, that architects raise their structures in imagination before they erect them in reality. At the end of every labor process, we get a result that already existed in the imagination of the laborer at its commencement. Laborers not only effect a change of form in the material on which they work; they also realize a purpose of their own that gives the law to their *modus operandi*, and to which they must subordinate their wills.[10]

Therefore, inasmuch as the psychogenetic element is decisive for the purpose of distinguishing human work, which is at the base of economic production, is it not contradictory to propose the concept of materialism to define it? All the more so because the most modern production has been more and more transformed by technology and science—that is, by work at the highest intellectual level?

Furthermore, even if the dialectic of the forces of production—as against the relationships of production—plays a leading role, it is itself more a cultural reality than a material process. "Superstructures" and "infrastructures" are therefore equally important as driving forces of historical evolution. It is impossible and inaccurate to separate them as does Marxist analysis. It is their unceasing dialectic that constitutes the real basis, the real evolution of history. The spatial imagery to which Marxism resorts dangerously falsifies the truth.

Such is the line of argument that Milovan Djilas develops in his remarkable critique of the famous Marxist synthesis.[11] He notes with reason:

> History is in essence a group action performed by nations with their lives at stake, and by thinkers who discover the inevitabilities, and by leaders who display clear practicable ideas and organizational abilities. The making of history is a creative act in which it is impossible to isolate, and still less to evaluate, the roles of its various factors. In any case, Marx and Marxism are the best testimony to the tremendous, unambiguous, and occasionally decisive roles played by ideas in history.[12]

The attempt to interpret the religion of the Old Testament and the Christian gospel in terms of economic production and the class struggle is certainly a point of the highest importance—on which the Marxist explanation particularly comes to grief. The pseudo scientific efforts in this vein that continue to this day would be laughable, were it not for the fact that they lead unwary readers into error.

It is legitimate and enlightening to point out that economic life and social conflicts did play a role in the history of ancient Israel, in the turmoil stirred up by the public ministry of Jesus Christ and in the heart of the apostolic church. From this point of view Marxist analysis is useful. But to look there for the *ultimate explanation* of the phenomenon under analysis is something that an objectively scientific approach cannot accept. The birth of monotheism, the essential components of prophetic faith and of the message of Jesus Christ, as well as those of the faith of the apostolic church—how can one claim to explain them by historical materialism without forcing history into a procrustean bed?

The Marxist conception of history is therefore not only a scientific process. It is that, true, but it is also a *philosophical extrapolation*. It is at once science of history and philosophy of history, and the philosophical element radically permeates the scientific element. Berdyaev describes it as "an economic metaphysics" or, more precisely, "an ontology."[13] It is science to the extent that it strives rigorously to discover the influence of economic production and social conflicts on the evolution of history. It is philosophy to the extent that it claims to explain under this rubric the totality of history. And to that extent scientific rigor compels us to reject it. From the rational point of view we must recognize in it *an* explanation of great importance (operating alongside others) but we must reject its pretension to be *the* explanation.

God in Human History

The *critique in the name of faith* presupposes the rational critique that I have just sketched. From its own point of view it will reinforce that critique by its conviction of the *intervention of God in history*, as creator and as actor in the drama of salvation. We cannot interpret historical evolution exclusively with rational keys. The word of God provides us with others that unlock unsuspected profundities.

Berdyaev said it magnificently:

History must not be understood as a purely human or a purely divine achievement, but rather as a reality to which both God and man contribute at the same time. Humanity partakes in the human nature of Christ. That is the fundamental insight of the Russian Christian mind of the nineteenth and twentieth century. It is the starting point of its understanding in history. The latter must be understood, not as an event apart, a symbolic, sacred event, but in its real divine-human process, in the tragic cooperation of God and man, cooperation whose force and intensity lead to the actual transformation of existence.[14]

History seen by faith is, finally, the history of an *alliance*—and ultimately of a *conflict* (recall Jacob's wrestling with the angel)—*between two fundamental partners: God and humanity*. God is clearly the master of history, but does not tyranically crush humankind. Humanity is also an actor in the historical drama, and completely so. The biblical God wants the human person to be free and responsible. Otherwise the entire theology of the covenant, as well as that of grace and sin, and that of the freedom of faith, would make no sense. Faith's critique will thus show forth the extraordinary value placed on human freedom by the word of God, one of whose summits is surely, as Olivier Clément notes, "the *fiat* of the Mother of God, which alone made possible the incarnation of the Word."[15] He rightly adds, from the divine-human point of view, "That is why the secret masters of history, though unaware of it, are those given to genuine prayer."[16]

The reformulation of the faith will thus be a *reformulation of the theology of history*, at once humble, audacious, and rigorous. *Humble*, because the action of God is its own secret. We know it only if God really wishes to reveal it to us. Often we can only guess at it. *Audacious*, because the theology of history throws light on the science and philosophy of history without distorting in any way their free action. *Rigorous*, inasmuch as it will not be developed *a priori* but on the basis of criteria that are at the same time authentically biblical in themselves and methodically applied to the most serious scientific analyses. There will be no question of suppressing the rational reading of history. On the contrary, it will always be presupposed and will serve to support the specifically theological undertaking. Scientific Marxist analysis will provide for its human density, that heavy burden of humankind's struggle to wrest from nature its subsistence by the sweat of its labor; the density also of the social conflicts that make up so much of written history.

The theology of history will also look for a reading of history but in a different way, like those instruments that detect light rays to which our eyes by themselves are insensitive and thereby make it possible to explore the darkness of the night. Thus, far from separating us from history and transporting us to an unreal world, it sends us back to it with unrelenting insistence.

As Vatican II put it,

> The church has always had the duty of scrutinizing the signs of the times and of interpreting them in the light of the gospel. Thus, in language intelligible to each generation, it can respond to the perennial questions that are asked about this present life and the life to come, and about the relationship of the one to the other. We must therefore recognize and understand the world in which we live, its expectations, its longings, and its often dramatic characteristics.[17]

The theologian of history who is familiar with, though critical of, Marxist analysis will be tempted less than others to be satisfied with mere words.

The theology of history will polarize more and more around "the secret of history," to use the expression of Henri Marrou,[18] for that is where its final meaning resides—namely, that it does not end in nothingness but in ultimate fulfillment: "the mystery of his will, according to his purpose that he set forth in Christ as a plan for the fullness of time, to unite all things in him" (Eph. 1:9-10). This meaning renders all others relative, while incorporating whatever truth they may contain.

The theology of history will rediscover the dynamic sovereignty of the kingdom of God under its aspect of completely gratuitous gift, as the salvation of humanity, as an invitation to conversion that is radical and endlessly renewed. It is an invitation to the renunciation of our prejudices, our egotism, our cowardice, our laziness. It is an appeal for a profound opening to God and to others, for a commitment to historical reality in order to transform it in the spirit of the gospel.

This evangelical urgency meets revolutionary urgency but at a very different level, that of radical personal conversion: "The time is fulfilled, and the kingdom of God is at hand; repent, and believe in the gospel" (Mark 1:15). While giving very serious attention to all the other subjects of history (especially to the human masses in their relationships, both hostile and peaceful), the theology of history will strive to understand the mystical body of Christ as "the true subject of history, just as the full growth of this body is the reason for and the measure of the period of time that is still going on."[19] The mystical body of Christ is called to act and to situate itself within that history of flesh and blood that is human history, where exploitation and oppression have so often counted so many victims and produced, as Marx put it, the "degradation . . . of the human race."[20]

Finally, the theology of history will rediscover and renew the bright possibilities of the theology of grace and sin as they were developed, for example, by St. Paul in that great theology of history that is the Epistle to the Romans. Without that theology we cannot understand in any depth the generosity, the devotion, the spirit of service, the willingness to sacrifice, that come alive so often and in so many ways in the very heart of the cruel history of humanity. Nor can we understand without it the cruelty, the egotism, the blindness of entire social groups and of so many individuals: cruelty, egotism, and blindness that resurface more than ever in the midst of revolutions that seem the most necessary.

As Berdyaev notes, the Israelites "were the first to conceive the world as historical fulfillment."[21] As he also notes, the "dynamism introduced by Christianity derived from its idea of the immediacy and uniqueness of events, which was foreign to the pagan world. The latter had, on the contrary, been dominated by the idea of the frequency and recurrence of events."[22] By this dynamic it enlists those who accept in truth the radical appeal to evangelical conversion, to "perform the impossible for the realization of the kingdom of God in this world"[23]—that is, to transform it in the spirit of the gospel.

Opium or Dynamite?

Marxism, I have pointed out, claims to give a total explanation, by way of historical materialism, of the genesis of religion as well as of the other aspects of social life. Here is a particularly clear text of Marx on this subject:

> Technology discloses humanity's mode of dealing with nature, the process of production by which it sustains its life, and thereby also lays bare the mode of formation of its social relationships, and of the mental conceptions that flow from them. Every history of religion, even, that fails to take account of this material basis, is uncritical. It is, in reality, much easier to discover by analysis the earthly core of the misty creations of religion than, conversely, it is to develop from the actual relationships of life the corresponding celestialized forms of those relationships. The former method is the only materialistic and, therefore, the only scientific one.[24]

Obviously, *the classic Marxist analysis of religion insists on being totally reductive.* It refuses to see in religion anything that might be divine. It strives simply to make manifest its "terrestrial core." In religious doctrine it sees only "misty creations" whose origin it explains by recourse to its general theory of the development of ideologies. Such an interpretation necessarily implies a negative evaluation of the religious phenomenon. At least as far as Karl Marx is concerned, that judgment is categorical.

"For Germany, the critique of religion is essentially completed; and the critique of religion is the prerequisite of every critique." It is with this triumphal statement that the young Marx (he was hardly twenty-six years old) opens his *Contribution to the Critique of Hegel's Philosophy of Right.*[25] Someone could have objected that religious practice was still very strong and Marx was rash to predict its demise in the near future. The objection would have made him smile. Such an appeal to public opinion would in no way have impressed him. What counted for him, from his point of view, was only the position of those whom he considered the cultural elite—that is, the Hegelian leftist posterity, whose star performer then was Feuerbach. Soon Marx would himself make a real break with it. He would become aware, as we have seen, that he was inaugurating a new era of thought and action, of imposing, so to speak, a new field of forces where all would be constrained to resituate themselves. But, in his eyes, there would never be a question of overlooking Hegel. He would regard him always as the unsurpassable summit of pre-Marxist thought—with a specific contribution, however, from Feuerbach.

At the time Marx was writing this treatise he was under the spell of Feuerbach. A few months earlier he had enthusiastically invited "theologians and speculative philosophers" to study him: "For you there is no other road to truth and liberty," he wrote to them, "than through Feuerbach."[26] True, he would soon make a sharp break with him as well; much less sharp, however, than he himself believed, at least in what concerns analysis of the religious phenomenon. All his life he would remain indebted to the Feuerbachian critique of religion. He would transcend it only indirectly, by introducing the genesis of what, following Feuerbach, he regarded as the religious illusion into the general framework of the Marxist explanation by way of his materialist conception of history.

Let us continue our reading:

> The wretchedness of religion is at once an expression of and a protest against real wretchedness. Religion is the sigh of the oppressed creature, the heart of a heartless world, and the soul of soulless conditions. It is the opium of the people.[27]

By itself the first sentence would seem to indicate that Marx recognized some positive content in religion: that of a sort of "challenge" to suffering. This is the interpretation of certain Marxists who are anxious for dialogue with Christians, such as Garaudy, or of certain Christians who want to reconcile Marxism and Christianity.

Unfortunately, the immediate context does not permit us to maintain this interpretation seriously: it would involve a real contradiction of the basic statement of the entire text, which leaves no doubt as to its meaning. Religion, for the author, has no other "value" than that of a drug, which relieves pain for a moment, it is true, by creating an artificial paradise. But it prevents one from grasping the true solutions that would make it possible really to escape from misery. It only provokes and accelerates the degradation of the individual by its continuation.

According to Gramsci, the identification of religion as "opium of the people" may have been suggested to Marx by his reading of Balzac, who had called lotteries the "opium of misery." We know, in fact, through Paul Lafargue, that he had such admiration for the author of the *Comédie humaine* that he intended to write a critical essay on him. The transfer of Balzac's expression to the field of religion could have been suggested by the impact created at that time by the argument of "Pascal's wager,"[28] whose existence Victor Cousin had just called attention to in the original manuscript of the *Pensées*, published in 1844.

On the other hand, according to the research of Reinhart Seeger, the Marxist expression was invented by Bruno Bauer. The tendency to compare religion to drugs was then in the air. Here, for example, is a passage by Moses Hess: "Religion is well able . . . to make tolerable the unhappy consciousness of servitude . . . just as opium does good service in painful illnesses. Faith in the reality of unreality and in the unreality of reality can indeed give the sufferer a passive happiness . . . but it cannot give the manly energy to free oneself from the evil."[29]

The comparison seemed obvious to Heinrich Heine, who, moreover, recognized in it a certain positive meaning: "I," he wrote, "have also my religion. Do not think that I am without religion. Opium is also a religion. . . . There is a closer relationship between opium and religion than most persons dream."[30]

In his contempt for religion Marx was very much a reflection of his time. Following his usual procedure, he immediately aligned himself with the most radical wing. I repeat: his interpretation of the religious phenomenon was purely negative. The identification with opium was for him the vilest of identifications. He saw in it only a dangerous illusion, which, instead of permitting us to attain happiness, could only contribute to keeping us the more in unhappiness. Therefore he saw no other solution than its abolition.

The lines I am about to quote, which follow immediately the statement of the famous expression we have been discussing, could not be clearer:

> The abolition of religion as the illusory happiness of the people is a demand for their true happiness. The call to abandon illusions about their condition is the call to abandon a condition which requires illusions. Thus, the critique of religion is the critique in embryo of the vale of tears of which religion is the halo.[31]

Marx's originality, however, soon asserted itself. Very quickly, in fact, he began to reproach Feuerbach for not having seen that the true cause of all alienation—therefore, in his view, of all religion—is a defective economic and social organization. More precisely, it is the exploitation of the mass of humanity that is inevitably caused by the private ownership of the means of production.

For Marxist thought it is economic alienation that gives birth to religious alienation. The latter in turn reacts on the former, which it helps to maintain and even to reinforce. That is why one must struggle directly against religion, notwithstanding the conviction that it will disappear by itself when all exploitation of workers has come to an end with the disappearance of the private ownership of the means of production. There is, therefore, reciprocal cause and effect between the economic factor and the religious factor, even though it is the former that is decisive in the end.

Thus we come to the basis of the Marxist explanation of the religious phenomenon by historical materialism. The explanation strips from religion all its original specificity and makes its own vision exclusive. It sees in religion only one ideology among others in the service of the ruling classes, which, furthermore, it serves in a doubly contemptible way: an ideology that justifies politico-economic exploitation and at the same time consoles its victims.

This radical critique Marx aimed, above all, at Christianity. We know, from a letter dated October 18, 1842, from a young Hegelian of the left, Georg Jung, that the position of the young Marx was violently anti-Christian: "Marx," he wrote, "considers the Christian religion as one of the most immoral."[32] Marx never wavered on this point. The only thing for which he was grateful to Christianity—and this only in spoken not written words—was that it taught us the love of children.[33]

Marx writes with irony, in the *German Ideology*, about the early Christians: "The early Christians owned nothing in this world and were, therefore, satisfied with their imaginary heavenly property and their divine right to ownership. Instead of making the world the possession of the people, they proclaimed themselves and their ragged company to be 'God's own possession' "(1 Peter 2:9).[34]

In *Capital* he exercises his irony by noting that "the sheep-nature of a Christian is shown in the resemblance to the Lamb of God."[35] He refers disparagingly to the Christian reading of the Bible in working-class circles.[36] He pictures Christianity, especially the Protestant variety, as the religion *par excellence* of that bourgeois society whose radical critique was his entire concern and whose inevitable disappearance he predicted. Naturally, from his point of view, it must disappear with the society to which it contributed its ideology.[37]

Has Marxist posterity remained as negative on the subject of Christianity? As far as Soviet and Chinese Marxism are concerned there is no doubt that they remained, on this point, entirely faithful to the spirit of the founding fathers. We have already seen the 1909 text in which Lenin affirms that Marxism "has fully taken over the historical traditions of eighteenth-century materialism in France and of Feuerbach . . . a materialism which is absolutely atheistic and positively hostile to all religion."[38] In 1917, in his *State and*

Revolution, he reacted vigorously against those party members who said they considered religion a private affair, members who have sunk to "the vulgar, 'free-thinking,' philistine level, ready to allow a nondenominational status, but renouncing all *party* struggle against the religious opium which stupefies the people."[39] At the present time one cannot perceive either in the Soviet Union or in China, on the part of officialdom, the slightest sign of an evolution toward a minimum of tolerance.[40]

Even Antonio Gramsci, though less dogmatic and more knowledgeable about Christianity, is scarcely less negative. Thus in his "Notes on Machiavelli" he can say that "Catholicism has been reduced in large part to a superstition shared by peasants, the sick, the elderly, and women."[41] He adds that "Catholic social thought has a purely academic value. It is necessary to study and analyze it as an element of a narcotic ideology designed to maintain persons in a state of passive expectation, of a religious nature, but not as a directly active element of political or historical life."[42]

In his *The Historical Materialism and Philosophy of Benedetto Croce*, Gramsci goes so far as to write: "Consistent Catholics—that is, ones who would apply Catholic standards to each act of their life—would look like monsters: which is, come to think of it, the most devastating and decisive criticism of Catholicism."[43] Of course we might ask what criteria he chose to justify this statement. St. Paul noted with pride that the early Christians passed easily for fools.

Other Marxists, fortunately, are far from having such a closed mind in regard to Christianity. It seems that Ernst Bloch is the one who opened the way. His basic approach to the subject consists in rediscovering and reaffirming on a higher plane, within Marxism, the dynamism of hope and action that characterizes religions, especially Judeo-Christianity. Such is the basic meaning of the famous dictum (already quoted) that he used as an epigraph at the beginning of his work, *Atheism in Christianity* (1968): "Only an atheist can be a good Christian; only a Christian can be a good atheist." The "atheist" of whom he speaks is exclusively the Marxist atheist, because only the Marxist appears to him coherent and consistent.

In my opinion it is highly significant that, even in a book as open-minded as this one, Bloch defines Marxism in terms of atheism. Furthermore, let us make no mistake: he is careful not to put the Marxist and the Christian on the same level, and he clearly does not want to see Christianity endure as it is. What he wants is what I have noted: a Marxist recovery of Christian dynamism; which does, however, come down to recognizing in Christianity a certain historical value, even if only provisional.

Roger Garaudy goes even further—as far as possible for someone who holds his philosophical positions. On the Marxist side, at least in the French-speaking world, he has become the representative *par excellence* for dialogue with Christians. The fact that he has been expelled from his party—not for that reason directly, but for his novel theories about socialism and his severely critical attitude toward the Soviet Union—has unfortunately limited his significance. In *The Alternative Future* [44] he has forcefully stated that religion is not necessarily an "opium" and that, in certain circumstances, Christianity has demonstrated a real revolutionary dynamic. He even concludes *Parole d'homme* with the statement, "I am Christian."[45] In reality, a close reading of this work shows that, despite his profound sympathy for Christianity, which he had, moreover, practiced intensely before becoming a Marxist, he is still far from adhering to the objective content of the Christian faith.[46]

I will also mention Milan Machovec. His book *Jesus for Atheists* [47] is delightful. Reading it can even help Christians to discover better and to love Jesus Christ. Although its author remains an atheist and therefore Christ can be for him only a human being, the reader senses that Machovec has been deeply moved by him. The book *God Is Not Yet Dead*[48] by another Czech neo-Marxist, Vitezslav Gardavsky, reveals an attitude that is quite as receptive, though within the same limits, to Christianity.

As for the communist parties in countries where they do not hold power, their attitude toward religion—as toward many other questions (the defense of various types of freedom, for example)—seems dictated mainly by circumstances, with the result that it is not easy to distinguish between what would be only political expediency (even though long-term) and a genuine change in thought as regards classical Marxism. Lacking proof to the contrary, the more likely hypothesis for analysis is the former. Many of these parties now practice the policy of "the outstretched hand," because they are aware of the evolution going on in the churches. They see in it the possibility of significant support for their revolutionary enterprise. Thus we read in a recent official work of the French Communist Party: "More than ever before we must . . . know how to listen to the questions, criticisms, proposals of Christians, as well as to explain our own ideas about common action, advanced democracy, and socialism."[49]

As early as 1936, at the height of the Stalinist period, Thorez had declared, "We have not asked Catholics to stop believing in God."[50] He had even made the solemn commitment: "The Communist Party clearly and resolutely disapproves of every kind of antireligious persecution. The Communist Party, when it comes to power, will guarantee to everyone the full liberty to believe or not to believe, to practice or not to practice religious rites."[51]

Let me add that up to now no communist party has itself renounced the materialist and atheist philosophy that goes back to the founders of Marxism. The following statement of Thorez says it clearly and, as with the other two quotations of his that we have just cited, it remains the official doctrine of the French Communist Party: "We solicit the collaboration of all persons of good will, without ourselves renouncing our own materialist conceptions, but also without demanding of Catholics that they abandon their beliefs."[52]

The address of Georges Marchais to the 22nd congress of the party offered nothing substantially new on this point, although it insisted on the possibility of collaboration between "Christian and atheist workers." Nor did his *Ap-*

peal to Christians of June 10, 1976, contain any significantly original statements on this issue.

Authentic and Spurious Christianity

If Christianity is an illusion and if it effectively paralyzes improvement of the human condition, how can one deny that Marx was right? He would have contributed in a decisive fashion toward opening the eyes of a humanity blinded by religious illusion, especially of the Christian variety. We reject this radical hypothesis, for our faith holds both to the truth of the Christian gospel and to its indispensable and beneficial help for the whole of humanity, because we believe with Deuteronomy 8:3, repeated by Jesus Christ when confronted by the Tempter, that the human person "does not live by bread alone, but by every word that proceeds from the mouth of God" (Matt. 4:4).

This frees us to accept more easily the *legitimacy of the Marxist challenge to the conservatism of historical Christianity*, at least in certain countries and at certain periods of history. In fact, the hasty generalizations too common not only among most Marxists but also among a fair number of Christians at the present time must be avoided. Even though his own historical documentation is somewhat questionable, Garaudy is right in stating that it was conservatism that was dominant, at the time of Marx, among Christians of Western Europe and, even if it has become clearly weaker since then, it is still common at the present time.

It is easy to substantiate this—for example, by reference to the attitude of French Catholics around 1848. Persons with open minds were not lacking, it is true (Maret, Ozanam, Lacordaire, Bishop Affre), but they remained isolated individuals whom the majority did not follow and did not even understand. The clergy strongly reflected its own class recruitment, all the more because its seminary training did almost nothing to expose future priests to social problems. There was a lower clergy, coming almost exclusively from rural areas, and a higher clergy whose mentality a serious historian has described as follows: "Petty bourgeois come at last to high dignities, intoxicated by them, and lacking that taste for the supernatural that might have moved them to sacrifice and make them solicitous for the needs of their people, good men at heart, with excellent attitudes, but so bourgeois."[53]

Let me emphasize their good faith, as does another historian in the case of two great laymen of the period: François Veuillot and Count de Montalembert. Adrien Dansette writes about them:

> The violently antisocialist sentiments of a Veuillot or a Montalembert are very different from those of a Cousin or a Thiers. They sincerely believed that religion was threatened equally with the social order, that social order whose destruction they thought would mean anarchy. There is not a shadow of class elitism in Veuillot and, if it is beyond question that Montalembert is influenced by his prejudices, it would be

a miscalculation to question his good faith; in his worst, most reactionary transports he believes always that he is fighting for Christ.[54]

The problem nonetheless remains: the objective scandal of turning a blind eye to social reality, of a Christianity mustered into the service of fear and conservatism. Montalembert stated his position: "I know of only one way to make those who are not owners believe in ownership: make them believe in God . . . who has dictated the Ten Commandments and punishes thieves for all eternity." We can understand why those on the left replied, "That is the way to destroy religion."[55]

When Louis Veuillot declared that "misery is the law for one part of society" and "that is the law of God to which we must submit," he was not aware that beneath the faith of a knight on horseback always ready to do battle for divine right he was uttering the worst blasphemy by endorsing what was simply injustice and human sloth.

Archbishop Gousset of Rheims attacked democracy. It is, he wrote, "the heresy of our time; it will be as dangerous and as difficult to root out as Jansenism."[56] As if autocracy and monarchy by divine right went necessarily and exclusively hand in hand with the gospel! Perhaps the worst was the eloquent bad judgment of a certain Father Combalot, a famous preacher and diocesan missionary of the time, for whom rebellious workers were "cannibalistic hordes" and their leaders "apostles of terrorism, plunder, and banditry."[57]

If these declarations exercised a considerable influence on the prevailing opinion among French Catholics of that time, they were just as much a reflection of that opinion. One can understand why the conservative bourgeois were sensitive on this score. They saw in that opinion an agreement with their own options for society. Such declarations by church representatives contributed a good deal toward weakening the anticlericalism of the bourgeoisie.

Adolphe Thiers, for example, who had been a fierce adversary of free education, now declared, "I formally demand something other than these detestable little lay schoolteachers. I want the brothers, although formerly I may have been opposed to them; I want to make the influence of the clergy once again all-powerful; I demand that the hand of the pastor be strong, much stronger than it is now, because I count heavily on him to propagate the good philosophy that teaches human beings that they are here on earth to suffer."[58]

When we realize that this was the mentality at the time of the publication of the *Communist Manifesto*, we can no longer be surprised at the indignation of the founders of Marxism with regard to the Christianity they knew of. Their main error was that they generalized unduly and believed that it was authentic Christianity.

What is important for the Christians of *our* time is to be aware of this conservatism, which is still too common, a conservatism that is fearful, closed to real problems and even to situations of injustice. It is also important that they denounce it and rid themselves of it, for it is a false god that lends weight to the Marxist identification of opium with a religion that seems to justify it. Above all it is important that they discover that it is in contradiction with the formidable dynamic of renewal that is at the heart of the gospel. However excessive it may have been, *the Marxist challenge to religious conservatism has been historically beneficial.* It would be regrettable if it were not taken very seriously.

When it is likened to opium, the Christian faith would be remiss if it accepted the accusation purely and simply. Christians would be right to point out to their accusers that Marxism also becomes opium only too easily. In the Soviet Union, for example, it continually serves to justify the political line of the day while forbidding the slightest criticism. And it conceals the crimes of Stalinism under the highly anesthetic veil of "the cult of personality." This argument is simply a clever maneuver to parry an attack. Marxists must learn to apply their analysis to the same phenomena that stem from Marxism instead of contenting themselves with using it as a grill for other societies.

This approach obviously depends only on *rational* analysis. From its *own* point of view the faith can object that, in its authentic New Testament meaning, it is nothing like opium, even if it may have been lived as such at certain stages of historical Christianity. It is true that the goal of Jesus Christ, as contrasted with that of Marxism, was in no way to take upon himself the political transformation of the world. The pseudo-scientific attempts that have been made to support the contrary interpretation have only served to reinforce what they opposed. Those analyses especially that have been made in terms of class struggle miss completely the point of the true question and even the correct perspective.

Jesus conceived his mission essentially as a mission of "salvation," in the sense of the establishment of a relationship of love between God and humanity through grace, conversion, and forgiveness, mediated by the preaching of the word of God, prayer, and the sacramental life—relationships inscribed in the very depths of human existence and terminating in the absolute future of the kingdom of God beyond the end of history. The inscribing is referred to by St. Paul in the theme of participation by baptism in the life of the risen Christ and the theme of filial adoption by God. It is referred to by St. John in the passages on the communication of eternal life.

However, for Christ, contrary to an interpretation too frequent among Christians in the course of the centuries, it was in no way a question of evading earthly existence. "The Christian egotism of salvation,"[59] for which Marx reproached Christians and which has in fact frequently characterized the lifestyle of Christians, is a corruption of the gospel. The commandment to love our neighbor is an essential element of gospel praxis.

As I shall explain later, Christians must strive to give their neighbors the concrete service that they need. And "the neighbor" is precisely every human being who has need of our concrete service. The commandment itself implies urgency and demands effectiveness.

In the parable of the good Samaritan, the priest and the Levite are the representatives of evasion-religion, opium-religion; the Samaritan is the representative of authentic gospel life (Luke 10:29-37). That life is recognized precisely by its effectiveness in the concrete service rendered to one's neighbor. The criterion obviously has a general significance. Even if the example given in the parable is of the individual order, the rule applies to the collective plane.

The perspective of the absolute future does not minimize the relative future. The eternal, from the gospel point of view, does not suggest that we forget the present. Quite the contrary, it compels us to take it even more seriously, for history does not end with nothingness but with an achievement that will surpass all our expectations.

As Leonhard Ragaz has said, the gospel proclamation of the kingdom of God, understood as it should be—that is, as a propellant dynamic for the profound transformation of individuals and society—understood as a power for the radical challenge of all our egotisms and all our injustices, is not "opium but dynamite."[60]

By a play on meanings we could even turn the famous Marxist accusation around, according to a perceptive observation of D. T. Niles, a Sri Lankan Christian:

> The gospel attaches importance to the struggle for existence and at the same time relegates it to a secondary rank. . . . It assigns to bread the task of assisting us to ensure genuine life, and frees the struggle for bread from the bitterness that it can provoke. It is true that religion is the opium of the masses, for true religion puts to sleep the desire for vengeance.[61]

Seen thus, as it should be, Christianity is not a depressant. It is a stimulant for humanization and—although it has deeper meanings as well—it stimulates us to take up the struggle for justice.

Once the authentic meaning of the Christian faith has been reestablished—against the Marxist view of it and that of a bastardized Christianity—as a dynamic for the transformation of the world at its most profound level, we can then dispute the organic relationship that Marx and his disciples thought they had identified between Christianity and bourgeois-capitalist society. "Christianity with its cult of the abstract person" would be, according to Marx, "the most fitting religious adjunct" of that society.[62]

I readily recognize that a fairly close relationship has existed between a certain kind of Christianity and this kind of society, but that Christianity was a corruption of authentic Christianity. In particular we shall see that one can hardly reproach it with such phrases as "the cult of the abstract person." The biblical perception of human nature could not be more realistic. However, as I have noted (in slightly different terms) what is most regrettable is that, with some exceptions, the churches have not sufficiently taken into account the most significant dynamisms of industrial society, with the result that the faith has not been sufficiently thought out and lived within those dynamics.

The Marxist prediction, endlessly repeated, that religion will disappear concurrently with other cultural characteristics of bourgeois society must also be disputed. Marxist theory claims, we know, that this event will occur progressively in a society of abundance that is culturally advanced and in which antagonisms between social classes will have come to an end. "The religious reflex of the real world," Marx assures us, "can, in any case, only then finally vanish when the practical relationships of everyday life offer to human beings none but perfectly intelligible and reasonable relationships with regard to their fellow humans and to nature."[63]

Inasmuch as the conditions fixed by the Marxist prophecy have not yet been realized, it is clearly not possible, from the sociological point of view, to conclude that it will or will not come true. From the same point of view we can only take notice of the fact that Christianity is far from disappearing in the Soviet Union, despite a multiform persecution that has lasted for more than half a century. Furthermore, we must note that in advanced industrial society of the liberal type there are signs of a renewal of the faith, even if the practice of religion has diminished quantitatively.

As for the faith itself, founded on confidence in the promises of the Lord of history, it remains convinced that, despite all the vicissitudes of that history, it will never disappear from the heart of humanity: "And I tell you, you are Peter, and on this rock I will build my church, and the powers of death shall not prevail against it" (Matt. 16:18).

Finally we must dispute the relevance of the explanation that is usually given for the radical hostility of the founders of Marxism toward Christianity—namely, that it was provoked by the corruption of the faith in their time, which prevented them from discovering its true evangelical nature. Of course it is not possible to discredit the argument entirely, because we do not know what they would have thought in the context of a Christianity that was not conservative and petty bourgeois. And this fact undermines the proposed explanation just as effectively because history cannot be done over.

We readily acknowledge that the corruption of Christianity played a real role in the genesis of the hostility shown by the founders of Marxism. That is certainly true of Engels. But it is no less certain, by their own admission, that the key to their anti-Christianity is found in a *philosophical stance*—namely, in their materialist and atheist convictions. This leads one to ask if, at least from a certain period onward, they would have been capable of opening their minds to the truth of an authentic Christianity. Their kind of analysis would probably have made it impossible. They would have seen it through tinted lenses.

This is surely true of contemporary Marxists who, if they wished, could encounter something other than corrupt Christian communities and could find works of theology and biblical interpretation that are of unquestionable value. The exclusive use of Marxist analysis in regard to religious phenomena constitutes, I believe, a screen that prevents the viewer from seeing the true facts.

Furthermore, *the axis of an interpretation of the faith must turn on a specific analysis—a theological analysis*. A theological analysis, of course, must take account of other kinds of analysis, such as Marxist analysis, but it must always remain true to itself, without subordinating itself to any other, because it rests on another foundation: the absolute reference point of the word of God in Jesus Christ.

A faith that is conscious of itself and that makes use of all the potentialities of intelligence in the analysis of its own experience, of the experience of the church through the centuries, and of the facts concerning the history of the Old and New Testaments—such a faith must reject the Marxist explanation of the genesis of Christianity by way of historical materialism. The Marxist explanation does not take account of facts that find their only fundamental explanation in the objective content of the New Testament faith, a faith that was later to be more precisely defined by dogmatic reflection that has continued through the centuries. Marxist analysis can be of real value in its diagnosis of facts, but its claim to provide the ultimate explanation of those facts has not been substantiated.

As for the Marxist accusation of "opium of the people," a *reformulation of the faith* must strive to rediscover and revise for our time the missionary dynamic and the social transformation dynamic that characterize New Testament Christianity. It will demonstrate that its respect for religious freedom and its acceptance of all that is true in other faiths and philosophies need not lead to the weakening of its missionary witness. And it will show that the two dynamics I named above are the two inseparable hemispheres of one gospel dynamic.

A genuine commitment to Jesus Christ is always a "conversion" in the sense that it is a profound change in relation to a previous way of life or a non-Christian situation. Logically, it will have repercussions in all the dimensions of a believer's existence; therefore also on the collective plane. The truth of this logical sequence dare not be overlooked.

If, therefore, authentic conversions multiply and if Christian communities embody the essence of the gospel, it will have a real and perhaps profound impact on the whole of society and could contribute to a genuine transformation of the world in the gospel sense. This evangelical dynamic will function both as a force for protest against society (against its injustice, its callousness, its egotism, its conservatism) and as an impetus to mobilize energy across the meaning of history guaranteed to us by the word of God in Jesus Christ.

We might review here the specific New Testament dynamics of the theological virtues. The *dynamic of faith*: a dynamic in the church and in each Christian springing from the decisive truth that comes to us from the word of God. The *dynamic of hope*: a dynamic of confidence, courage, and action, facing both toward the future of history and toward the absolute future of the kingdom of God. The *dynamic of love* (or charity): a dynamic that can humanize history through or in spite of the realities of conflict. More on this later. From the human point of view it is enough to add now that the effectiveness of the gospel dynamic that impels us toward a transformation of the world depends on the responsibility of Christians within history. They can be faithful or unfaithful to their mission. They will have to answer for it before the Judge of history.

The Utopia of the Classless Society and the Absolute Future of the Kingdom of God

Here we have then, face to face, a philosophy of history and a theology of history—because the Christianity under attack has no intention of dying and because, in its more dynamic wing, it eagerly accepts the challenge.

The Marxist philosophy relies on a new kind of science—although, by reason of the promethean excess of its pretensions, it is more in the nature of a questionable projection of science. The Christian theology does not directly appeal to science, but it does give it full rein. It itself stands on another level.

The Marxist philosophy predicts and prepares for a seductive future. The Christian theology does not dispute it directly on this point. It leaves to rational criticism the job of pronouncing judgment on such matters. What, however, it does quarrel with is Marxism's desire to lock humanity within a terrestrial future, as if behind the impenetrable walls of a prison.

Both schools of thought, in any case, are turned toward the future. The contemporary interest in the future, though passionately pursued as much by non-Marxists as it has been by Marxists, certainly owes much to Marxism. Roger Garaudy is right in line with Karl Marx when he writes, "The future is not an already written script in which we have only to play our roles. It is a work that we have to create."[64]

Advanced contemporary culture has acquired a dynamic sense of history that radically questions all thought that is nonhistoric—for example, the following observations of Pascal, despite their striking profundity:

> Let each of us examine our thoughts, and we will find that they are all occupied with the past or the future. We can scarcely think of the present; and if we think of it, it is only in order to find our bearings for mapping out the future. The present is never our goal; the past and the present are our means; the future alone is our goal. Thus we never live, but we hope to live; and inasmuch as we are always preparing ourselves to be happy it is inevitable that we never are happy.[65]

Certainly Pascal is right in respect to those who do not know how to seize the fullness of the present moment and are always somewhere else—a danger that the great activists always face—but he was wrong in not seeing that the very fullness of the present is a component of the future.

On both sides also we encounter a *utopia*, not in the unrealistic and illusory sense that has prevailed for so long, but in the positive sense of a *concrete utopia* so admirably elaborated by Ernst Bloch, who thus rediscovered the original meaning of the *Utopia* of St. Thomas More, to which Marx himself paid homage, at least indirectly.[66] Christianity firmly rejects the charge of illusion that Marxism directs at its transcendent utopia.

Classless Society?

The Marxist schema still remains fundamentally the same as the original Marxist schema. According to the founders of Marxism, the industrial proletariat, which in their eyes represents the ultimate oppression that a class can undergo, has a destiny—written in facts—progressively to encompass the entire population of industrial society, save only a handful of capitalists. Therefore, when the proletarian revolution carries the day and finally destroys the capitalist class, society will be reduced to one single social class. It will become a classless society.

It will then be necessary at all costs to prevent new classes from arising, or at least new *antagonistic* classes—a nuance of official Soviet doctrine to explain why the undeniable existence of social classes in the U.S.S.R. does not contradict the "orthodox" theory. Such prevention is necessary because otherwise new struggles would arise between them, with their heavy toll of injustice and oppression.

The mission of the working class will therefore be to found a truly *new society*, and it will in fact found it, a society defined as "an order of things in which there are no more classes and class antagonisms."[67] This classless society will be final. Why?, one might ask. Will the clock of history be finally stopped? The response of the founders of Marxism is always the same: the victorious proletarian revolution will finally have eliminated the private ownership of the means of production. Because in the Marxist perspective the existence of social classes is uniquely bound to such ownership, the disappearance of the unique cause will necessarily mean the disappearance of the effect. This *utopia of the classless society* is essential to the Marxist projection.

The major texts of the founders of Marxism on this subject remain the most rich and fertile, whereas those of their disciples are too often but colorless repetitions, so that the reader wonders about the quality of the conviction behind them.

The *German Ideology* exalts the personal fulfillment that citizens will enjoy in the classless society of the future, which the two coauthors call the *communist society*. They describe it in terms of such concepts as development, originality, freedom, interdependence, and solidarity.

"This development," they explain, "is determined precisely by the connection of individuals, a connection which consists partly in the economic prerequisites and partly in the necessary solidarity of the free development of all, and, finally, in the universal character of the activity of individuals on the basis of the existing productive forces."[68]

What do they mean by this last unclear expression, "the universal form of the activity of individuals?" No doubt it refers to that characteristic, so important in their eyes, that involves the *elimination of the division of labor* in the classless society of their utopia. To understand why they envisioned such a goal, we must recall that they were thinking of the kind of work that they observed in the industrial society of their time. The majority of workers were—by reason of the lack of technology and the indifference of most employers toward their personal fulfillment—forced to accept a brutalizing labor, when a great many of them, formerly craftsmen or small farmers, had practiced interesting, though insufficiently remunerative, occupations. It was evidently of that joyless labor of the majority of the workers of his time that Marx was thinking when he wrote in the *Economic and Philosophic Manuscripts of 1844* of that "division of labor that changes a person into an abstract being, into a machine tool . . . in order to reduce it to a physical and intellectual monster."[69] Was he not right to denounce such a state of affairs?

In his *Contribution to the Critique of Political Economy* (1857-1858), Marx, contemplating the future, exults in the vision of the prodigious explosion of creative capacities that humanity will then enjoy: "The full development of human mastery over the forces of nature," he assures us, "those of so-called nature as well as of humanity's own nature. The absolute working-out of his creative potentialities . . . the development of all human powers as such the end in itself, not measured on a *predetermined* yardstick."[70]

That is a very modern perspective on creativity. In his *Critique of the Program of the German Labor Party ("the Gotha Program")* (1875), he introduces a supplementary distinction between the *first phase* of communist society, "when it has just emerged after prolonged birth pangs from capitalist society" and is consequently marked by inevitable imperfections, and its *higher phase*. In celebrating the latter, the visionary Marx abandons himself to a splendid lyricism:

> In a higher phase of communist society, after the enslaving subordination of the individual to the division of labor, and therewith also the antithesis between mental and physical labor, has vanished; after labor has become not only a means of life but life's prime want; after the productive forces have also increased with all-round development of the individual, and all the springs of cooperative wealth flow more abundantly—only then can the narrow horizon of the bourgeois right be crossed in its entirety and society inscribe on its banner: From each according to their ability, to each according to their needs![71]

As for the following text from *Capital*, it is only in appearance that scientific precision weakens its enthusiasm:

> Let us now picture . . . a community of free individuals, carrying on their work with the means of production in common, in which the labor power of all the different individuals is consciously applied as the combined labor power of the community. . . . The social relationships of

the individual producers, with regard both to their labor and to its products, are in this case perfectly simple and intelligible, and that with regard not only to production but also to distribution.[72]

Notice the emphasis he placed at the same time on freedom, the perfection of economic organization, and the clarity of social relationships. Marx formulates all this in antithesis to capitalist society, which he indicts as being dictatorial under a mask of democracy, squandering the forces of production by reason of the anarchy inherent in a competitive system, and confusing all social relationships.

I could easily quote other texts. I have chosen only a few among the most significant from different periods of Marx's life in order to demonstrate that for him his utopia was an essential vision. I will conclude with the following quotation from Engels in his *Anti-Dühring* (1877-1878):

With the seizing of the means of production by society, production of commodities is done away with, and, simultaneously, the mastery of the product over the producer. Anarchy in social production is replaced by planned, conscious organization. The struggle for individual existence disappears. Then for the first time the human person, in a certain sense, is finally marked off from the rest of the animal kingdom, and emerges from mere animal conditions of existence into really human ones. . . . Only from that time on will humans, with full consciousness, make their own history—only from that time on will the social causes set in movement by them have, in the main and in a constantly growing measure, the results intended by them. It is the ascent of the human person from the kingdom of necessity to the kingdom of freedom.[73]

What a contrast, one might object, between the historical present and the utopian future! That is the reaction of Cottier when he notes that Marxist thought "juxtaposes to a merciless diagnosis of liberal capitalism—which appears as *the* evil—a paradisiac dream of the harmonious city."[74] This reasonable objection effectively puts in question the scientific objectivity of such thinking. We note, however, that Marx himself has deliberately chosen this contrast.

We might equally question, with Father Dognin, the materialist credentials of such theorizing: "We have here nothing less than a takeover of the economy by the spirit, by the human conscience, one might almost say, by 'political prudence'. . . . We are compelled to point out that Marx, who is materialist in his philosophy, is not at all so in his economics, or again, that materialist for today, he is not at all so for tomorrow."[75] Although the statement is pertinent and Horkheimer is too quick to ridicule remarks of this kind, we should remember that Marxist "materialism" contains a genuine richness of thought even amidst its contradictions.

Utopia?

For my part, I shall take seriously the Marxist utopia as just described. I see there, though under a guise that is clearly too idyllic, some fundamental insights that are good and certainly realizable, at least in part. There is, for example, the desire for manual work that will be more fulfilling in itself by offering workers a variety of activities and by stimulating workers' creative interest in their own work; the possibility of combining manual activity and intellectual activity, which is today fairly often the case with technicians; an increase in leisure activity, of a genuine cultural quality; the possibility of a significant decrease in social inequalities; the guarantee of a reasonable living standard for the entire population; a better organization of the economy that would ensure greater productivity.

Nowadays we are more and more aware of such objectives—which appeared "utopian," in the sense of "wishful thinking" in the nineteenth century. Important progress has been made toward their realization in some advanced industrial societies: improvement and diversification of jobs, shortening of the workweek, development of technical schools, increase in the number of engineers and technicians of all kinds, introduction and lengthening of paid vacations, unemployment insurance, subsidies to the handicapped and elderly, and the like. This does not mean that we have already arrived at a satisfactory level. More progress is desirable and much more could be achieved, even in the near future, if those who held political and economic power really wanted it and if the privileged classes were ready to accept the necessary sacrifices.

The objection to the Marxist utopia on the grounds of its being unrealistic is therefore not convincing, in my opinion. True, its formulation is much too idyllic, and, for that reason, dangerous to the extent that one takes it literally. It is even highly possible that Marx and Engels sincerely believed in it, carried away as they doubtless were by their revolutionary enthusiasm. Is this not *the* characteristic of doctrinaire innovators? Perhaps their primary purpose was to mobilize the masses, whose need of myths and dreams is proportionate to the depth of their suppression. In any case, I believe, as noted, that we must learn how to discover and recognize the truth in their fundamental insights.

The same is true of their dream of the so-called *classless society*. What the founding fathers envisioned was essentially the suppression of class privileges—so obvious in their day in the case of the aristocracy and the bourgeoisie—and thereby the suppression of antagonistic relations between social groups. Interpreted in this way, utopia is not a chimera. Without wanting to dream the impossible in the foreseeable future—and therefore without imagining that there will never again be conflicts—and without pursuing a visionary egalitarianism, we could no doubt create a society that had no social differences in the sense of privileges that would appear to be unjust and insupportable to the groups that do not share them. To this extent the Marxist utopia challenges the conservatism, egotism, class consciousness, pessimism, cowardice, and the lack of imagination and courage on the part of many.

We cannot reproach the founding fathers of Marxism with having believed that this was going to happen by itself. They were very much aware that their utopia could not take place without the creation of a new type of person: at once free, responsible, creative, and in solidarity with others. Again one might object, is this not—again and especially—dreaming? Not necessarily, I would respond. Fortunately persons of this kind do exist. Why should we not reasonably hope that, thanks to better education and appropriate changes in social structures, their number might increase significantly?

Up to now, in my agreement with what I consider the sound insights of the Marxist utopia, I have taken my position on the rational plane. From *the viewpoint of the faith* my agreement will be even warmer, though within the precise limits that I have defined.

In the first phase of western industrial society Christians were not, alas, the least conservative, the least pessimistic, or the least selfish, whether they were petty bourgeois or capitalist employers. For a long time those Christians known as "progressive" have been only a handful and have been held suspect by their peers. Even today a theologian or a preacher who formulates a serious critique of our predominantly capitalist society is easily accused of communism in certain Christian circles.

If we recognize in every human being their preeminent dignity as created "in the image of God," if we believe in the universal fellowship of all human beings in God, if we have understood that the great universal directive of the New Testament regarding interhuman relations is that of *egalitarian sharing* practiced in an attitude of responsibility and creativity, how can we refuse to accept the basic insights I have just described?

How can we fail to consider it a dictate of our faith that we work with all our strength to promote these principles to the full extent possible? It is true that in formulating these "insights" as I have done, I have reduced somewhat the Marxist utopia, in favor of a greater realism. Nevertheless their insights do constitute the essence of that utopia. Their articulation must, in my opinion, lead to a vision that will mobilize our energy.

A *rigorous critique* of the Marxist utopia, however, is necessary in regard to its specific application, on both the rational and the religious level.

From the *viewpoint of reason* there are objections of various kinds, and they are serious. Certain goals and proposals of the Marxist utopia are clearly unrealistic and even mystifying in the sense that they are presented to the masses as scientific objectives.

Paul Fabra asks:

> What will society look like once Marx has rooted out of it that protean Capital that takes on now the form of commodity, now the form of money? He will have deprived it of everything that has made of it a society of subtle mechanisms. What remains will be no more than a Robinson Crusoe world in which wages are abolished, money probably

suppressed (that is not clear), and where everyone—why not?—will receive according to their needs, without our being told how those needs
are defined nor why they should stop being unlimited, which would
exclude in advance the possibility of satisfying them.[76]

The objection holds, at least in regard to Soviet ideology, which has never
ceased to brandish—though without, it seems, all that much conviction—the
famous slogan, "to each according to their needs." What they criticized
Khrushchev for is merely to have made promises that were too precise for a
future that was too near.

I should like to comment—in a way that is favorable to its promoters—on
the famous thesis regarding the *progressive disappearance of the state* in the
utopian society. Let me recall that, for the founders of Marxism, "political
power, properly so called, is merely the organized power of one class for
oppressing another."[77] Let it be granted that in such a society there might no
longer be such phenomena as collective oppression or serious collective antagonisms.

Such a goal is not in itself unrealistic. However, how can it avoid all types
of personal and group conflict? How can it escape entirely the demands of
constraint? Would that not be to imagine a society that is idyllic beyond all
the bounds of reason?

Besides, was not the Marxist conception of power too narrow? Is there not,
in fact, a specific political minimum that is founded on the most fundamental
demands of life in common? Is not this political minimum confused, in
Marxist thinking, with the minimums involved in the organization of
economic life?

It seems to me that such a negative conception of the state leads to the
creation of a superstate such as we have seen, and continue to see, in all
communist regimes. Practice takes its revenge—unfortunately on living persons—for a theory that has been too carelessly conceived for a future that is
fundamentally mythical.

In a more general sense this is *the myth of a new golden age* that has been
proposed to us in scientific trappings, complete with a new preestablished
harmony. It is the same myth of the naturally virtuous and sociable human
being in the idyllic Arcadia of ancient utopians. Only this time, thanks to the
radical transformation produced in society and in humanity itself by the proletarian revolution, it is sited not in the past but in the future of a superindus-
trial society.

It is difficult to understand how a theory that wanted to be so thoroughly
scientific could be nourished on such a myth and in turn have proposed it with
such assurance. Is that not proof at once of an extreme naivety and of the
existence of needs that go beyond science, which the most convinced materialists conceal within themselves? In my opinion, this is not an innocent
myth, for history proves that it can give rise to all sorts of mystifications and
engender the worst disappointments.

On the other hand, the realization of the Marxist utopia always assumes a society of abundance and even of superabundance. Is this not to assume as self-evident a situation that the present state of science is far from guaranteeing? Even if we have reason to reproach them for a certain pessimism, the studies of the Club of Rome are impressive enough to be taken seriously.[78] They show at least that the earth's resources are not inexhaustible and that the potentialities of science and technology do not extend to the production of miracles. It would certainly be possible—although at the price of radical changes in structure and mentality around the world—to guarantee one day a minimum standard of living for all of humanity. But it would be far from that superabundance that the Marxist utopia presupposes. Here again the myth is dangerous.

At heart does not this utopia, which wants to be so radically revolutionary, transpose into that future classless society the bourgeois dream (or rather, petty bourgeois dream) of capitalist society, a dream based on a society of superconsumerism? I have said that considerable progress can be made in the direction of a decent material life for all. But, for reasons dictated by realism and from a more human perspective, it seems to me that the accent ought to be placed on the qualitative rather than the quantitative aspects of life.

No regime up to now has claimed that it has realized the higher phase of communism, which means that the complete utopia remains always in a limbo of promise. Many do claim, however, to have realized by and large the lower phase, that of socialist society. Noncommunist analysts, even the most sympathetic, although recognizing some positive and even impressive achievements, are far from sharing their official enthusiasm. François Perroux, for example, states baldly that historical communism "is a statist society . . . a society divided into masters of machines and servants of machines."[79]

At the end of some remarks on power, Raymond Aron, identifying himself explicitly as a sociologist, concludes: "I simply observe that proletarian regimes are not those where the proletariat is in power; they are those in which the leaders of the state declare that they govern in the name of the proletariat, even if the flesh-and-blood proletarians have different ideas from those of their leaders."[80]

According to the Yugoslav Marxist Svetazar Stojanovic, the working class in a Soviet Union of the Stalinist type

> is totally dominated and considerably exploited. . . . It does not even enjoy those rights that it could exercise in a capitalist regime, such as choosing one's employer or discussing the conditions of work or the level of wages. From this point of view, one can make an analogy between Stalinism and feudalism: in Stalinism it is not only the capacity for work, but in a certain sense the workers themselves who find themselves reduced to a thing.[81]

Father Bigo sees in the proletarian revolution the substitution of "the absolutism of the collectivity" for "the absolutism of property."[82]

For a long time now it has often been observed that the alleged dictatorship of the proletariat is, in reality, a dictatorship over the proletariat. Western Marxists hardly appreciate such objections to historical deficiencies. If they are communists, they deny them or at least minimize them. Or they try to explain them in terms of special historical circumstances, adding immediately that a communist regime in the West, planted on democratic cultural traditions, would be altogether different. If they do not belong to a communist party, they respond that true Marxism has nowhere been realized up to now. I think, on the contrary, that a scientific analysis ought to take all the facts into account and that it is precisely history that permits us to discover the real significance of theories.

From the *viewpoint of faith* we must note first with Berdyaev that "revolutionary communism has a very strong eschatological element in it. The time and hour are nigh, a gap in time is approaching."[83] Recalling the famous axiom of Engels, which I have already quoted, on "the ascent of the human person from the kingdom of necessity to the kingdom of freedom," Berdyaev continues: "History ends and superhistory begins."[84]

Marxists will reject any diagnosis that in effect contains objections. As formulated, however, the texts on the Marxist utopia cannot entirely escape Berdyaev's objections. We have seen that, from the rational viewpoint, to assure them a minimum degree of realism, these texts must be given an interpretation that severely reduces their content.

From the viewpoint of faith, the critique must be even stronger. It is only the absolute future promised by God to humanity that will make a break with history. Whatever may be the changes that will occur in the present time—changes of structure or mentalities—it will remain itself a difficult history, full of conflict, marked profoundly by sin—which does not mean that significant improvements are impossible. In no way does this erode the ground for hope. It recognizes the only true ground for hope in a historical future: a *realistic hope.*

We must note also with Berdyaev that the communist utopia "gives in to the temptations Christ refused, the changing of stones into bread and the kingdom of this world."[85] The objection joins the previous one by way of a reference to the gospel account of the temptations, which is itself an expression of the categorical rejection by Jesus Christ of the politico-messianic ideology of most of his compatriots. Its characteristics included realization in this life and fantasies directed toward the most materialistic human dreams of extreme abundance, marvels, and unlimited power. Although the Marxist utopia is essentially of the promethean type, it offers some basic similarities to this ideology. From the Christian viewpoint, it calls for similar reservations. It is the more dangerous because, as Dostoevski remarkably saw, in the *Legend of the Grand Inquisitor*, it will be tempted to want to legislate the total happiness of humanity, even against its will, and thus to create totalitarian structures.

We will note also, with Father Refoulé, that "Marxism looks for . . . salvation and liberation neither from a transcendent intervention nor a conversion of heart, nor exclusively from a transformation of society or the progress of history. It withholds its confidence from the person and lavishes it on institutions, which it expects to produce happiness and altruism."[86] Let us understand this clearly. What we fault Marxism for is not that it advocates socio-political liberation. It is, on the one hand, that it presents it as true eschatological salvation and, on the other, that it puts the emphasis too exclusively on revolutionary changes of structure, to the slighting of the human person.

Paradoxically it is Milovan Djilas—a non-Christian and for a long time one of the historical leaders and one of the most prestigious theoreticians of communism—who has formulated from the viewpoint of faith the most biting critique of the Marxist utopia. Here is his basic formulation:

Communism, once a popular movement that in the name of science inspired the toiling and oppressed peoples of the world with the hope of creating the kingdom of heaven on earth, has launched, and continues to launch, millions to their deaths in pursuit of this unextinguishable primeval dream.[87]

He comments further:

How could they [the communists] think or act otherwise when they have been named by a higher power, which they call history, to establish the kingdom of heaven in this sinful world to reign over weak human creatures? Luther believed that the sinless person would have no need of laws, while Calvin tried to create such a person by force. The communists would be in the right if their sinless—that is, "classless," society were possible, and if they could possess exhaustive knowledge of the laws of society and history and drive the living social reality along in accordance with these laws. But perhaps it is as well that the perfect communist society is no more a possibility than Luther's sinless person—for with sinful persons and unperfect societies we can be sure of not sinking into apathy and we can continue to be creative human beings.[88]

These statements call for a long discussion, which we are pursuing, in fact, all through this inquiry. I have already said that from my point of view the fundamental myth at work in Marxism, and even at the heart of its scientific procedure, is the *promethean myth*. But it does not exclude necessarily the presence and action of other myths. Study of its utopia seems to manifest clearly, as Milovan Djilas points out, the myth of the kingdom of God; that is to say—for the distinction is all-important—not the gospel teaching on the kingdom of God, which is at the opposite pole, but the politico-messianic myth of the kingdom of God, categorically rejected by Jesus Christ. His rejection of it led to the defection from his cause of the great majority of his compatriots, to the implacable hostility of the ruling classes of his people and, finally, to death on the cross.

Faith and the Future

However vulnerable it may be to criticism, the Marxist utopia, taken in all the seriousness of its challenge, can contribute to a reformulation of the faith that can make it possible to grasp more concretely *the components of its essential and authentic eschatological dimension.*

Faith in the absolute future of the kingdom of God will lead logically to thought and action directed toward *the building of the historical future,* under our own responsibility as human beings and Christians. The following remark of Gerhard Ebeling is profound: "Luther dared to say of *fides* that it is *creatrix divinitatis in nobis,* faith is the creation of divinity in us. . . . So we may dare to speak of faith that creates the future."[89]

Nourished as he is on the hope-filled thought of Ernst Bloch, Jürgen Moltmann suggests to Christians that they work for the "world of possibilities, the world in which we can serve the truth and righteousness and peace that have been promised and that will come." He argues magnificently that "the task of the Christian church" is to "disclose to the world the horizon of the future of the crucified Christ."[90]

There is no doubt that the faith must enter with all its resources into that hopeful attitude that we discover on all sides at the present time—and, as I have noted, to a significant degree under the influence of Marxism. Entirely oriented toward the absolute future of the kingdom of God, as it was in its original impact, how could faith not commit itself to the construction of that historical future in which already the seedbed of the absolute future is being prepared? For itself there is the grace of a new impulse: that of putting to work the potentialities that were still dormant in the heart of the New Testament revelation, for they were waiting for a time of historical ripening.

In this way Christians will rediscover the essential eschatological dimension of their faith, not as a passive attitude of waiting, but as a dynamic and powerfully stimulating orientation of their thought and action. This was undoubtedly what St. Paul meant when, for example, in his Epistle to the Romans he strove to move his readers with the assurance that "we ourselves, who have the first fruits of the Spirit, groan inwardly as we wait for filial adoption, the redemption of our bodies. For in this hope we were saved" (8:23-24). This dynamic expectation, in his eyes, must embody itself in action and certainly you would have greatly astonished him if you had suggested that it should be limited to personal or ecclesial life. "The kingdom of God," he makes clear in the same epistle, "is not a matter of eating and drinking, but of justice, peace, and the joy that is given in the Holy Spirit" (14:17). Justice and peace have political dimensions.

Jürgen Moltmann is right to insist that, in discussing the great events of the divine promise, the most common eschatological interpretations ignored "their directive, uplifting, and critical significance for all the time spent here, this side of the end, in history."[91] And he is right when he further points out that eschatological hope correctly understood becomes "a historical force that can inspire creative utopias by its love for suffering humanity and its failed world in their encounter with the unknown but promised future of God."[92]

It is true that this powerful mobilizing dynamic itself challenges us to exercise our responsibility and our creativity. As Wolfhart Pannenberg notes, "It is not without significance that, with his message of the nearness of the rule of God, Jesus turned to the individual; he did not come forward as a social or political reformer."[93] Does not this freedom offer a great opportunity for historical action that is appropriate and effective?

Here is where faith in the *resurrection of Jesus Christ* comes in, understood in all its New Testament dimensions, as brought out in a series of questions nicely put by Jürgen Moltmann. It is not only an intellectual faith: "What can I know of the historical facts?" It is also an "ethical and existential question, 'What am I to do?' " It is equally an "eschatological question, 'What may I hope for?' "[94]

Such a faith personally engages believers and moves them to action. The conqueror of death—of that most frightening necessity, which seems to seal the nothingness of the human individual and the human species—inaugurates the reign of freedom, as noted by André Dartigues: "The resurrection of Jesus did not inaugurate a new order within the framework of the ancient necessity; it destroyed that necessity."[95]

As St. Paul so strongly emphasized (1 Cor. 15), the resurrection of Jesus by itself calls for faith in the resurrection of the dead, which it is essential to interpret in its exact meaning as the end of history and the arrival for humanity of the absolute future of the kingdom of God. It cannot be understood in the sense of the arrival of the Marxist utopia and the classless society, as suggested, for example, by Fernando Belo, to the neglect of all serious exegesis.[96]

Wolfhart Pannenberg notes, with greater accuracy, that "The link between the fulfillment of the kingdom of God and the general resurrection of the dead reminds us that all political renewals of society inspired by eschatological hope are only capable of realizing a remote analogy to the peaceful order of the kingdom of God."[97]

The relativization that characterizes our political projects is, on the contrary, a warning against their risks of inhumanity. In every way it is true that our faith orients us toward the time beyond time and history. "For here we have no lasting city," the Epistle to the Hebrews assures us, "but we seek the city that is to come" (13:14). Still there is no question here of an escapist hope that would move us to take no interest in history. The result would be that the actors on the stage of history would have no alternative but the stoic despair of the myth of Sisyphus, of "those who think clearly and have ceased to hope," in the words of Albert Camus.[98] Or they would have a hope immovably riveted to earth's horizon, as with Marxist hope.

Christian hope properly understood, a hope that is founded on the expectation of the absolute future of the kingdom of God, will on the contrary sustain with all its strength those who live it and challenge them to the construction of the historical future. Perhaps some Christians needed the shock of Marxism before they could understand this clearly.

NOTES

1. In *Critique of Hegel's "Philosophy of Right,"* trans. Annette Jolin and Joseph O'Malley (New York: Cambridge Univ. Press, 1970), p. 132.

2. Cf. *Reading Capital*, trans. Ben Brewster (London: NLB, 1970), p. 59.

3. *For Marx*, trans. Ben Brewster (London: Penguin, 1969), p. 168.

4. Cf. Maurice Dobb, ed., *Contribution to the Critique of Political Economy* (New York: International Publishers, 1970), pp. 20-21.

5. *Anti-Dühring* (Moscow: Foreign Languages Publishing House, 1959), p. 367.

6. *Reading Capital*, p. 133.

7. Quoted by Henri Niel, *Karl Marx* (Paris-Bruges: DDB, 1971), pp. 163-64.

8. Cf. *For Marx*, p. 113.

9. Cf. Samuel Moore and Edward Eveling, trans. (Chicago: Encyclopedia Britannica, 1952), p. 83.

10. Cf. *Capital*, p. 85.

11. *The Unperfect Society*, trans. Dorian Cooke (New York: Harcourt, Brace and World, 1969), pp. 133-49.

12. *The Unperfect Society*, pp. 142-43.

13. *The Russian Revolution*, trans. Donald Atwater (London: Sheed and Ward, 1931), p. 64.

14. *Christianisme, Marxisme* (Paris: Centurion, 1975), p. 35.

15. *Questions sur l'homme* (Paris: Stock, 1972), p. 126.

16. Loc. cit.

17. Constitution *Gaudium et Spes*, No. 4: "Renewing the Earth," in *Catholic Documents on Peace, Justice and Liberation*, ed. David O'Brien and Thomas Shannon (Garden City, N.Y.: Doubleday-Image, 1977), p. 180.

18. *Time and Timeliness*, trans. Violet Nevile (New York: Sheed and Ward, 1969), p. 24.

19. *Time and Timeliness*, p. 36.

20. *Capital*, p. 130.

21. *The Meaning of History*, trans. George Reavey (London: Bles, 1936), p. 28.

22. *The Meaning of History*, p. 33.

23. Nicholas Berdyaev, *Christianisme, Marxisme*, p. 45.

24. Cf. *Capital*, p. 181, footnote 3.

25. In *Critique of Hegel's "Philosophy of Right,"* p. 131.

26. "Luther as Arbiter between Strauss and Feuerbach" (signed "A Non-Believer"), in *Anekdota* (February 13, 1843): MEGA, I, 1/1, p. 175. (Note the play on words: Feuerbach means literally "stream of fire.") [Ed.—More recent editions of the collected works of Marx and Engels reject the Marxian authorship of the 1843

work quoted here: see *Collected Works*, Vol. 1 (New York: International Publishers, 1975), p. xxxiii.]

27. "Contribution to a Critique of Hegel's 'Philosophy of Right,' " in *Critique of Hegel's "Philosophy of Right," "* p. 131.

28. "If God does not exist, the skeptic loses nothing by believing in him; if God exists, the skeptic gains eternal life by believing in him."

29. *Einundzwanzig Bogen aus der Schweiz* (Zurich-Winterthur: G. Herwegh, 1843), quote by Helmut Gollwitzer, *The Christian Faith and the Marxist Critique of Religion*, trans. David Cairns (New York: Scribner's, 1970), p. 16.

30. Heinrich H. Houben, *Gespräche mit Heinrich Heine*, 2nd ed. (Potsdam, 1948), pp. 770-71; cf. trans. in Gollwitzer, *The Christian Faith,* p. 18.

31. "Contribution to the Critique of Hegel's 'Philosophy of Right,' " p. 131.

32. Here is the complete quotation: "Dr. Marx, Dr. Bauer, and L. Feuerbach are joining forces to found a theologico-philosophical journal. Good old God will do well, therefore, to surround himself with all his angels and to indulge in self-pity, for these three men will surely expel him from his Paradise and, besides, put him on trial. Marx, for one, considers the Christian religion to be one of the most immoral; still, though a hopeless revolutionary, he is one of the most penetrating minds that I know": MEGA I, 1/2, 261-62, quoted by Charles Wackenheim, *La faillite de la religion d'après Karl Marx* (Paris: PUF, 1963), p. 49.

33. We know this from a confidence of his youngest daughter, corroborated by the testimony of a worker, F. Lessner, a friend of the family: "I remember," she wrote, "his telling me the story of the carpenter's son put to death by the rich people. Never, I believe, neither before nor since, has this story been so well told. Many times I heard him say, 'In spite of everything we can forgive Christianity a great deal because it taught us the love of children' " (in Karl Marx, *Eine Sammlung von Erinnerungen* "[A Collection of Memories"], 1934, p. 116, quoted by Wackenheim, p. 50).

34. Cf. *Collected Works*. Vol. 5 (New York: International Publishers, 1976), p. 188.

35. Cf. *Capital*, p. 21.

36. *Capital*, p. 47.

37. *Capital*, p. 35.

38. "The Attitude of the Workers' Party to Religion," in *Collected Works*, Vol. 15 (London: Lawrence and Wishart, 1963), p. 402.

39. New York: International Publishers, 1943, p. 64.

40. Translators' Note: In recent years the communist leadership in China seemed to be permitting more religious activity than had characterized China under Mao. The Soviet Union had earlier allowed some degree of restricted religious worship. We interpret Father Coste's statement as referring to tolerance in the official ideology. The French word we have translated "tolerance" is *ouverture*.

41. *Note sul Machiavelli, sulla politia e sullo Stato moderno* (Turin: Einaudi, 1966), p. 237.

42. *Note sul Machiavelli*, p. 238.

43. *Il materialismo storico e la filosofia di Benedetto Croce* (Turin: Einaudi, 1972), p. 28.

44. Trans. Leonard Mayhew (New York: Simon and Schuster, 1972), pp. 74-77.

45. Paris: Robert Laffont, 1975, p. 265.

46. Xavier Dijon, "*Parole d'homme*. A propos du livre de Roger Garaudy," in *Nouvelle Revue Théologique* 97 (1975), pp. 970-75. "One must acknowledge," he

concludes at the end of his critique of the book "however astounding the journey of this former Stalinist may be, Roger Garaudy fits precisely within the atheistic tradition of Hegel, Feuerbach, and Marx. And, when it comes to fundamentals, when it comes to uttering a human word, can one be simultaneously a Christian and a Marxist?" (p. 975). He further remarks, however—and rightly!—"This book challenges us."

47. *Jesus für Atheisten* (Berlin-Stuttgart: Kreuz Verlag, 1973); *Gesù per gli atei* (Assisi: Citadella Editrice, 1973).

48. *Gott ist nicht ganz tot* (Munich: Kaiser, 1971); Eng. trans., *God Is Not Yet Dead* (Harmondsworth, Eng.: Penguin, 1973).

49. Roland Leroy, Antoine Casanova, André Moine, *Les marxistes et l'évolution du monde catholique* (Paris: Editions sociales, 1972), p. 114.

50. *Les marxistes*, p. 127.

51. *Les marxistes*, pp. 130-31.

52. *Les marxistes*, p. 128.

53. Quoted by Roger Aubert, *Le pontificat de Pie IX* (Paris: Bloud et Gay, 1963), p. 45.

54. Adrien Dansette, *Histoire religieuse de la France contemporaine*, Vol. 1 (Paris: Flammarion, 1948), p. 365.

55. In *Moniteur* (September 21, 1848), quoted by Aubert, *Le pontificat*, p. 48.

56. Quoted by Aubert, *Le pontificat*, p. 49.

57. A. Ricard, *L'abbé Combalot*, pp. 392 and 395, quoted by Aubert, *Le pontificat*, p. 49.

58. *La Commission extraparlementaire de 1849* (Paris, 1937), p. 31, quoted by Aubert, *Le pontificat*, p. 50.

59. "On the Jewish Question," in *The Marx-Engels Reader*, ed. Robert C. Tucker (New York: Norton, 1978), p. 52.

60. Quoted by Gollwitzer, *The Christian Faith and the Marxist Criticism of Religion*, p. 20.

61. *Die Botschaft für die Welt* (Munich: 1960), pp. 38-39, quoted by Gollwitzer, *The Christian Faith*, p. 21.

62. Cf. *Capital*, p. 35.

63. Cf. *Capital*, p. 35.

64. *The Alternative Future*, p. 102.

65. *Pensées*, No. 84 (Lafuma numeration); cf. trans. by Martin Turnell (New York: Harper and Brothers, 1962), p. 132.

66. *Capital*, p. 365, footnote 2.

67. *The Poverty of Philosophy* (1844), in *Collected Works*, Vol. 6 (New York: International Publishers, 1976), p. 212.

68. *The German Ideology*, p. 439.

69. *Economie et philosophie* (1844), in *Oeuvres: Economie*, Vol. 2 (Paris: Gallimard, 1968), p. 27.

70. *Grundrisse*, trans. Martin Nicolaus (New York: Vintage, 1973), p. 488.

71. Cf. *The Marx-Engels Reader*, ed. Robert C. Tucker, p. 531.

72. Cf. *Capital*, pp. 34-35.

73. Engels, *Anti-Dühring*, pp. 390-91.

74. Georges M. Cottier, *L'athéisme du jeune Marx* (Paris: Vrin, 1969), p. 340.

75. Paul D. Dognin, *Initiation à Karl Marx* (Paris: Cerf, 1970), pp. 267-68.

76. *L'anti-capitalisme. Essai de réhabilitation de l'économie politique* (Grenoble: Arthaud, 1974), p. 67.

77. *The Communist Manifesto*, in *The Marx-Engels Reader*, p. 490.

78. René Coste, "Stratégie pour demain, analyse, éthique et prospective, " in *Défense nationale* (July 1975), pp. 111-23.

79. *Industrie et création collective*, Vol. 1 (Paris: PUF, 1964), p. 86.

80. *La lutte des classes* (Paris: Gallimard, 1964), p. 53.

81. *Critique et avenir de socialisme* (Paris: Seuil, 1971), p. 59.

82. *Marxisme et humanisme*, 3rd ed. (Paris: PUF, 1961), p. 157.

83. *The Russian Revolution*, pp. 74-75.

84. *The Russian Revolution*, p. 75.

85. *The Russian Revolution*, p. 60.

86. *Marx et Saint Paul* (Paris: Cerf, 1973), p. 51.

87. Cf. *The Unperfect Society*, p. 16.

88. Cf. *The Unperfect Society*. p. 131.

89. *The Nature of Faith*, trans. Ronald Gregor Smith (London: Collins, 1961), p. 176.

90. Cf. *Theology of Hope*, trans. James W. Leitch (New York: Harper, 1967), p. 338.

91. Cf. *Theology of Hope*, p. 15.

92. *Théologie de l'espérance* (Paris: Cerf, 1970), p. 395. [Translators' note: The quotation is from an Appendix that does not appear in the English translation by Leitch.]

93. *The Apostles' Creed in the Light of Today's Questions*, trans. Margaret Kohl (London: SCM, 1972), p. 177.

94. *Theology of Hope*, p. 166.

95. André Dartigues, *Le croyant devant la critique contemporaine* (Paris: Centurion, 1975), p. 123.

96. Fernando Belo, *Lecture matérialiste de l'Evangile de Marc* (Paris: Cerf, 1974), p. 391; Eng. trans., *A Materialist Reading of the Gospel of Mark* (Maryknoll, N.Y.: Orbis Books, 1981), p. 288.

97. *The Apostles' Creed*, pp. 177-78.

98. *The Myth of Sisyphus and Other Essays*, trans. Justin O'Brien (New York: Knopf, 1955), p. 92.

Chapter 4

Marxist Anthropology and Christian Anthropology

The ambition of Marxism, as we shall see, is to produce a new type of human being in full bloom, at least in the context of the classless society of its projected utopia. This ambition is shared by Christianity—and Christianity does not localize it in relation to the absolute future of the divine promise, but in relation to the initial conversion to Jesus Christ and the sacramental experience of baptism, which together signify a radical transformation of existence. "You have put on the new nature," St. Paul wrote to the Colossians, "which is being renewed in knowledge after the image of its creator" (3:10).

It could certainly be objected that there are radical differences in the levels of meaning and in the concrete goals of Marxist anthropology as compared with Christian anthropology. The overall goal remains nonetheless identical in purpose: the total fulfillment of the human being. Therefore a comparison is called for and it promises to be revealing.

It is true that Marxist humanism has been radically called into question not only by its usual adversaries, but also by some of those who have lived for a long time within its orbit and who have even been among its most prestigious theoreticians. We can cite, for instance, Milovan Djilas:

> It seems to me that we are witnessing the twilight of every kind of humanism that starts off with doctrinaire and theoretical hypotheses about the human being; this applies particularly to communist humanism, which no one has ever explained properly, or ever will, although communists overflow with love for the abstract "person of the future" while they are disenfranchising and neglecting the human being around them.

As far as he personally is concerned, he declares that he has "moved toward a new, undoctrinaire, unidealized, existential humanism."[1]

For their part the founders of Marxism were violently opposed to what they believed to be the Christian conception of human nature. We can establish this from the reckless charge of Karl Marx against "the social principles of Christianity" and his vitriolic comments on the story of Fleur-de-Marie in

Eugène Sue's novel, *Les Mystères de Paris*. Since then Marxism, even when its opposition is expressed in a less violent way, has not ceased to reproach Christianity for what Marx called "its cult of the abstract person."[2] This is a reproach at least partially merited by the historical behavior of Christians. Has not the time come for them to open themselves, on the level of anthropology, to a new understanding of the gospel?

Social Relationships and the Human Essence

If there is an essential characteristic of Marxist anthropology, it is surely that the human being is considered as the confluence or nexus of the social relationships that are realized in its psycho-biological individuality. This is true to the point that that anthropology seems to be identified with the field of forces that those relationships constitute in the human person. And it is true to the further point that the ontological reality underlying human psycho-biological individuality seems to be completely forgotten, at least in the theoretical presentations that have been given to us. It is easy to conclude that this was already the intuition of the young Marx when he employed the concept of *generic being*, although he was quick to repudiate it and Althusser considers it to be pre-Marxist. "The human being," Marx explained, "shows itself to be a conscious generic being—that is, a being that relates itself to its species as to its own proper nature, or to itself as a generic being."[3]

True, this was still a philosophical and abstract formulation. The young thinker was then insufficiently aware of the economic and sociological dimensions of human reality and he had hardly begun to see the importance of class conflict, on which he would soon concentrate all his attention. Should we, like some of his interpreters, be satisfied to regret this? It is rather the contrary that I regret: not that he should have opened himself to certain concrete dimensions of reality, but that his new discovery should have moved him to relegate to the shadows that full dimension of human nature that dictates that human individuals, despite all the social antagonisms in which they find themselves, are bound to the whole of humanity by the deepest fibers of their being.

Does, for example, the fact that someone is an employer or an employee prevent them from being ontologically a human person? Does the fact that two persons confront each other in the class struggle cancel the possibility of all respect and all dialogue between them? I shall return to these serious questions. I wanted only to emphasize at this time that Marx's first inquiry retains a lively interest for anyone who would wish to undertake a new anthropological formulation. It is significant that it is this early formulation that neo-Marxists of the "revisionist" school prefer to explore.

On the other hand, perhaps Marx never did forget completely his first perspective. Take, for example, the following text on *alienated labor* as he wrote it during that first inquiry into the question of the generic human person:

The object of labor is, therefore, the realization of generic human life: the human person replicates itself not only intellectually, as in consciousness, but also actively, in exterior reality, and therefore it contemplates itself in a world that it has created. In tearing away from workers the object of their production, therefore, estranged labor tears away from their generic life, their generic objectivity. It transforms their advantage over animals into the disadvantage that their inorganic body—their nature—is taken away from them.[4]

We could compare this text with many others in *Capital* where Marx criticizes the capitalist system not only for exploiting workers but also for preventing them from realizing their human potential. Was he not right? The critique of capitalism is valid only if it is founded on the fundamental dignity of every human being and the unity of humankind. But then we are brought back to the first Marxist inquiry. If you try too hard to reconcile the mature Marx with the Marx of the early works, you risk undermining the very foundations of the Marxist revolutionary enterprise.

We might say as much of the text in which the young Marx compares the *positive humanism* of communism with the "theoretical humanism" of atheism, which, however, he is careful to include, although wishing to surpass it dialectically: "Atheism is humanism mediated with itself through the annulment of religion, whereas communism is humanism mediated with itself through the annulment of private property. Only through the annulment of this mediation—which is itself, however, a necessary premise—does positively self-deriving humanism, *positive humanism*, come into being." Let us not forget the qualification that immediately follows these lines, according to which atheism and communism are "the first real coming-to-be, the realization become real for the human being of the human essence—of the essence of the human being as something real."[5]

We can agree that this manner of expressing himself is too Hegelian and that it is not exactly a brilliant display of clarity, but we should also realize that we are already situated in a revolutionary context, with the suppression of private property and the call for a practical listing of objectives. In any case, it is human fulfillment in its full potential that Marx is looking for here, with the express intention of breaking the locks that keep the human person from its realization.

My insistence that we not lose sight of Marx's original anthropological inquiry—both because it seems to me to be provocative and because it remains present in his later work—does not mean that we fail to recognize, with Althusser, what he has called an "epistemological break" between the earlier and the later writings. The significance of this break is located precisely in the domain of anthropology, understood in the broad sense of a conception of human nature. According to Althusser, the great discovery of Marx was to see that history is "a process with neither subject nor end(s)."

At any rate, this is the heart of Althusser's interpretation, his most profound conviction, which he never ceases repeating, with only minor variations. "History," he insists in a recent text, "is truly a 'process with neither subject nor end(s),' whose given circumstances, where persons act under the determination of social relations, are the product of the class struggle. Therefore history does not have a subject, in the philosophical meaning of the word, but a motor: the class struggle."[6] He also thinks that we ought to "dispense completely with the theoretical services of a concept of the human being, which seems to him "useless from a scientific point of view . . . because it is not scientific." According to him, this would be the attitude of Marx himself, who in his mature works would "never ever again introduce as *theoretical* concepts the concepts of human nature or humanism; but other, quite new concepts, the concepts of mode of production, forces of production, superstructure, ideology, and so forth."[7]

Althusser's concern for scientific rigor, which leads him to speak of "Marx's theoretical anti-humanism,"[8] goes so far as to make him suspicious with regard to an expression such as "real or socialist humanism." He admits only that it could "serve as a *practical, ideological* slogan insofar as it is exactly adequate to its function and not confused with a quite different function." In any case, in "no way" does he admit that it could "abrogate the attributes of a *theoretical* concept."[9]

Was this scientific dehumanization already the work of Marx? I think that Althusser is fundamentally right, but that his mentor was fortunately more complex. Not only did Marx's first inquiry remain as an underlying element of his entire work, even though hidden, beyond the famous "break," but the most vibrant and convincing pages of his most basic book of theory, *Capital*, are precisely those in which he denounces the dehumanization of industrial workers, as a result of the inhuman conditions of work and of life that had been imposed on them by the harshness of capitalism in the nineteenth century.

It is nonetheless true that *Marx passed from an anthropological conception that was essentially philosophical to an anthropological conception that was socio-philosophical.* I deliberately use a composite formula to describe this second conception, for I believe that it remains philosophical even though it embodies a highly scientific component of the sociological type. A statement such as the one I am about to quote remains clearly on a scientific level and its wording is noteworthy: "The human being is in the most literal sense a *zoon politikon*, not merely a gregarious animal, but an animal that can individuate itself only in the midst of society."[10] The distinction embodied here between "the political" and "the social" puts in its proper place the excessively broad conception of the former that is so fashionable at the present time. I cannot say the same, from my viewpoint, of the famous Thesis 6 on Feuerbach where "the essence of the human person" is defined as "the ensemble of the social relations,"[11] which is considered, rightly, as the most lapidary and synthetic statement of this new idea.

Marxist theoreticians never stop waxing ecstatic on this subject. It will suffice to quote Lucien Sève:

It is precisely on this point that in 1845-46 Marx and Engels made the crucial breakthrough to the radically new philosophy that Marxism is, when they arrived at the concept that the human essence—whose elucidation was the quixotic goal of speculative philosophy—is nothing other than the ensemble of social relationships that human beings necessarily establish among themselves, and first of all, in the material production of their existence.[12]

This quotation is significant. It has the merit of forcefully emphasizing that the final Marxist formulation of the essence of the human person remains philosophical at its core and that science constitutes only one element of it. This statement does not imply in itself that the conception has any less value, although I do have to question it. My purpose is only to reveal its true character. Science does not permit one to formulate such a conception while pretending to remain on its terrain. From the point of view of science it is an extrapolation.

Let me recall here the same sentence that I quoted earlier from the famous passsage of the *Contribution to the Critique of Political Economy*, which I called "a synthetic exposition of Marxist analysis by Marx himself": "It is not human consciousness that determines human existence; it is social existence that determines human consciousness." Let us link this statement—in my opinion of decisive importance in Marxist theory and, from all the evidence, a corollary of Thesis 6 on Feuerbach—with the principal components of Marx's doctrine of class struggle.

It seems to me that the following interpretation suggested by Pierre Bigo is well founded:

There is no other consciousness than class consciousness—consciousness that is either reactionary or revolutionary. No element foreign to a perspective on class enters into consciousness. Consciousness is defined strictly in terms of economic structure and, therefore, ultimately in political terms.[13]

In this hypothesis we are far beyond the simple statement that consciousness is strongly conditioned by class membership, a statement that would be perfectly accurate. What we have here, in reality, is a statement of the philosophical order on "the essence of consciousness," defined by class membership—defined still more precisely by the position occupied in the relationships of production, with all the social antagonisms to which the individual is subjected by that very fact. Bigo's interpretation, it seems to me, proceeds logically from the dynamic of Marxist theory.

Here is a particularly clear passage from *The German Ideology*:

The phantoms formed in the brains of human beings are also, necessarily, sublimates of their material life-process, which is empirically verifiable and bound to material premises. Thus morality, religion, metaphysics, and all the rest of ideology, as well as the forms of consciousness corresponding to them, no longer retain the semblance of independence. They have no history, no development. Human beings, engaging in material production and pursuing material interaction, alter, along with the world around them, their own thinking and the products of their thinking. It is not consciousness that determines life, but life that determines consciousness.[14]

Having explored one of its principal articulations, which is clearly related to an element of philosophical materialism that we have already had the opportunity to spotlight on several occasions, we thus find ourselves back at historical materialism.

Transcendence or Historical Necessity?

Despite the severe criticisms that I shall be compelled to express, I recognize that Marxist anthropology contains an important element of truth in the emphasis it puts on the *social dimensions of the human being*. Certainly this is a fact widely recognized by the human sciences today. But we should not forget two other facts. First, that if this is so, it is partly due to an obvious influence of Marxist analysis in the various scientific disciplines. Second, that the founders of Marxism, without having entirely been the initiators on this point, have greatly contributed toward demonstrating that the human personality is profoundly conditioned by the complex field of social relationships in which it is involved.

In fact, if sociology was not born with the founders of Marxism, they have contributed a great deal to it and rare are the sociologists today who would completely ignore their contribution. Of all the scientific analyses, whether of the classical or psycho-sociological school, it is certainly the one that most emphasizes the social dimensions of the human being. From this point of view one of the important contributions of Marxism is its highlighting of the strongly conflictual character of social relationships throughout the period of history under study. (Perhaps it has done so to excess; I shall return to this point.) It also had the merit, more than any other analysis, of helping to discover the great importance of the phenomenon of social classes and their antagonisms within industrial society. (Here again doubtless to excess, as we shall see.)

We cannot say that it has done so good a job in analyzing the realities of nation and race—by reason of its lopsided polarization around class struggle. But, when one understands to what extent the human being is marked by social relationships, it is easy to understand that ethnic or racial identity will have profound repercussions on personality, especially when ethnic or racial groups confront one another in a limited geographical space.

Similar analyses of all political and economic relationships will have to be made, as also of cultural relationships, wherein the impact of language on the formation of personality should be given special notice.

The study of history, constructed by the interaction of all these social relationships through the course of time, will no longer appear simply as a matter of scientific curiosity, but as the analysis of the temporal dimensions of human personalities and of the terrain that fashions them. Personal psychology (including psychoanalysis, of course) is no longer the study of an individual turned in upon itself, but that of the human personality shaping itself through its social relationships. Robinson Crusoe on his island had in fact brought with him the society that had fashioned him and that he had internalized.

You may have noticed that I have been using metaphors evocative of the construction of a house or the shaping of pottery. I have done so with a view to hinting at what all these analyses are converging toward: the notion that the human personality, although an individual and individualized reality, fashions itself concretely through the complex interaction of multiple social relationships. To speak philosophically of the social dimensions of the human being is to use language with ontological import.

By reason of its content of rational truth Marxist anthropology represents a challenge to the Christian faith. It is of the highest practical importance to understand that *theological discourse*—even when it is speaking authentically of the word of God and the most fundamental truths of the faith—is structured both in its formulation and in the comprehension of its hearers and readers by particular social dimensions of culture, language, ethnic and racial membership, and social class. This means that it can be significant for some and not for others, and that its claim to universality, even if it be legitimate, must accept the humble limitations of its diverse particularities. Even though they may have a strong faith and strive to bear witness to it with firmness, pastors and theologians who understand this will be less dogmatic in their affirmations as well as in their condemnations. They will be moved to look for language that is better adapted to particular hearers or readers. They will also accept more easily other formulations of the faith, except when competent and profound study convinces them of their inaccuracy.

There is another challenge here that touches us even more deeply. The *Christian individualism*, which has so deeply marked the last centuries of the history of the church, is here called into question. This is the individualism of the concept of salvation reflected in the verse "I have only one soul to save" of a popular French hymn. It became an egotistical and solitary pursuit, bereft of any concern for evangelization. It was the individualism that went hand in glove with an isolationist Christian life in which no attention at all was given to communitarian interests. It saw participation in the Eucharist as a purely individual and interior concern, in contrast with the lifestyle taught by Jesus Christ, which is essentially communitarian. It was the individualism of a great many Christians who gloried in their (supposed) uninvolvement in political life and who were careful, often under the loftiest of pretexts, not to participate in any collective undertaking, as if evangelical charity should be confined to the strictly personal realm.

On the doctrinal level—that of the official teachings of the church—neither the significance of structures (whether helpful or harmful) nor the conditioning of mentalities was in general understood clearly enough. The result was that social doctrine usually stopped halfway, despite the good intentions of its framers.

In the end, we are compelled to take seriously our *fellowship in God*. We must accept it as a dimension that structures our relationships with our fellow humans. And we must accept the mandate that we continually concretize that fellowship on both the interpersonal and the collective plane. Perception of the social dimensions of the human person calls for perception of the social dimensions of the faith. The apostolic church admirably understood this for its time. It is up to the church of our time to understand it as well, in the light of new potentialities. The more we think about it, the more we see how much the individualism inherent in liberal ideology has scarred the concrete life of the churches.

My criticism of Marxist anthropology is no less firm, and above all I question its synthetic formulation in Thesis 6 on Feuerbach. I readily agree with Lucien Sève that it is not the human *individual* that is identified therein, with the totality of its social relationships, but rather the human *essence*. However, does this distinction suffice to counter the radical objection that such an identification raises? Must not the human essence be recognized as identical in all human beings? Is it not precisely what makes an individual a human being? To be capable of forming human social relationships, is it not necessary to be a human person—not necessarily a "finished" person, but one capable of properly human achievement, one composed of spirit and body, naturally endowed with the capacity for intelligence, volition, and feeling?

Is not an anthropology that looks for its basis exclusively in social relationships a building without sound ontological foundations, a tree without roots? The most orthodox Marxist interpretation compels me to insist on this radical objection, against all those who would seek to blunt the point of the famous thesis by claiming that it means only that persons are *conditioned* by their social relationships.

It is enough to see how Lucien Sève argues against "the idea that the human person is not reducible to social relationships," an idea that he maintains—emphatically and ironically—is "particularly dear to all speculative humanist interpretation of Marxism,"[15] which he repudiates. If we read a few lines of his argument, we will get the point:

> This cannot in the least justify the idea that philosophical humanism always seeks to convey in its formula, "individuals are not reducible to social relationships," and is even its *raison d'être*—that is, the idea that as far as what is most essential, most intrinsic, and most eminent in them, human beings are *not* the product of history but *transcend* it, that

within their innermost being they are not *determined* by, but only *influenced* by, the social relationships in respect of which they retain an essential *freedom*.[16]

This idea is *par excellence* the one that historical materialism was formulated *against*. Marxism is not, as such, a "philosophy of freedom"; it is the scientific theory of historical necessity and, at the same time, of the concrete liberation of humankind. I have already acknowledged the truth that it contains in this regard. My objection to it remains basic.

Let others not object that we are here concerned only with a theoretical question! I would respond that this theory has decisive practical consequences: it provides the foundation for the Marxist identification of human beings with their social class, as well as the theory and practice of absolute class struggle. The following observations of Berdyaev summarize very neatly the Marxist conception on this subject:

> Marxism is interested so exclusively in class that it does not see the individual: in every thought and estimation of the human person, the Marxists see only class, with its special class interests. Thought is only an expression of class, and is of no value by itself. Bourgeois, capitalist reason is a different thing from proletarian, communist reason. And there can be no agreement between these two kinds of reason, only war to the death.[17]

I agree with his criticism, and without in any way lessening my solidarity with the working class, to which I belong by social origin. "It is not the discovery of truth that results from a person's class situation," Berdyaev notes, "but rather the deformation of the truth and downright falsehood. Truth is revealed when persons overcome the limitations of their class situation, because this class situation determines not the whole person but merely some of its aspects."[18]

Turning to the practical domain, what are we to think about the dictatorship and totalitarianism that have characterized all communist regimes to the present day? True, they may be only caricatures of true human sociality, but are they not the concrete consequences of a theory that defines the human essence in terms of the totality of social relationships? I do not mean that they are *inevitable* consequences of such a theory, but only that it *can* lead to them.

In any case, what theoretical defense can someone in an oppressive society invoke against it? In Marxist analysis, there is no defense for someone who invokes freedom from within a socialist society. It simply is not permitted. And persistence will be met with chastisement.

Besides, how can there be any legitimate complaint in a society that is so totally liberative? (I am not forgetting that neo-Marxists of the "revisionist" school have had the courage to question this "dogma." Adam Schaff has resolutely posed the problem of alienation in socialist society.)[19]

In theory, in a liberal society, it is the right of the individual that takes precedence. In practice, it is often the right of the strongest. In a Marxist society the individual is never right in any confrontation with society. On this precise point of my criticism anyone can easily grasp the frightful clarity of the following observations of Berdyaev about Lenin, which applied even more to his immediate successor and remain true for the highest levels of the Soviet bureaucracy:

> Lenin did not believe in the human person. He recognized in it no sort of interior principle. He did not believe in spirit and the freedom of the spirit, but he had a boundless faith in the social regimentation of human beings. He believed that a compulsory social organization could create any sort of new person you like—for instance, a completely social person who would no longer require the use of force.[20]

For the same reasons Stalin's vaunted formula, "human beings, that most precious capital," is extremely dangerous, for it reduces the human person to the level of an object with which one may do what one wishes—give it or sell it—and still regard it as precious. In the context in which Stalin pronounced it, does this statement not betray his conviction of the total control of the state over the individual? It is true that liberal ideology also speaks often of "human capital." Here again the human person risks being reduced to the level of an object. Words are never innocuous.

The critique from *the viewpoint of faith* can be stated briefly, however great its import. It appeals to the dignity of the human person as "the image of God," with the freedom willed by the creator, the profound transformation made possible by evangelical conversion, and personal participation in the divine life inaugurated by the risen Jesus. These biblical themes reinforce with all their weight the rational criticism of the dwarfing of the human essence to its social dimensions.

As for *the reformulation of the faith*, I can again limit myself to a brief reflection. It is obviously the evangelical doctrine of the fellowship of all human beings in God and the Pauline teaching of the (Mystical) Body of Christ that our present responsibility as Christians should lead us to rediscover and apply to our time in all their theological density and practical relevance. Some decades ago Catholic theology and the official teaching of the papacy had magnificently restored to a position of honor the doctrine of the Mystical Body. Perhaps it has become a little blurred in our minds at the present time, doubtless because Catholics find it too abstract, too little relevant to the political scene, or because they are reluctant to appeal to a language that appears mythical ("mystical") to non-Christians.

How can we not applaud the discovery of the consequences or political effects of a true human fellowship? The "fellowship" (*fraternité*) of the French republican trilogy was too often only a vague sentimentalism and it could conceal a genuine mystification in promoting a collaboration of classes to the real detriment of the exploited classes. It is essential that Christians break away from such an attitude, into which they have too often fallen, and that they open their minds to the structural changes that the world of today calls for. But that is no reason for consigning to the shadows their greatest riches of thought and of spiritual life.

We should try to grasp, in all their anthropological relevance, the profundity of Karl Barth's observations on Jesus Christ, "the man for others,"[21] and on his "cohumanity":

> Jesus has to let his being, himself, be prescribed and dictated and determined by an alien human existence (that of his more near and distant fellow humans), and by the need and infinite peril of this being. He is not of himself. He does not live in an original humanity in which he could be far more glorious perhaps, in virtue of his divine determination. No, the glory of his humanity is simply to be so fully claimed and "confined" by his fellows, by their state and fate, by their lowliness and misery. . . . If there is indeed a powerful *I* in Jesus, it is from this *thou*, from fallen Adam, from the race that springs from him, from Israel and the sequence of its generations, from a succession of rebels, from a history that is the history of its unfaithfulness.[22]

We might perhaps discover in this passage a certain implicit reference to the conceptualization of Marxist anthropology. In any case, what it says integrates social relationship perfectly, without being reduced to it, and points to a model of life in the total gift of self and the most all-embracing fellowship imaginable.

Human Personhood

The fact that Marx defined the human essence in terms of social relationships did not prevent him from producing elements of a humanism that was at once attractive, original, and provocative. This is true in his more mature works, but especially in his early writings, when he had not yet come to a definition that was so restrictive and so heavy with consequences.

The young Marx was already a revolutionary. Although his strategy was still very vague, he already envisioned a transformation of society in depth, which he expected to produce *the true human being*: "Society produces humankind in the entire richness of its being—produces the *rich* humankind *profoundly endowed with all its senses*—as its enduring reality."[23]

How could we refuse to accept this magnificent formulation, even if we do not read into it exactly the same objective content as the young atheist thinker? Let us admire also, in the same context, the analysis of what he understood by the education of the senses, and especially by such happy expressions as "the human sense of the senses" and "the humanness of the senses":

> Only through the objectively unfolded richness of humankind's essential being is the richness of subjective *human* sensibility (a musical ear, an eye for beauty of form—in short, *senses* capable of human gratifications, senses confirming themselves as essential powers of the human person) either brought into being or cultivated. For not only the five organic senses but also the so-called spiritual senses—the practical senses (will, love, etc.); in a word, *human* sense, the humanness of the senses—come to be by virtue of their object, by virtue of *humanized* nature. The forming of the five senses is a labor of the entire history of the world down to the present. The sense caught up in crude practical need has only a restricted sense. For the starving person, it is not the human form of food that exists. . . . The objectification of the human essence, both in its theoretical and practical aspects, is required to make the human person's *sense human*, as well as to create the *human sense* corresponding to the entire wealth of human and natural substance.[24]

It does seem that it is the materialist conception of the young author that moved him to include the will and love in what he called "the practical senses," but we are not obliged to share his materialism.

Along with the definition of the human essence as the totality of social relationships, the other important characteristic of Marxist anthropology is the concept of the human person as *homo faber*, as producer, as producing its personality through work. This characteristic converges with the first. From this point of view Marx is very much of his time—one of the most characteristic thinkers of industrial and technical society. In this he proves himself a true disciple of St. Simon, and technocrats of the liberal school will agree with him. Observe, for example, how he expressed himself in *Capital* in reference to Benjamin Franklin: "The use and fabrication of instruments of labor, although existing germinally in certain species of animals, is specifically characteristic of the human labor process, and Franklin therefore defines the human being as 'a tool-making animal.' "[25]

Let us say then, using the accepted Latin expression, *homo faber*. The consistent materialist that Marx wanted to be insisted that we see the human being as producer of the indispensable means of its biological existence: food and clothing. "Human beings can be distinguised from animals," we read in *The German Ideology*, "by consciousness, by religion, or anything else you like. They themselves begin to distinguish themselves from animals as soon as they begin to *produce* their means of subsistence, a step that is conditioned by their physical organization. By producing their means of subsistence, human beings are indirectly producing their material life."[26] (We could ask in passing why it was only the human species that made this "step forward." Was it not because it alone was radically endowed with potentialities that were completely lacking in other species?)

The producer is obviously the *worker*. It is on the worker that Marxism has especially focused its attention, because, according to Marx, humankind situates itself essentially in the context of industrial society. For ideological reasons he focuses principally on the manual worker, or at least on the one who works directly on matter. Marxist theory will go so far as to speak of a *self-creation* of humankind by its work. That was already the position of the young Marx, who did not hesitate to give credit for it to Hegel, while reproaching him for a conception of his intuition that was too abstract, too narrow.

"The outstanding thing in Hegel's *Phenomenology*," Marx acknowledged, "and its final outcome—that is, the dialectic of negativity as the moving and generating principle—is thus first that Hegel conceives the self-genesis of humankind as a process, conceives objectification as loss of the object, as alienation and as suppression of this alienation. He thus grasps the essence of *labor*, comprehends objective humankind—true because real—as the outcome of its *own labor*."[27]

We should not be surprised, in the light of this, to read in the same work the following observation on the fabrication of universal history: "Because for socialists the entire so-called history of the world is nothing but the begetting of humankind through human labor—nothing but the coming-to-be of nature for humankind—socialists have the visible, irrefutable proof of their *birth* through themselves, of their *process* of *coming-to-be*."[28] The old Engels wrote without flinching, "Labor created humankind itself."[29] This conception therefore could only remain central for their disciples.

These are noteworthy insights, we might say, on the essential role of work in the fashioning of personality—or its dehumanization, if the work is purely repetitive or too painful. That is true and I shall return to it. But we should note that one can speak of self-creation only in an atheistic context and that the expression contains in itself a polemical atheistic thrust. "The only practicable emancipation of Germany," wrote the young Marx, "is the emancipation based on the theory that holds that the human being is the supreme being for humankind."[30]

Later he will abandon this language of Feuerbachian manufacture, which still seemed to him to imply a certain transcendence. For that was surely his essential rejection: the *rejection of all transcendence*. We have already encountered Marxist atheism. It will suffice then to note that Marxist humanism is an *atheistic humanism*. It involves a deliberate intention to exalt human nature. We can acknowledge its positive intention but, in its concrete form, is it not as illusory as it is dangerous? Listen, for example, to the frenzied directive of Gorky: "We must make humankind understand that it is the creator and the master of the world, that it is on humankind that the responsibility falls for all the evil of the earth, but that it is to humankind also that the glory belongs for all the good in life."[31]

If the human essence is defined by the totality of social relationships, it is *society* that is exalted, in the final analysis. But what if society is oppressive?

Without forgetting this question, we welcome with pleasure the concept of *the integral individual* in *Capital*—literally, the totally developed individual (*das total entwickelte Individuum*), which Marx opposed to the fractured or partial individual (*Teilindividuum*). The fragmentation of the human person, the setting up of obstacles that prevent the human fulfillment of workers, is possibly the greatest reproach that he addressed to the capitalist industrial society of his time.

Conscious as Marx was of the evolution of technology and situating it in his own perspective of an advanced industrial society of the *socialist* type, he foresaw a higher technological level where it would be necessary to call for the diversification of tasks and for creativity:

> Modern industry, indeed, compels society, under penalty of death, to replace the detail-worker of today, crippled by lifelong repetition of one and the same trivial operation, and thus reduced to a mere fragment of a human being, by fully developed individuals, fit for a variety of labors, ready to face any change of production, and to whom the different social functions they perform are but so many modes of giving free scope to their own natural and acquired powers.[32]

Naturally, inasmuch as we are dealing here with a materialist perspective, we must not imagine that this concept would sanction what might be a spiritual component of the human being that would not be at root the product of biological matter and that might subsist after death. Even a Marxist as open to Christianity as Garaudy comments ironically on "the pretended immortality of Plato's soul."[33] Although he says he includes the Christian hope of "eternal life" in his thinking, for him it is a question "not of *another* life, but of a certain quality, a certain density and intensity of this life."[34] He is precise: "Eternity does not exist in another life. Not in another world. Not outside time."[35]

It is a fundamental characteristic of Marxist anthropology that it rejects the immaterial nature of the soul, as Lucien Sève explains: "For historical materialism the denial of the soul as a 'nonmaterial substance' is definitely established of course, and there can be no question of reverting to it."[36] That does not mean, he explains, that Marxists refuse to speak of the soul. What is necessary he says, is to try to arrive at "rigorously grasping what constitutes the *rational kernel* of the notion of the soul, the *scientific concept* of soul— namely, *the dynamic of nonphysiological relations that give life to a personality*. From this point of view a concept of the soul is not only fitted to function in materialist theory but—I will even say—materialism cannot dispense with it without becoming meaningless."[37]

Let me add that Marx did not necessarily reject the concept of human nature, but he reacted strongly against every rigid interpretation and he insisted especially on emphasizing the historical dimension. That was a point, for example, on which he thought the philosophers of the eighteenth century were found wanting (not without reason, it is true).[38]

We cannot speak of Marxist anthropology without making reference to the problem of *alienation*, which has recently given rise to passionate controversies. As Franz Grégoire explains:

> Alienation *(Entäusserung, Entfremdung)* means in the language of Marx, which he borrowed from Hegel, the separation of what ought to be united, with conflict between the separate elements. The term that in current French best conveys this idea is *"divorce."* The end of alienation is "reappropriation" *(Aneignung)* or "reconciliation" *(Versöhnung).*[39]

For the school of Althusser this would be a pre-Marxist concept that the more mature Marx later abandoned. In any case, it would not enter into the conceptual apparatus of Marxism properly understood.

We might note with Maximilien Rubel the transition from the concept of alienation, much used in the manuscripts of 1844, to that of *reification (Verdinglichung)*, which occurs gradually in the manuscripts of 1857-58, but does not reach a final formulation until *Capital*. But he notes that "the ethical meaning of the concept of alienation will pass intact into the concept of 'reification,' applied to human relations under the rule of a capitalist economy."[40] I think so also.

Apart from some differences in vocabulary, I would readily agree with Ernest Mandel in the following analysis: "It is in the transformation of the theory of alienation from an anthropological conception, metaphysical and resigned, into a historical conception, dialectical and revolutionary, that lies, in brief, the significance of the enormous amount of work in the field of political economy that Marx carried out."[41]

We are continually running into the ethical dimension in Marx's work. In *Capital* is it not the fact that it has been thought out in terms of alienation that provides the percussive force of his denunciation of the dehumanization of capitalist society?

I shall conclude by raising the problem of *human subjectivity*, on which Garaudy has greatly insisted in reaction to the Althusser school and as part of his claim that he has rediscovered the true Marx. In a magnificent passage he writes: "This, then, is the new task of socialism. It must provide each and every person with the real opportunity to become a person—that is to say, a creator—at every level of their social existence, whether economic, political, or cultural."[42] Elsewhere, in terms that recall the concept of "development" in the encyclical *Populorum Progressio*, he proposes as the "ultimate goal of socialism" the "full flowering of the human person and of all persons."[43]

As a good Marxist he tries to justify his vision by reference to scientific and technological progress: "The technology of the last part of the twentieth century, that of computerization, can create conditions for an explosion of human subjectivity."[44]

We do not lack for texts of Marx in favor of subjectivity. Or we could just as well quote Lenin. For example: "The minds of tens of millions of those who are doing things create something infinitely loftier than the greatest genius can foresee."[45] We can readily welcome such a perspective, but can we reconcile it easily with the definition of the human essence as the totality of social relationships, or with the revolutionary praxis prescribed by the founders of Marxism and applied by its historical leaders?

Dehumanization

I have already admitted that despite its troublesome concept of the human essence, which reduces it to the totality of social relationships, and despite some serious reservations that I am compelled to express, *Marxist anthropology has an undeniable richness* that can be remarkably provocative for thought and action. I agree with Pierre Bigo:

> There is an affirmation of humanity in Marx. And this humanism is so essential to the Marxist political economy that you cannot tear it out without destroying the structure. The great achievements of that political economy, all related to the discovery of the meaning of work, lose their significance if you remove that background. . . . It is not really the adventure of production that interests Marx, the accumulation of material riches; it is the human adventure involved therein.[46]

With Bigo I would emphasize particularly the striking significance of the philosophy of work that is involved here: "It is not production in itself that is exalted; it is the human person at work. The grandeur of humankind at work. The misery of humankind at work. All the dynamic of Marxist thought is in that contrast, which calls to mind Pascal."[47]

The more one studies the writings of the founders of Marxism, the more one realizes that the theoretical antihumanism of Althusser, under the pretext of scientific rigor, intellectualizes them in the negative sense of the word, impoverishes them, devitalizes them. The founders' writings also sought scientific precision. Even if we do not agree with all their argumentation, we must agree with their legitimate indignation at the painful conditions of work in their time and at the resultant dehumanization of the working class. Without them perhaps we would not have understood it so well.

All work that is oppressive, endlessly repetitive, brutalizing, joyless—all these phenomena still so common in industrial society—must be denounced. With all urgency we must look for ways, if not to eliminate it entirely—probably not possible in every case—then at least to reduce it significantly, if only by shortening the length of the workweek. We are far from paying as much attention to this problem as it deserves. Practiced efforts in this direction remain woefully inadequate.

On the other hand, unemployment is too easily accepted in advanced industrial society of the liberal type. We are too easily satisfied with the guarantee of a modest subsidy for the unemployed. If the human person is dehumanized by reason of detrimental work conditions, the absence of work is also dehumanizing. Here again the founders of Marxism were on target.

This is something that will touch Christians in their inmost being only if they take their faith seriously. How deplorable it is, for example, that in the nineteenth century they were so insensitive to the dehumanization that the industrial production system caused for so many workers and their families. Worse still, certain theological circles blundered into an erroneous justification of the harshness of work on the basis of the biblical teaching on the consequences of original sin. What in the Bible was "confession" and "denunciation" of the sins of humankind, of the oppression and exploitation practiced by the powerful, became in those theological circles "legitimation" and "mystification," because their adherents did not understand the true prophetic—and critical—significance of the biblical teaching. How could they not perceive the blasphemy on their lips? It was because they read the Bible in the light of an uncritical acceptance of the ideology of capitalist society.

Death

My critique of Marxist anthropology, however, will be exacting. First, *from the standpoint of reason.* Berdyaev writes:

> The Hegelian conception [of history], as well as the Marxist conception, with their totalitarian demands, ignore the victory over death, forget the eternal tragedy of existence. Thus faith that grows in the Marxist soil of this conception of history, faith in the final resolution of conflict between the person and society, the person and history, faith in the complete rationalization of human life, is illusion and utopia. This faith stems from the subordination of all that is personal and individual to what is universal and general.[48]

The basic criticism will therefore be directed both at the reduction of the human essence to the totality of social relationships and at philosophical materialism, which defines the human spirit as the product of biological matter. I have already emphasized the first and will return to it again.

The issue of philosophical materialism raises at once the problem of *death.* On this point the thought of the founders of Marxism is terribly limited. In the immense corpus of the writings of Karl Marx there seems to be only the following text: "*Death* seems to be a harsh victory of the species over the *determinate* individual and seems to contradict their unity. But the determinate individual is only a determinate *generic being*, and as such mortal."[49]

Was the practical Marx willing to deal only with problems about which he had some comprehension? No doubt. Earlier I alluded to Engels's observation about the relentless march of the human species toward death. His description is one of somber despair:

> Millions of years may elapse, hundreds of thousands of generations be born and die, but inexorably the time will come when the declining warmth of the sun will no longer suffice to melt the ice thrusting itself forward from the poles; when the human race, crowding more and more about the equator, will finally no longer find even there enough heat for life; when gradually even the last trace of organic life will vanish; and the earth, an extinct frozen globe like the moon, will circle in deepest darkness. . . .[50]

What good is it, then, to struggle for justice, for the promotion of the human person? True, the present moment is important, but if I die defeated in the struggle? I shall have sacrificed myself for future generations, yes, but for nothing, in the end? "After all, it is only death that wins," Stalin is reported to have said to General de Gaulle.

It is true that Marxism can generate a stoic attitude in the face of death. Jacques Duclos confided to an interviewer:

> I am afraid of illness, but I am not afraid of death. I accept it with the serenity of the sages of antiquity. Let it come when it wishes; I know that it must come. When you have no fear of death, I find that you are freed from a great many anxieties.[51]

For her part Rosa Luxemburg wrote to a friend, Sonia Liebknecht: "I hope that I shall die at my post, on the barricades or in prison."[52]

The description of the death of the "red hero" by Ernst Bloch has a somber and poignant grandeur:

> Confessing to the moment of his assassination the cause for which he has lived, he advances clearly, cooly, consciously toward that Nothingness in which he was taught to believe as a free spirit. . . . The heaven toward which the martyrs raised their arms in the midst of the flames and smoke, this heaven does not exist for the red materialist; and yet he or she dies as confessor of a cause and their nobility can be compared only with that of the early Christians or a John the Baptist.[53]

From the materialist perspective that he still professes, Garaudy has written some beautiful pages on death.[54] We read there: "Death has nothing to take from the one who has known how to be detached from everything that had made one a singular, possessive particularity, and not an active, loving, joyful participant in the indivisible life of all."[55] This sense of detachment is in itself magnificent and partially Christian. But faith in the divine promises revealed in Jesus Christ provides us with a perspective very different from this stoic grandeur.

Creativity and Alienation

Let us pursue our rational critique.

The Marxist accent on *human creativity* is on target. Until recently theology had not given it adequate consideration, even though it has a noteworthy foundation in the Bible. Marx's exaltation of creativity, however, does not settle the question of its origin or of that of creation itself. There is at least one text of Marx on this subject that seems to reveal a lack of intellectual honesty.[56]

The concept of the *integral individual* is equally fertile. But does not philosophical materialism make of the human person a truncated individual? We need not go so far as Jean-Marie Domenach, who has noted that "the question of personal existence and its relation to the collectivity is not even raised by Marx."[57] I shall be less severe. It is enough to say that the question is inadequately—and badly—posed, by reason of Marx's philosophical materialism as well as his conception of the human essence. In any case, I certainly agree with Domenach that "it is not only a question of the meaning of our life and of our death," but "it is also a question of the tie that binds us to others, and of our sacrifices for them—that is, of our militancy."[58]

I have already said that Marx was right to accuse the capitalist society of his day of promoting the *alienation* or *reification* of workers (and eventually of the capitalists enslaved to money). I think we must extend the indictment to all industrial society, and to all bureaucratic society that concern themselves too little with work conditions. All serious analyses agree on the judgment that Soviet society is at least as much at fault—and even more, from the viewpoint of bureaucracy—as the advanced industrial society of the West.

I have said and say again: the problem of the harshness of certain types of work, and especially of the repetitive and boring character of certain others, is difficult to resolve in industrial society. Furthermore, the inevitable and, in the end, beneficial development of a more and more complex network of relationships seems to give birth to an equally inevitable proliferation of bureaucracy, with paralyzing consequences for freedom and initiative on the part of persons and local groups. How can we limit this to reasonable proportions?

Human Rights

A rational critique must also raise the question of *human rights* in Marxism. Marx limited himself to ironic remarks on the subject. For him "the so-called rights of the individual, as distinct from the rights of the citizen, are simply the rights of a member of civil society—that is, of egotistic humankind, of the individual separated from others and from the community.''[59] These are basic charges, which he repeated variously in a sarcastic tone. "None of the supposed rights of the human person," he assures us, ". . . go beyond the egoistic individual, the individual as such, as a member of bourgeois society—that is, as individuals separated from the community, withdrawn into themsevles, wholly preoccupied with their private interests and acting in accordance with their private caprice.''[60]

What about private property, the cornerstone of liberal ideology? "The right of property is, therefore," Marx retorts, "the right to enjoy one's fortune and to dispose of it as one will, without regard for others and independently of society. It is the right of self-interest.''[61]

And what about personal security, which occupied such an important place in the demands of the revolutionaries of 1789? The young theoretician of a new kind of revolution was no more tender on this subject: "The concept of security is not enough to raise civil society above its egoism. Security is, rather, the *assurance* of its egoism.''[62] And here is the supreme indictment from Marx's pen: "It is the human person as bourgeois and not as citizen who is considered the *true* and *authentic* person.''[63]

I have no difficulty in acknowledging that Marx was right in denouncing the narrow concept of human rights contained in liberal ideology: its individualism, as well as the oppression, exploitation, and mystification that it could conceal, for it had been conceived and designed for the profit of bourgeois property owners. But was not such a negative critique—without any reservation to safeguard a possibly positive element in what he was attacking—at once unjust and dangerous? *Unjust*, because democratic freedoms were not an empty phrase for the advanced nations of the West, even in the nineteenth century, despite the too real exploitation of the workers of that time. The popular classes of those days were not deceived on this score. *Dangerous*, because it cleared the way for dictatorship and totalitarianism, due to the lack of statutory protection for personal freedom. True, one may sing its praises ideologically and exalt democracy, but if no laws are provided or guaranteed juridically or practically, the worst kind of mystification is the result.

Confronted with what happened, for example, under the regime of Stalin, Giulio Girardi reacts—with insight—as follows:

The system we are examining is humanistic in central motivation, but comes to be embodied in an antihumanistic regime. This is not the result of pure chance. It cannot be attributed to human weakness or adverse circumstances. The fact that, up to the present, this situation has come about wherever communism has come to power, is explained by the fact that the principle of *praxis* is the sole criterion of value.

The gravest threat to Marxist personalism is not the community spirit, therefore, but the party spirit; not that the individual is sacrificed to the community, but that the majority is sacrificed to a minority. The dictatorship of the proletariat is exposed to the danger of becoming the dictatorship of the party over the proletariat, and, by the same token, of some personalities or party groups over the party.[64]

These observations are accurate, but I believe that the fundamental explanation lies in the very ambiguities of Marxist humanism.

Love

The critique from *the viewpoint of faith* will give priority to the unconditional defense of the human person, as demanded by Berdyaev: "What counts most in Christianity is the human person; for it the human soul is more precious than all the splendor in the world. For Christianity, the human person has an unconditional value."[65] With him again we must relate this question to love, a very concrete love of neighbor:

> The human personality has for Christianity an absolute value. The human soul has more value than all the kingdoms of this world. The spiritual life of the human being no longer belongs, in its integrity, to society, whatever be the form of that society; it is bound to the church and not to the state; it belongs to the kingdom of God and not to the kingdom of this world. At the base of Christianity is love of neighbor, love of humankind. At the base of Marxism there is denial of that love of God and neighbor. Marxism loves neither God nor humankind.[66]

It is true that individuals must accept the responsibility to devote themselves, and even to sacrifice themselves, for society, and political leaders have the responsibility of looking after "the common good." Also, love must find concrete form in structures; otherwise one falls into abstraction and does not take proper account of the real conditions required for promotion of the human person. By the same token, society must have profound respect for the person and leave it wide scope for free action.

While remaining open to the necessary criticisms and corrections, a responsible Christian faith must therefore be utterly sensitive to the threats that Marxist anthropology, in both its theoretical and practical aspects, represents for the human person. For the same reasons it will gladly recognize that the reevaluation of the person and of subjectivity made by neo-Marxists of the "revisionist" school has been a (partial) response to its exigencies on this subject.

Atheism and Personhood

We must also question the *atheistic dimension* of Marxist anthropology. In irrevocably closing humankind in upon itself, does it not foreclose an essential openness? Is there not at least a terrible risk that, as Berdyaev writes, "Communism is inhuman, for denial of God leads to denial of humankind"?[67]

We recall also the profound theological vision of the Book of Genesis, which shows that rupture with God brings with it the most violent ruptures between human beings, because they no longer have that center of agreement in which to meet. One can object, it is true, that individuals have fought each other violently over diverse concepts of divinity and even of Christianity. The soundness of the objection does not diminish the truth of the Bible's judgment. Such hostilities were, and are, in complete contradiction with the spirit of the gospel.

Once again Christians are sent back to the sources of their faith. Once again they are called to repentance and to the lucidity that can help them avoid ideological contaminations in contradiction with it. An example would be the unqualified condemnation of a political adversary, according to the perceptive remarks of Maurice Clavel in a recent television interview:

> I recalled that early Christianity was spread around the world by a former executioner, and an executioner of Christians, St. Paul. This means that at the height of my political struggle against a Franco or a Pinochet I cannot . . . consider them as a different species from my own, or as someone already damned; nothing is certain, nothing is final before the final hour. And so much the worse, I agree, if that weakens me. So much the worse if I cannot give way to unrestrained anger, if I am divided between the temporal and the spiritual. I will maintain that division. Otherwise we have the Inquisition; we know that it exists on many sides.[68]

Consistent Christians cannot, phariseelike, take the place of God. They concede to everyone the possibility of conversion and of sincerity.

Reformulation of the faith will not be afraid to welcome any authentic theological approach:

> John of the Cross, I ask you,
> Other than a Corregidor
> What is humanity and what is love,
> What is night and what is day,
> John of the Cross?
>
> John of the Cross, I ask you
> Not to speak for the Inquisitor
> But to illumine the dark night
> With your light,
> John of the Cross. . . .

These are the words of a Marxist poet, Aragon.[69] It is significant that he addressed himself not to a saint of action, as one might have expected (a St. Vincent de Paul, for example), but to one of the most characteristic mystics of Christianity, therefore to someone representative of what, at first sight, seems diametrically opposed to Marxism.

To respond to this challenge, let us concentrate on the concept of *person*, seen in its full theological meaning, but also, as we shall note, in all its human density. The originality of Christian thought on the human person is especially luminous in comparison with Greek thought. For the latter, especially under its Platonic form, what was primary was the one and the universal. The multiple was always secondary. Particular beings—including human beings—are only individuals. They result from the fragmentation of an archetypal Idea by matter. (Apart from this last formulation, of the "idealistic" kind, note a strange, possible rapprochement with Marxist thought. We shall be less surprised when we recall Marx's admiration of Aristotle and the great importance in his symbolism of the myth of Prometheus, of Greek origin. It does no injury to Marxism to note the striking similarities between socialist society and the Platonic City.)

Christian thought, by contrast, sees in the human being not just an individual but a person. As Cardinal Ratzinger remarks, "This passage from individual to person contains the whole span of the transition from antiquity to Christianity, from Plato to faith. This definite being is not at all something secondary, giving us only a fragmentary glimpse of the universal, which is the real. As the minimum it is a maximum; as the unique and unrepeatable it is something supreme and real."[70]

Originally the word "person" *(prosopon)* belonged to the language of the theater, where it designated the mask that made an actor the incarnation of someone else. This is the word that Christian thought adopted, but infused into it a distinctive meaning, foreign to ancient thought, which western culture henceforth would place under the name of person.

This discovery, of such great significance for civilization, was made through the theological process that sought to think as precisely as possible both about the living God who through an act of self-disclosure had been revealed in Jesus Christ and about Jesus Christ himself. In order to think about the triune God, Christians discovered that the person must be thought of as a "relational being," which immediately provided an opening to the social dimensions of the human person, without reducing it to that. Jesus Christ is thought of as "the man in whom personalization and socialization no longer exclude each other but support each other."[71] He is "the exemplary man, the man of the future, through whom it becomes evident how much humankind is still a coming-to-be creature—a being still, so to speak, waiting to be realized—and what a short distance humankind has even now progressed toward being itself."[72]

A faith that combines belief in the dignity of the human individual as "the image of God," as in Genesis, and belief in the identification willed by the sovereign judge of history with the most miserable, as in the famous scene of the last judgment in St. Matthew—such a faith gives to respect for the human person an astonishing depth and urgency. "Even though it were economically useless, socially irrecoverable, psychologically beyond all communication," writes Adolphe Gesché accurately, "this human being, in the name of the Transcendence who created it in his image and likeness, has an absolute and inalienable right to be respected."[73] He adds with no less reason, "Faith tells me that there is more on this earth than what is profitable, marketable, useful, and the like. *Res sacra homo*: there is in humankind a supreme resistance to my shameful power to dispose of him according to my calculations and my reasons."[74]

Olivier Clément notes with great insight: "Love is always a preference. Christ prefers each one of us. He addresses each one to say, 'It is you whom I prefer.' For him each one of us is an absolute."[75] This means that the one who lives by this spirit, by the example of Christ, will strive to love concretely every human being, even the one who acts as an enemy. Moreover, the theology of conversion, from within the context of the theology of salvation, teaches us that "nothing is fatal, irremissible, irrevocable, irreparable, irremediable, even though everything else (sociology, economics, war, violence, etc.) tells us that there is fatality, the inexorable, the irremediable."[76]

These are only some aspects, among the most fundamental, of the theology of the person. They are enough to show how imprudent and unjust are the "Marxist Christians" who insist that theological discourse that does not incorporate Marxism is out of date. They also show what admirable theoretical and practical riches Christian anthropology places at our disposal. By its philosophical reduction of the human being to its social dimensions Marxism irremediably compromises the human person. Christian faith, on the contrary, saves it, while situating it at the most profound of its social dimensions, because it reveals to it the fellowship of all human beings in God. What is important is that this faith be thought through and lived, with the help of all the human sciences, striving for the maximum in personal and social effectiveness.

The Marxist Profile and the Christian Profile

The profile resulting from the *Marxist* view of the human person has already been sketched in essential outline. The evocation of a visual image—we could almost say "model"—is all the more appropriate inasmuch as the Marxist conception is not simply theoretical. It means to give birth to a new version of humankind. By the same token, thanks to my own method of reflection, I have begun to sketch the profile resulting from the *Christian* view of the human person by way of contrast. There remains only to add some important lines to our two sketches so that we can distinguish them unmistakably.

The Christian conception of the human person, we know, also seeks to be practical as well as theoretical, and the gospel also envisions the formation of a new type of humankind. If there are similarities, the dissimilarities are even sharper. A number of Christians—and not only those who call themselves "Marxist Christians"—would like to emphasize the similarities and practically blot out the dissimilarities, in company with the "Christian communists" of the mid-1800s. As we are going to see, the attitude of the founders of Marxism, and Marx especially, was exactly the reverse. Their tendency was rather to insist on a total dissimilarity. For them the Marxist profile had nothing in common with the Christian. To a certain extent they made their projections in radical antithesis to the Christian conception. Did they view the Christian image through distorted lenses? That is another matter. But perhaps, despite their errors on the subject, they were, in the final analysis, correct. Is their thesis of a radical dissimilarity not the correct one?

I emphasize that we are talking about "conceptions" or "theoretical profiles" of humankind, and not about concrete persons. The Marxists whom we meet—especially those who do not belong to "the apparatus"—are not necessarily persons shaped by theory—a theory that they claim to profess but often do not know well, in fact. As for Christians, they know from their own experience of sin that they can realize only in an imperfect, and often ambiguous, way the kind of new person heralded by Jesus Christ.

As I mentioned at the beginning of this chapter, I shall develop this comparison, beginning with the attacks of Marx on "the social principles of Christianity" and his own version of the story of Fleur-de-Marie. That way we shall see better what idea he himself had of the Christian view of human nature and why he abhorred it to such a degree.

It was in an 1847 article entitled "The Communism of the *Rheinischer Beobachter*"[77] that he made his famous attack on "the social principles of Christianity." The occasion of his article was an attack in the *Rheinischer Beobachter* on the new communist conception advocated by Marx and Engels. The newspaper had been founded in Cologne shortly before by the Prussian government with a view to stirring up the workers of the Rhineland against the bourgeoisie. The attack directed against Marxist communism upheld the viewpoint of a monarchical Christian socialism. Its author was the young Hermann Wagener, then consistorial assessor at Magdeburg. The imprudent writer was not aware that he had taken on such a formidable opponent and that his name would be remembered thanks only to the retort of his adversary. As for Marx, who did not like to be contradicted and who saw himself attacked on a particularly sensitive point, by reason of his aversion to Christianity, he could only be delighted to find such a whipping boy in the person of "Herr Consistorial Assessor." He went on the attack with gusto in a brilliant article that revealed a journalistic talent of the first order.

"What is the alpha and the omega of the Christian faith?," the young consistorial assessor asked himself. He answered, "The dogmas of original sin and redemption. And therein lies the solidarity of humanity in its highest potential: one for all and all for one." This response was not a happy one, for it focused Christianity on sin, and left its social significance highly ambiguous.

It was easy for Marx to wax ironic—and not with a light touch—on "the revenues from the heavenly domains of original sin and redemption, which . . . equal zero" and on their inability to placate the hunger of the people. "We also pray, in the Lord's Prayer," Wagener had written, " 'Lead us not into temptation.' " Marx countered by reminding his readers of the authoritarian and merciless attitude of the Prussian bureaucracy toward the working class: "And *we*, gentlemen, we bureaucrats, judges, and consistorial assessors of the Prussian state, practice this consideration by having persons broken on the wheel, beheaded, locked up, and flogged to our heart's content, thereby 'leading' the proletariat 'into the temptation' to have us later similarly broken on the wheel, beheaded, locked up, and flogged. Which will not fail to occur."

In a general way, Wagener invoked the gospel to support his political theses, which could only make the young atheist revolutionary react strongly, because his objective was precisely to deliver humanity from what he regarded as religious illusion.

"The gospel recommends this," Marx responded. "This is recommended by everything in general, only not by the terrifyingly barren condition of the Prussian state treasury, this abyss, which, within three years, will irrevocably have swallowed up the fifteen Russian millions. The gospel recommends a great deal besides, among other things also castration as the beginning of social reform of oneself."

Figuring that he had sufficiently torn the theological argument of his adversary to shreds, Marx could return to the target he was really aiming at: Wagener's attempt to convince the working class that they had the support of the monarchy and that it was therefore necessary to support it in return. Marx wrote, "The monarchy, declares our consistorial assessor, is one with the people." It is easy for him to reply that that was a delusion: "Of all political elements the people is by far the most dangerous for a king. Not the people of which Frederick William speaks, which offers thanks with moist eyes for a kick and a silver penny; this people is completely harmless, for it only exists in the king's imagination. But the real people—the proletarians, the peasants, the plebs—is, as Hobbes said, *puer robustus, sed malitiosus,* a robust, but ill-natured youth, who permits no kings, be they lean or fat, to get the better of him." He then recalls the executions of Charles I of England and Louis XVI. He then concludes confidently, "That is what happens when kings *appeal to their people.*"

It was necessary to outline with sufficient detail the general context of this article in order to understand the exact significance of Marx's violent diatribe against "*the social principles of Christianity.*" If he attacked them with such rage, it was above all because he considered Christianity as anti-revolutionary in its essence. But it was also to undermine one of the ideological foundations of the Prussian monarchy, which hid its authoritarianism and its political and social conservatism behind the screen of "a Christian state." What he wanted at that point for Prussia was a bourgeois revolution as a necessary step toward the socialist revolution whose theory he was beginning to elaborate. From his point of view the monarchy could only delay it by deluding minds with the empty appearances of reform. Consequently he attacked Christianity on its own count and also as the ideology of a particular historical form of political behavior.

"If only those who have the vocation for it develop the social principles of Christianity, then the communists will soon fall silent," the consistorial assessor had rashly written. Here is the complete text of the slashing reply that he inspired Marx to write:

> The social principles of Christianity have now had eighteen hundred years to be developed, and need no further development by Prussian consistorial assessors.
>
> The social principles of Christianity justified the slavery of antiquity, glorified the serfdom of the Middle Ages, and are capable, in case of need, of defending the oppression of the proletariat, even if with somewhat doleful grimaces.
>
> The social principles of Christianity preach the necessity of a ruling and an oppressed class, and for the latter all they have to offer is the pious wish that the former may be charitable.
>
> The social principles of Christianity place the consistorial assessor's compensation for all infamies in heaven, and thereby justify the continuation of these infamies on earth.
>
> The social principles of Christianity declare all the vile acts of oppressors against the oppressed to be either a just punishment for original sin and other sins, or trials which the Lord, in his infinite wisdom, ordains for the redeemed.
>
> The social principles of Christianity preach cowardice, self-contempt, abasement, submissiveness, and humility, in short, all the qualities of the rabble, and the proletariat, which will not permit itself to be treated as rabble, needs its courage, its self-confidence, its pride, and its sense of independence even more than it needs its bread.
>
> The social principles of Christianity are surreptitious and hypocritical, and the proletariat is revolutionary.
>
> So much for the social principles of Christianity.

The reading of this text leaves no doubt as to the interpretation that I have already proposed. What the young revolutionary was questioning was *Christianity in its gospel essence* and not simply its historical deficiencies or the ideological use of the gospel for conservative ends. It is more than probable that those deficiencies and ideological misuses had falsified his own interpretation of the original Christian message. But it remains nonetheless true that it was this message that he attacked in the end and it was this message that he reproached for being not only an illusion but a factor for dehumanization.

Such an attitude, it might be noted was not original at that time. A large part of the intelligentsia then shared this viewpoint. Nietzsche would have been able to endorse a good part of the Marxist diatribe. As for Marx himself, it is his fundamental opposition to the original Christian message, as I have analyzed it, that explains his relentless struggle against all those who pretended to unite socialism and Christianity and to justify the former by the latter.

The principal proof of this is in the *Circular against Kriege.*[78] It was actually

Weitling who was aimed at by way of Kriege, the latter being his disciple and friend. Weitling had earlier been exalted to the pinnacle by Marx and Engels. Engels had even written of him that he should "be considered the founder of German communism."[79] Later the turnabout was complete. "Faith," Marx and Engels wrote, "is the last thing required for the achievement of communism." They criticized Kriege, "who in Europe always claimed to be an atheist," for seeking "to foist off all the infamies of Christianity under the signboard of communism and ends, in perfect consistency, with *humankind's self-desecration.*"

Irony mingles constantly with tight argumentation in which they denounce the inconsistency of their adversary's analyses of the proletariat, analyses in which Kriege brandishes—they say—"the following mythologico-biblical images: . . . Prometheus bound, the Lamb of God that bears the sins of the world, the Wandering Jews." (You will note the imprecise character of this reference: the first and the third have nothing biblical about them.)

Marx and Engels were far from being entirely wrong in their violent opposition to the "Christian communists" of their time, who were as inconsistent and mistaken in their use of the Bible as they were in their political and sociological analyses. I would almost agree with Engels in his following comment about them (he was aiming at the French in particular):

> One of their favorite axioms is that Christianity is communism. . . . This they try to prove by the Bible, the state of community in which the first Christians are said to have lived. . . . But all this shows only that these good persons are not the best Christians, although they style themselves so; because if they were, they would know the Bible better, and find that, if some few passages of the Bible are favorable to communism, the general spirit of its doctrines is, nevertheless, totally opposed to it.[80]

The fundamental reason for the attitude of the two founders of Marxism toward the Christian communists remains the reason that I have noted: their low regard for original Christianity itself. That is why they fought so energetically to protect the revolutionary movement they were founding from what they considered a dangerous contamination.

Fleur-de-Marie

The notations of Fleur-de-Marie in *The Holy Family*[81] are even more revealing of their thought on the subject that concerns us and vitriolic in a somewhat different way. It is about a young prostitute, they tell us, a victim of the misery of her social class. Although she lives in a degrading situation, "she preserves a human nobleness of soul, a human unaffectedness, and a human beauty that impress those around her." She "shows great vitality, energy, cheerfulness, elasticity of character—qualities that alone explain her human development in her *inhuman* situation." The two authors insist on her human qualities. She "is a girl who can vindicate her rights and put up a fight."

In what concerns good and evil, she is not locked into abstractions. Her ideas are more simple and more sane: "She is *good* because she has never caused *suffering* to anybody, she has always been *human* towards her *inhuman* surroundings."

Here is then a person whom bourgeois society has not succeeded in corrupting directly, although it has placed her in an inhuman situation: "In *natural* surroundings the chains of bourgeois life fall off Fleur-de-Marie; she can freely manifest her own nature and . . . is bubbling with love of life, with a wealth of feeling, with human joy at the beauty of nature."

The thesis is clear: the human person is good in itself; it is only society that corrupts it (in this case society of the bourgeois type); morality has no need of abstract norms. We see here the myth of the perfectly exemplary proletarian.

Unfortunately for her, the young girl meets Monsieur Rodolphe, who wants to convert her. He entrusts her to Madame Georges, "an unhappy, hypochondriac, religious woman," and to the Abbé Laporte, "who has grayed in superstition." The priest places her immediately in a context of sin and expiation. He "decides to make Marie *repent*; inside himself he has already *condemned* her."

Because of her past, marriage for her is out of the question. With "unctuous eloquence," the priest distorts everything of which he speaks. He "must soil her in her own eyes, he must trample underfoot her moral capacities and gifts to make her receptive to the supernatural grace he promises her, *baptism*." He succeeds only too well. Little by little she discovers her "degradation."

The two authors comment: "That means that she owes to the Abbé Laporte and Madame Georges the replacement of the human and therefore bearable consciousness of her debasement by the Christian and hence unbearable consciousness of eternal damnation. The priest and the bigot have taught her to judge herself from the *Christian point of view*."

That is not all. This "heartless priest . . . grayheaded slave of religion" pursues his "hypocritical sophistry." He has succeeded only too well so far. Having reduced her to a tortured conscience, he will not be satisfied until he has made her enter a convent. Not only does she become a religious, she even becomes an abbess as the result of Rodolphe's intrigues. Because of this coerced vocation, convent life is a catastrophe. It drives her to the grave.

This is how the two authors explain the process: "Christianity consoles her only in imagination, or rather her Christian consolation is precisely the annihilation of her real life and essence—her death. Rodolphe changed Fleur-de-Marie first into a repentant sinner, then the repentant sinner into a nun, and finally the nun into a corpse."

Let us make no mistake: for them the fable has a much greater significance than the questioning of forced vocations or the deviations of Christian asceticism, which have only too often occurred. On that we could agree with them.

In their mind—as in that of Nietzsche when he attacked those priests of "muffled melancholy"[82]—it was Christianity itself, taken at the summit of evangelical self-denial, that they meant to indict because it was there that, in their eyes, it most clearly revealed its corrupting influence.

Their thesis was: Christianity is even more degrading than the most degrading of inhuman situations. Their demonstration had been conducted in masterly fashion.

Is the person envisaged by Marxism therefore the fully human one? And is the Christian person the one who is dehumanized, inefficient, condemned to the inner torments of a conscience delivered over to illusion and guilt? The affirmative response to both questions is clearly the thesis of the founders of Marxism. Members of the communist parties of the West are fortunately much less negative at present on the subject of the Christian ideal. One can even read or hear frequent appreciations of a positive nature on this subject, and not only from a Garaudy, who sees, for example, in the life and death of Christ, "through the limitations of the period that formed its image, the noblest model of liberty and love, of the opening of humankind to an infinite destiny."[83]

"What a shock in the history of the societies around the Mediterranean," exclaims Pierre Juquin, a member of the Central Committee of the French Communist Party, "when they said to the slave: you have a soul! Frequently in history faith has been the vehicle for the raising of revolutionary consciousness."[84]

Enrico Berlinguer, secretary general of the Italian Communist Party, notes with satisfaction that "there is an ever greater possibility of agreements and meetings between the workers' movement and the Catholic movement in activities to promote peace and justice in the world."[85]

Georges Marchais, in his address to the twenty-second congress of the French Communist Party, is no less happy to state that "the economic and social consequences of the crisis bring together Christian and atheist workers in daily struggles" and, despite episcopal warnings, which he identifies as anathemas, he proclaims: "We nonetheless pursue our efforts to encourage every form of rapprochement."[86]

Many similar quotations could be added. The disagreements remain, nonetheless. The two types of human being are very different, even if one takes into account the differences in fundamental points of view: on the one hand, politics; on the other, faith.

Ideals, Ideology, and Projections

However violent may have been Marx's indictment of the Christian view of the human person in his attack on "the social principles of Christianity" and in his interpretation of the story of Fleur-de-Marie, I will accept it for its value as a challenge.

It is certain that he did not understand the true significance of Judeo-

Christian revelation on all points where he accused it of promoting dehumanization. Nowhere is "heaven" presented as "the compensation for all infamies," or "the vile acts of oppressors against the oppressed" as "a just punishment for original sin."

How could the founder of Marxism, we wonder, have forgotten the insistent and frequent attacks of the prophets against injustice, not to mention those in the Epistle of St. James. Furthermore, evangelical charity constantly supposes justice, of which it is the crown. As for "original sin," if it is, from the viewpoint of faith, the final explanation of the sin of oppressors and exploiters, it is exactly for that reason that it is in no way its justification. Quite the contrary; it is its radical indictment. We ask ourselves if such accusations are due to the ignorance or the bad faith of their author. In any case, they are inaccurate.

Without accepting them we can more easily understand the charges of "cowardice," of "self-contempt," of "abasement," of "submissiveness," as well as the negative reading of "humility," which is also included among "the qualities of the rabble." A reader who had not taken the trouble to enter into the correct perspective of the Sermon on the Mount could, in fact, interpret some of its counsels in this way. We could say as much for the Marxist interpretation of Christian repentance in the story of Fleur-de-Marie. Here again the superficial reader of certain biblical texts could commit a similar error of interpretation. Nietzsche reacted in the same way.

Was their error of interpretation due to the ambiguity of the texts? I deny it. The texts are clear for anyone who knows how to read them objectively and is sensitive to their high human value. The texts in question do not demand any special competence in the field of exegesis. The most probable explanation is that Marx and Nietzsche, by reason of their philosophical options, had become incapable of opening their minds to certain gospel values.

I will adhere to this critique, even at the level of interpretation—I repeat—not only because the founders of Marxism brought a radical charge against the Christian ideal embodied in the original message of Christianity and not simply against the historical practice of the church over the years, but also because that radical charge remains, to a great extent, in contemporary Marxism. (We shall see the decisive reason for this a little later.) That said, it is easier to recognize that the Marxist charge is pertinent to the history of the church. But not entirely, I add immediately.

It would be easy to prove that the charges raised by the founders of Marxism and their disciples have not been verified always and everywhere. Christianity, for example, has never purely and simply "justified the slavery of antiquity," as Marx claimed. During the first centuries of the history of the church—the period when slavery remained a common practice—it was the teaching of St. Paul that prevailed. His teaching, it is true, was not a revolutionary demand for the immediate suppression of slavery. (In the historical context, that would have been the expression of a total lack of realism and would only have rendered the condition of the slaves even worse, because any revolt on their part would have been easily crushed.) St. Paul's teaching was an ethical demand for a humane and even comradely treatment of slaves, capable of leading to their emancipation when that step appeared realistic.

Christian repentance and the religious vocation are far from having always been that kind of guilt-ridden, dehumanized phenomena that are denounced in the story of Fleur-de-Marie. How often they have been lived as a magnificent human fulfillment! It remains true that theology, preaching, and the prevailing mentality of Christian milieus have too often borrowed from a conservative ideology in which the Bible was, wrongly, invoked in behalf of a "social order" that too often profited only the ruling and dominant classes. This was not always because of bad faith, but because, through laziness of spirit, Christians did not see the possibilities of a better order. This was clearly the case in the nineteenth century. In the same way Christian asceticism—and perhaps especially during that same period—was too often conceived in a guilt-ridden, dehumanizing way—for example, in certain religious communities where the ideal seemed to be to oppose every desire for whatever corresponded to the tastes of their members.

In view of all these historical facts, the Marxist accusation is legitimate. By its cutting power it has the great merit of helping Christians to understand that the historical "Christian humanity" was only a caricature of the authentic "Christian humanity" of the original Christian message and especially of its supreme example in Jesus Christ. I must add that the resurgence of the authentic Christian ideal has been pursued with remarkable success for half a century now by currents of Christian humanism and personalism, culminating in their magnificent articulation in the *Pastoral Constitution on the Church in the Modern World* of Vatican II.

"What then, in your opinion, is the Marxist ideal to which you want to oppose the Christian ideal?" I will answer this question immediately, and thus open the critical phase of my study. I am convinced that *the type of person that Marxism dreams of creating is the "ideal person" of advanced industrial society*. It is the person who is rational, methodical, scientific, happy at work, disciplined within a perfectly regulated organization, living in abundance, riveted to an earthly horizon. It is the brilliant manager, of which there are already millions of examples, in the Soviet Union as well as in North America and Western Europe. It is the person shaped according to a generalized model—that dictated by the organization of universities and graduate schools, by administrative and industrial practice, by the ambitions of the young and their families, by the movies, by illustrated magazines and posters. We could as well say: the technocrat, who, in the East as well as the West, claims to be a stranger to ideology and exclusively preoccupied with efficiency. Let me put it still more clearly: Marxism dreams of creating the type of person advocated by industrial society of the capitalist variety—but much better than that society can produce and with a guarantee that, thanks to the revolutionary change that it will effect, everyone will be able to become such a person.

Maurice Clavel notes with insight this profound resemblance, which Marxism is very unwilling to recognize, even though it is at the core of its dynamic:

> What is at the heart of the history of the West is first and foremost the liberation or advent of *humankind*—by the humanization of nature and the naturalization of humanity—and not of humankind in general or even the proletariat in particular, still less Marxism, but . . . the bourgeoisie, capitalism! Yes, at bottom, in truth, it is really capitalism that first makes us *humans*, that emancipates us. And that is why Marx yields sometimes to the temptation to sing its praises. And that is why the continuing battle strategy of Marxism . . . will be to represent the bourgeoisie as purely and simply grasping. . . . Whereas the really important thing is to ravish from it—let us say perhaps to steal from it—the spark, *its* spark![87]

Already at the time of Stalin, Berdyaev had called attention to "an americanization of the Russian people, the production of a new type of practical person for whom daydreaming and castle-building passed into action and constructiveness, of a technician, a bureaucrat of a new type."[88] Marxist analysts do not like to hear about this convergence. To counter such talk they insist on the differences in social practices.

I would in no way deny these differences, but I do believe that the "symbolic archeology" of the Marxist person that we have been discussing explains the central dynamic of industrialization of the Marxist and the Marxist-Leninist type. It helps especially to understand why capitalist technocrats and communist technocrats get along so well, despite differences in the ideologies and the social practices with which they are identified.

A great many of our contemporaries no longer want this kind of person, either in the East or in the West. This explains the wide readership of Herbert Marcuse's *One-Dimensional Man*.[89] There are many who perceive, at least in a confused way, that the role model of advanced industrial society overdevelops certain human potentialities (the technical intelligence of *homo faber*) to the detriment of others just as vital (emotional fulfillment, the quality of thought, and the equanimity of *homo sapiens*). They reject the frenzy of professional and "worldly" activity that leaves time neither for reflection on essential questions nor for love nor for enjoyment of what gives life its charm. They see to what extent the abundant society creates more and more artificial needs to the detriment of essential needs and of solidarity with all humankind. The challenges they formulate are often sketchy and insufficiently realistic, even the challenges of an Ivan Illich, because humanization for the mass of humanity does at present depend on the spread of science and technology. And the return to life on the land or to archaic handicrafts so highly praised by some (especially intellectuals of bourgeois origin) is now a luxury that is possible for only a very small number of persons. But these challenges do contain an important element of truth, especially in the case of

Ivan Illich, as I have noted earlier in reference to the new willingness to pose questions.

It is this element of truth that I shall consider from *the viewpoint of faith.* Christians who want to make their own the present period of history in the spirit of the gospel will reject neither scientific and technological progress nor rationality and method, nor organization, nor abundance. Quite to the contrary, they will seriously commit themselves to these things. But they will not make of them their ultimate objective. They will know how to save time for reflection, prayer, and friendship. They will give themselves to the service of others in solidarity and fellowship. Far from confining themselves to an earthly horizon, they will be the ones who are open to the infinite perspectives of the absolute future of the kingdom of God, while being actively present— as the dynamic of evangelical charity requires—in the effort to make this world more just, more human, more comradely.

The Christian wants also to be an active member of advanced industrial society in this phase of history, but without the conceptual narrowings that mutilate that society and are, in the final analysis, factors of dehumanization. It is for all Christians to understand that this is the type of person that a consistent faith invites them to emulate.

In this way the analysis of our times and especially the acceptance of the Marxist challenge will permit theology to develop an *original anthropology.* It will incorporate certain potentialities in the original message of the gospel that until now have been largely ignored. Jesus Christ is the anti-Prometheus, for, contrary to the hero of the famous Greek myth so prominent in the hostile ideologies of advanced industrial society, not only does he accept with joy his total dependence on the Father, but he also finds in it his ultimate fulfillment. This, in fact, is the fundamental significance of the story of the temptation.

The Christian of advanced industrial society will therefore be a person truly given to the present, but who, within a historicity that is consciously assumed, will be open in depth and joy to the God of Jesus Christ, in a relationship that, instead of alienation and oppression, will mean a life of dynamic fulfillment. That is the primary meaning of the first beatitude in Matthew: "Blessed are the poor in spirit, for theirs is the kingdom of heaven" (Matt. 5:3): the sense of dependence, at once radical and humanizing, on the God who through an act of self-disclosure was revealed in Jesus Christ.

But evangelical poverty has another meaning just as essential, and inseparable from the first: that of openness to others, of acceptance of everything in them that is different from us, of respect for their freedom, of availability to them, of unselfish service, of sincere love, capable of overcoming even the hostility of others toward ourselves. The supreme example of this again is Jesus Christ: he was the one totally open to others, totally unselfish, totally loving, whose very death sealed this total availability, for "there is no greater love than this: to lay down one's life for one's friends" (John 15:13).

Following his example, Christians of advanced industrial society will be the ones who commit themselves to giving their scientific and technological competence, their activity characteristic of *homo faber*, to the service of others. They will commit themselves to stand in readiness to take part personally in the building of structures designed to intensify justice and solidarity in human society.

Let me emphasize that such persons, even when seeing and wishing themselves poor before God, in full dependence on God, will see and wish themselves, as did Jesus Christ, fully responsible and stimulated to take action. Dostoevski said it tellingly, if somewhat grandiloquently: "Now, changing my life, I am being reborn into a new form. Brother, I swear to you that I shall not lose hope, and shall preserve my spirit and heart in purity. I shall be reborn to a better thing. That is my whole hope, my whole comfort."[90]

Christian conversion is not seen only as a gift by those who live it, but also as a responsibility and an ongoing process, an attempt to make real the spirit of the gospel in all the dimensions of their existence. Before God and before their fellow humans, they see themselves as free and they are ready to accept all the risks of that freedom, their mistakes and their failings, as well as the hostility of which they may well become the object, and precisely because of their fidelity to the gospel.

They will recognize themselves in the following statement of André Philip:

> I believe that the essential thing is to be oneself. It is to be a free person, free from bending before any reality, whether it be the static reality of the past or the dynamic reality of the present, free from yielding either to custom or to fashion or to the winds of history, but, at every moment, free to analyze reality, to define the means of acting on it, and to dialogue with others, our brothers and sisters.[91]

And they will experience something quite foreign to the Marxist, the truth that the gift "of simple adoration is humanity's highest possibility, [that] it alone forms its true and final liberation."[92]

Delusion, Marxists will say. But Christians will confirm it by their own experience, by their own practice as human beings freely and consciously living their faith in Jesus Christ. Men and women are striving to live according to the model of the Christian person. They do not seek, first of all, to argue with Marxists, but rather to show them by their words and by their actions what that model is in its authentic embodiment.

NOTES

1. Cf. *The Unperfect Society*, trans. Dorian Cooke (New York: Harcourt, Brace and World, 1969), p. 258.

2. *Capital*, p. 35.

3. *Economic and Philosophic Manuscripts*, in *Marx-Engels Reader*, p. 76.

4. Cf. *Economic and Philosophic Manuscripts*, pp. 76-77.

5. Cf. *Economic and Philosophic Manuscripts*, pp. 120-21.

6. *Réponse à John Lewis* (Paris: Maspero, 1973), p. 76. The reader should note the critique—as virulent as it is pertinent—of the principal theses of Althusser undertaken by Adam Schaff in *Structuralisme et marxisme* (Paris: Anthropos, 1974).

7. *For Marx*, trans. Ben Brewster (London: Penguin, 1969), p. 244.

8. *For Marx*, p. 229.

9. *For Marx*, p. 246.

10. *Introduction to the Critique of Political Economy*, in Karl Marx, *Grundrisse*, trans. Martin Nicolaus (New York: Vintage, 1973), p. 84. See a similar statement in *Capital*: "The reason for this is that the human person is, if not as Aristotle contends, a political, at all events a social, animal" (Cf. p. 159).

11. *The German Ideology*, in *Collected Works*, Vol. 5 (New York: International Publishers, 1976), p. 4.

12. Cf. *Man in Marxist Theory and the Psychology of Personality*, trans. John McGreal (Atlantic Highlands, N.J.: Humanities Press, 1978), pp. 50-51.

13. *The Church and Third World Revolution*, trans. Jeanne Marie Lyons (Maryknoll, N.Y.: Orbis, 1977), p. 156.

14. *The German Ideology*, pp. 36-37.

15. *Man in Marxist Theory*, p. 109.

16. *Marxism et théorie de la personnalité*, p. 154.

17. Cf. *The Realm of Spirit and the Realm of Caesar*, trans. Donald A. Laurie (New York: Harper and Bros., 1952), p. 127.

18. Cf. *The Realm of Spirit*, p. 128.

19. "To Marx it was an axiom that, since economic alienation is the basis of all other forms of alienation, its elimination—by the abolition of private ownership of the means of production—would automatically put an end to every other kind of alienation. But is this the case? Is alienation impossible under socialism? Or can it perhaps arise from other sources than private property? This is the question that makes alienation an outstanding problem not only in the context of capitalism, but also of socialism" (*Marxism and the Human Individual*, based on trans. by Olgierd Wojtasiewicz [New York: McGraw-Hill, 1970], p. 107).

20. Cf. *The Origin of Russian Communism*, trans. R.M. French (London: Geoffrey Bles, 1955), pp. 127-28.

21. *Church Dogmatics*, Vol. 3/2 (New York: Scribner's, 1960), p. 212.

22. Cf. *Church Dogmatics*, pp. 214-15.

23. Cf. *Economic and Philosophic Manuscripts*, in *Marx-Engels Reader,* p. 89.

24. Cf. *Economic and Philosophic Manuscripts*, pp. 88-89.

25. Cf. *Capital*, p. 86.

26. Cf. *The German Ideology*, p. 21.

27. Cf. *Economic and Philosophic Manuscripts*, p. 112.

28. Cf. *Economic and Philosophic Manuscripts*, p. 92.

29. Cf. *Dialectics of Nature* (Moscow: Foreign Languages Publishing House, 1954), p. 228.

30. Cf. *Contribution to the Critique of Hegel's "Philosophy of Right,"* in *Critique of Hegel's "Philosophy of Right,"* trans. Annette Jolin and Joseph O'Malley (New York: Cambridge Univ. Press, 1970), p. 142.

31. Cf. quoted by Georges M. Cottier, "Marxisme et messianisme," in *Nova et vetera* 49 (1974), p. 153.

32. Cf. *Capital*, p. 240.

33. *Parole d'homme* (Paris: Laffont, 1975), p. 48.

34. *Parole d'homme*, p. 246.

35. *Parole d'homme*, p. 50.

36. *Man in Marxist Theory*, p. 225.

37. *Man in Marxist Theory*, p. 225.

38. *Introduction to the Critique of Political Economy*, p. 83.

39. *La pensée communiste* (mimeo.), (Louvain: Anc. Librairie Desbarax, n.d.), p. 13.

40. Maximilien Rubel, *Karl Marx. Essai de biographie intellectuelle* (Paris: Rivière, 1971), pp. 327-28.

41. *Formation of the Economic Thought of Karl Marx*, trans. Brian Pearce (New York: Monthly Review Press, 1971), p. 207.

42. Cf. *The Crisis in Communism*, trans. Peter and Betty Ross (New York: Grove, 1970), p. 42.

43. Cf. *The Crisis in Communism*, p. 149.

44. *The Crisis in Communism*, p. 20.

45. *Concluding Speech to the Third All-Russia Soviet Congress* (January 1918), in *Collected Works*, Vol. 26 (London: Lawrence and Wishart, 1964), p. 474.

46. *Marxisme et humanisme*, 3rd ed. (Paris: PUF, 1961), pp. 132, 135.

47. *Concluding Speech*, p. 132.

48. *Christianisme, Marxisme* (Paris: Centurion, 1975), p. 47.

49. Cf. *Economic and Philosophic Manuscripts*, p. 86.

50. *Dialectics of Nature*, p. 49.

51. Christian Chabonis, *Dieu existe-t-il? Non, répondent . . .* (Paris: Fayard, 1973), p. 190.

52. Gilbert Badia, *Rosa Luxemburg* (Paris: Editions sociales, 1975), p. 694.

53. *Das Prinzip Hoffnung*, Vol. 3 (Frankfurt: Suhrkamp, 1969), pp. 1378-79.

54. *Parole d'homme*, pp. 47-63.

55. *Parole d'homme*, p. 61.

56. *Economic and Philosophic Manuscripts*, pp. 91-92.

57. "L'histoire n'est pas notre absolu," in *Lumière et vie,* Nos. 117/118 (1974), p. 150.

58. "L'histoire n'est pas," p. 150.

59. Cf. *On the Jewish Question*, in *Marx-Engels Reader*, p. 42.

60. Cf. *On the Jewish Question*, p. 43.

61. *On the Jewish Question*, p. 42.

62. Cf. *On the Jewish Question*, p. 43.

63. Cf. *On the Jewish Question*, p. 43.

64. *Marxism and Christianity*, trans. Kevin Traynor (New York: Macmillan, 1968), p. 111.

65. *Christianisme, Marxisme*, p. 30.

66. *Christianisme et réalité sociale* (Paris: "Je sers," 1934), pp. 51-52.

67. *The Russian Revolution*, trans. Donald Atwater (London: Sheed and Ward, 1931), p. 81.

68. In *Le Nouvel Observateur* (October 13, 1975).

69. *Le fou d'Elsa* (Paris: Gallimard, 1963), p. 353.

70. Cf. *Introduction to Christianity*, trans. J.R. Foster (New York: Seabury, 1979), p. 113.

71. *Introduction to Christianity*, p. 179.

72. Cf. *Introduction to Christianity*, p. 170.

73. "Le discours théologique sur l'homme," in *Nouvelle Revue Théologique* 97 (1975), p. 809.

74. "Le discours théologique," p. 810.

75. *Questions sur l'homme*, p. 62.

76. *Adolphe Gesché*, "Le discours théologique sur l'homme," p. 810.

77. Published in No. 73 (September 12, 1847) of the *Deutsche Brüsseler Zeitung*. Cf. English trans. in *Collected Works*, Vol. 6 (New York: International Publishers, 1976), pp. 220-34.

78. This circular is dated May 11, 1846; English trans. in *Collected Works*, Vol. 6, pp. 35-51.

79. "Progress of Social Reform on the Continent," published in *The New Moral World* (November 1843); see *Collected Works*, Vol. 3 (New York: International Publishers, 1975), p. 402.

80. Cf. "Progress of Social Reform," p. 399. Cited in F. Grégoire, *La pensée communiste*, p. 85.

81. Cf. (Moscow: Foreign Languages Publishing House, 1956), pp. 225-35.

82. *Thus Spake Zarathustra*, in *The Portable Nietzsche*, ed. Walter Kaufmann (New York: Viking, 1968), p. 204.

83. *Humanisme marxiste et religion*, in *Marxistes et chrétiens. Entretiens de Salzbourg* (Paris: Mame, 1968), p. 91.

84. Interview in *Hebdo-TC* (January 2, 1975).

85. *La proposta comunista* (Turin: Einaudi, 1975), p. 12.

86. In *La Croix* (February 5, 1976). In his *Appeal* of June 10, 1976, he is particularly enthusiastic in listing the common points of agreement between communists and Christians, perceiving "broad common aspirations" shared between them: "No!," he exclaims, "it is not on the basis of a temporary strategy or ideological confusion that we strive passionately to draw together all those desiring the liberation of humankind—communists because it is demanded by their socialist ideal, Christians because it is demanded by their evangelical ideal, both because they want fellowship and justice." What a contrast here with the *Circular against Kriege* and how far we have traveled! However, on one side and the other, do we mean, *practically*, the same thing when we use the same words?

87. *Qui est aliéné?*(Paris: Flammarion, 1970), p. 261.

88. Cf. *The Origin of Russian Communism*, p. 142.

89. *One-Dimensional Man* (Boston: Beacon, 1966). See also his *Eros and Civilization* (New York: Vintage, 1962).

90. Letter of December 22, 1849, to his brother Michael, quoted by Constantin Motchoulski, *Dostoïevski* (Paris: Payot, 1963), p. 117; English trans. in Fyodor Dostoevski, *Letters and Reminiscences* (New York: Knopf, 1923), p. 11.

91. *André Philip par lui-même ou les voies de la liberté* (Paris: Aubier, 1971), p. 150.

92. Cf. *Introduction to Christianity*, p. 219.

Chapter 5

Love and Class Struggle in History

Up to now, for reasons of method, I have taken only a sketchy look at the question of a *social dynamic*, except in the course of examining the ultimate explanation of history by Marxist analysis. Even then, my point of view was too limited, because more is needed than an understanding of history. What is especially needed is to approach the social dynamic with a view to its transformation, by way of a social critique and the development of a social practice of a new kind.

For the present historical period, faced with a world where oppression and exploitation still hold sway, Marxism is of course mainly interested in a *revolutionary dynamic*. Its particular feature, among all the other revolutionary dynamics, is the development of a deliberate strategy and tactic for a takeover by the revolutionary class (conceived as the vanguard of the oppressed and exploited masses) by means of class struggle. This struggle, according to Marxism, constitutes the historical axis of social dynamics, and *has* done so ever since the establishment of the private ownership of the means of production, and *will* continue to do so until the elimination of such ownership.

But once the revolution has triumphed, what will then be the driving impulse of history? The texts on the Marxist utopia announce for that time, as seen earlier, a remarkable explosion of creativity, but their perspective seems quite as unhistorical as it is dangerously idyllic. Soviet doctrine does not cease to advocate revolution for capitalist countries, but it envisions only improvements in countries that are legitimately socialistic—that is, that follow its own model. As for Chinese doctrine, in launching its famous cultural revolution, it came out for permanent revolution, even in red China. It is true that nowhere have they attained that superior phase of socialist society expected in the utopia.

The social dynamism advocated by Christianity is of a very different kind, for its axis is *love*. Not only Marxists will object that this is not a political dynamic and that it is even dangerous on that level. The objection is an old one and is shared by the great majority of political analysts and activists. Would not the dynamic of class struggle and the dynamic of love be absolutely incompatible? Perhaps it would be necessary to examine that question a little more closely.

A Christian such as Jean Girette who, after having been an executive at the highest level, became a worker out of evangelical concern for the poor, tells his readers: "The day that you begin to look at things from below, after having for a long time looked at them from above, everything changes; there is a complete reversal of perspectives."[1]

This is also the claim of Marxism: that of seeing everything from the viewpoint of the oppressed and the exploited, or at least from that of the revolutionary class (their vanguard), the industrial proletariat, according to the founding fathers. Would the Marxist viewpoint and the evangelical viewpoint therefore be the same? A certain number of Christians are quick to agree.

It is true that the "good news" of the advent of the kingdom of God was first announced to the poor (the vast majority of the Jewish people at that time), although not so as to exclude leaders and wealthy persons who were prepared for "conversion," and recognizing further that "conversion" was always required of the poor themselves. It is also true that he who proclaimed that advent was not content simply to live by preference with the poor but that he was himself materially poor and that he was committed to that poverty. It is true finally that he wanted the community of his disciples to be poor both economically and from the standpoint of power. He gave them firm directives: material poverty, humility, and no use of coercive means.

From all the evidence these are decisive characteristics of the original message of Christianity. Let me add—and this is also a characteristic of the greatest importance—that this was asserted from the standpoint of God: God, not only as defender of the poor, but especially as one who proposes to all humanity that it should establish filial relations with the divine.

The examination of these two approaches (the Marxist approach and the Christian approach) will lead us to pose the ultimate questions of morality from the original perspective of each: the dynamic of class struggle on the one hand, and that of love (evangelical charity) on the other.

Truth and Pitfalls of the Marxist Theory of Class Struggle

Marx was not the first to expose and analyze the phenomena of class conflict and it is not necessary to be Marxist to recognize them, although, in our day, it may be difficult to study them without reference to Marxism. He readily acknowledged that he had predecessors, but he strongly insisted on his originality in the matter and his disciples are convinced that he elaborated the only true scientific theory about them.

The simplest way to see how he understood it is to begin with the reading of his letter of March 5, 1852, to Joseph Weydemeyer:

And now as to myself, no credit is due to me for discovering the existence of classes in modern society or the struggle between them. . . . What I did that was new was to prove: (1) that the *existence of classes* is bound up with *particular historical phases in the development of production*; (2) that the class struggle necessarily leads to the *dictatorship of the proletariat*; (3) that this dictatorship itself constitutes the transition to the *abolition of all classes* and to *a classless society*.[2]

The first element of Marxist originality takes us back to the fundamental axiom of historical materialism, according to which it is production (the infrastructure defined as the dialectic between forces of production and relationships of production) that explains in the last instance all historical reality: let us say—to return to the basic concept of the present chapter—the whole social dynamic of history.

For Marx it is class struggle that constitutes the true axis of social dynamics, at least during the period that began with the establishment of the private ownership of the means of production. This period, according to his scientific forecasts and his revolutionary perspective, will end with the substitution of social ownership. This shows that it is a *historical* phenomenon—therefore relative and contingent.

It also sets the stage for a revolutionary enterprise, over against the ideology of a capitalist society that insists that industrial production necessarily demands that there be, on the one hand, capitalist owners of the means of production and holders of political power over them and, on the other hand, wage earners working for their masters' profit and executing their will. A simple explanation is thus offered us, which pretends to clarify the entire process.

From the moment that these two social categories confront each other, their interests are antagonistic. The owners' interest is to extort the maximum of surplus value possible—that is, to make their employees work as hard as possible and to pay them as little as possible. They also want to preserve this privilege of exploitation and command, and transmit it to their posterity. In consequence, it is to their advantage to make common cause with others who share their interest in maintaining this lopsided situation.

The wage earners' interests, on the contrary, will be to work as little as possible and to earn as much as possible. It follows that they too must join together to take collective action.

Social classes and class struggles are therefore born of the same movement, which follows from the fundamental antagonism that is engendered by a certain type of production relationships. And they will endure, however complex their history may be, as long as does the private ownership of the means of production.

With the second component of Marx's originality we find ourselves at the heart of his revolutionary dynamic, inasmuch as the dynamic of class struggle has been described for us as *necessarily* leading to the *dictatorship of the proletariat*. The adverb is of the greatest importance. What kind of necessity is involved here? For Marx it was a question of a *necessity of revolutionary practice* (for the goal of radical transformation of society in a socialist direction) *founded on a historico-sociological necessity*.

He was too much aware of the realities of life to imagine naively that the unfolding of the revolutionary process would just happen automatically and that it would not be necessary to pursue it by way of strategies, tactics, responsible decisions, and an appropriate organization. But he was convinced that the revolutionary practice that he proposed corresponded exactly to the evolution of industrial society of the capitalist type—which he believed himself qualified to evaluate with certainty—and that, for that very reason, it was sure to succeed.

To return to his theory of the dictatorship of the proletariat, there is no doubt that he always considered it as an essential piece of his larger theory on the revolutionary seizure of power. It would be easy to assemble quotations on this subject dating from every period of his life. The most important is his peremptory statement in the *Critique of the Gotha Program* (therefore a few years before his death):

> Between capitalist and communist countries lies the period of the revolutionary transformation of the one into the other. There corresponds to this also a political transition period in which the state can be nothing but the *revolutionary dictatorship of the proletariat*.[3]

As for the practical measures that he proposed, it seems that he always held to those he recommended in *The Communist Manifesto*, although they need not be considered a panacea. They revolve around the suppression of the private ownership of the means of production and the substitution of social (or collective) ownership, in the context of a centralized system conceived as a generalized planning mechanism. "The proletariat," wrote the young revolutionary theoretician, "will use its political supremacy to wrest, by degrees, all capital from the bourgeoisie, to centralize all instruments of production in the hands of the state—that is, of the proletariat organized as the ruling class."[4]

He saw in this only a temporary stage, convinced as he was that state control would come to an end of itself with the advent of a classless society. That, at least, is what he asserted.

Was he aware that his abstract logic could set off an irreversible and unfortunate process, as demonstrated by the history of those regimes that claim loyalty to him? How could he fail to see that such a generalized system of state control would almost inevitably give birth to top-heavy bureaucracies and that these tend to perpetuate themselves indefinitely?

What is certain is that all communist regimes to date have included in their programs the basic list of measures advocated by *The Communist Manifesto*, with some slight variations. And their official teaching holds firmly to the theory of the dictatorship of the proletariat, as understood by Lenin:

> They who recognize *only* the class struggle are not yet Marxists; they may be found not to have gone beyond the boundaries of bourgeois reasoning and politics. To limit Marxism to the teaching of the class

struggle means to curtail Marxism—to distort it, to reduce it to something acceptable to the bourgeoisie. A Marxist is one who *extends* the acceptance of class struggle to the acceptance of the *dictatorship of the proletariat.*[5]

As for the third element of Marxist originality—that is, in the intent to be realistic and even scientific, the perspective of the utopia of the classless society—I have already given it considerable attention.

The text that I have just commented on has already given us a glimpse of the fact that, for Marx, the dynamic of history has been a dynamic of class struggle, at least in the history dominated by the private ownership of the means of production. I must insist on this point, recalling Althusser's thesis that "class struggle is the motor of history,"[6] which is the perfect summary of the teaching of the founding fathers.

"The history of all hitherto existing society is the history of class struggles," we read in *The Communist Manifesto*.[7] The lines that follow this peremptory statement are famous. In a few sentences that are no less peremptory, the young revolutionary theoretician encloses in his schema of class struggle the entire history of Western Europe, from "ancient Rome" to "modern bourgeois society," wherein "society as a whole is more and more splitting up into two great hostile camps, into two great classes directly facing each other: bourgeois and proletariat."[8]

The text of the Marxist founders that is at once the most precise and the most inclusive on this subject can be found in Engels's *Anti-Dühring*:

> The new facts made imperative a new examination of all past history. Then it was seen that *all* past history was the history of class struggles; that these warring classes of society are always the product of the modes of production and of exchange—in a word, of the *economic* conditions of their time; that the economic structure of society always furnishes the real basis, starting from which we can alone work out the ultimate explanation of the whole superstructure of juridical and political institutions, as well as of the religious, philosophical, and other ideas of a given historical period. But now idealism was driven from its last refuge, the philosophy of history; now a materialistic treatment of history was propounded, and a method found of explaining humankind's "knowing" by its "being," instead of, as heretofore, its "being" by its "knowing."[9]

Three essential theses of Marxist analysis are here found in joint relationship: (1) the reduction of all conflicts—and, finally, of all history—to the one dynamic of social conflict; more precisely, to the dynamic of class struggle; (2) the ultimate explanation of the entirety of social life by economic production; (3) the linking in one equation of this double analysis of history by class struggle and economic production as the materialistic conception (or science) of history, or again—following the concept that I have already explained—as historical materialism.

In this conceptual framework two questions are particularly important: that of class consciousness and that of the limitation of social classes, and therefore of their number.

In regard to *class consciousness*, as in the case of Georg Lukacs,[10] the explanations are generally more ideological than scientific. The approach taken by Marx, in his notes on the peasant owners of small farms,[11] is nevertheless provocative. In his view a social class is fully constituted only if, in addition to an identity of position in the production process, it has acquired an adequate consciousness of its objective interests and some sense of undertaking common action to make them prevail.

As for the *limitation* or *number of classes*, the doctrine is far from being fixed, either in the founders of Marxism or their successors, despite their constant reiteration of the tendency toward bipolarization, which makes them especially reluctant to recognize the existence of middle classes.

In any case, for Marxism the linking of all social conflicts to the dynamic of class struggle is an essential thesis, entirely scientific and true, as expressed by Engels:

> It was precisely Marx who had first discovered the great law of motion of history, the law according to which all historical struggles, whether they proceed in the political, religious, philosophical, or some other ideological domain, are in fact only the more or less clear expression of struggles of social classes. . . . This law . . . has the same significance for history as the law of the transformation of energy has for natural science.[12]

Such a conception of the dynamic of class struggle naturally opens the way for a *revolutionary dynamic*: as a revolutionary goal and at the same time an interpretation of the dynamic of history itself. For Marx, in fact, revolution is the driving force of history, as the rupture marking the victory of the revolutionary class and inaugurating its domination up to the moment when it permits itself to be supplanted: "Not criticism but revolution is the driving force of history, also of religion, of philosophy, and all other kinds of theory."[13] Or again, using an image popular in the symbolism of early industrialization, "Revolutions are the locomotives of history."[14]

The thesis is further developed in a grandiose revolutionary description of the totality of historical evolution:

> No social order is ever destroyed before all the productive forces for which it is sufficient have been developed, and new superior relations of production never replace older ones before the material conditions for their existence have matured within the framework of the old society. Humankind thus inevitably sets itself only such tasks as it is able to

solve. . . . In broad outline, the Asiatics, ancient, feudal, and modern bourgeois modes of production may be designated as epochs marking progress in the economic development of society. The bourgeois mode of production is the last antagonistic form of the social process of production. . . . The prehistory of human history accordingly closes with this social formation.[15]

Such an interpretation of history, one might note, is remarkably optimistic. We sense here the confidence characteristic of the philosophy of the Enlightenment and the famous axiom of Hegel: "What is rational is actual and what is actual is rational."[16] Marxism sees itself as a gigantic revolutionary enterprise capable of transforming social reality in such a way that it becomes entirely conformed to the *revolutionary rationality* that will take charge of the future—a titanic, promethean enterprise of intelligence that will master and manage the evolution of history.

But is humanity so rational? It would be easy to offer analyses that suggest a very different interpretation, unless one wants to justify at any price the historical fact: so many crimes and violent acts that reveal nothing else but madness and human passions. Perhaps Marx meant to speak only of his own revolutionary rationality. Let us leave the question open.

The division of history into four periods, four modes of production, has been consistently maintained in Marxist analysis. In light of the vast and complex conglomeration of history, is that division not a little artificial? In the Marxist revolutionary perspective these periods constitute only the "prehistory" of humanity. History in the true sense of the word will begin with the social revolution—a radical and final revolution—that germinates in industrial society of the capitalist type and that the new revolutionary class (the industrial proletariat) will bring to completion.

Engels predicted:

[The] solution of the contradictions: the proletariat seizes the public power, and by means of this transforms the socialized means of production, slipping from the hands of the bourgeoisie, into public property. By this act, the proletariat frees the means of production from the character of capital they have thus far borne, and gives their socialized character complete freedom to work itself out. Socialized production upon a predetermined plan becomes henceforth possible. Development of production makes the existence of different classes of society thenceforth an anachronism. In proportion as anarchy in social production vanishes, the political authority of the state dies out. Humanity, at last the master of its own form of social organization, becomes at the same time the lord over nature, its own master—free. To accomplish this act of universal emancipation is the historical mission of the modern proletariat.[17]

The dynamic of the class struggle, by its supreme revolutionary action, thus emerges into the utopia of the classless society. "Orthodox" or "heterodox" (in relation to the original Marxism) as far as concerns the designation of the revolutionary class, Marxists all converge in the prediction of this climactic fulfillment.

If we agreed with this analysis of history as well as with its conception of the world and Marxist anthropology, logically we would agree with Marxism in considering the class struggle as the *foundation of morality*. I have just mentioned one of the essential elements of the Marxist theory of class struggle. I shall examine it in the two sections that follow, especially in the final one. That is why I here limit myself to the sociological, historical, and political aspects of that theory.

The Christian Response

The *element of truth* in Marxist theory is *beyond question*. Before any other and better than any other it brought to full light and analyzed acutely the following phenomena:
• The reality and primary importance of social classes in industrial societies.
• The reality and importance of their conflictual relationships, which earlier political and religious ideologies had tended to conceal—and which too often they still conceal—either deliberately or by reason of inadequate analysis.
• The impact of class affiliation not only on households and lifestyles, but also on mentalities, cultures, and scales of values.
• The extreme social inequalities that persist in western industrial society, in spite of a genuine and general improvement in standards of living and culture—inequalities that are often hidden by an ideology that emphasizes equality of opportunity, to the benefit of the ruling classes or groups and to the detriment of the lower classes.
• The sufferings and frustrations of the working class, as well as its need and potential for collective action to improve its lot.
• The mystification of politics, which, under the guise of national unity, has a tendency to favor the ruling classes or groups.

The class struggle is not necessarily that struggle to the death that Marxist theory would maintain and that it advocates in its revolutionary practice. When real social progress has been realized and the lower classes do not lack for necessities, they are more likely to perceive their solidarity with other classes of society in the body politic. Without renouncing the struggle, unions will more easily accept periods of social armistice, especially in times of economic crisis when they see that certain demands would risk driving business to the wall.

Thanks to the mass media—notably to the fact that the same programs on television and radio and the same movies are seen and heard by all—certain cultural standards become common to the entire population. It would be simplistic to maintain that they are the exclusive expression of the ideology of the ruling class, which it has cleverly injected everywhere. It remains nonetheless true that the entire life of industrial society, even of the advanced variety, is marked by the dynamic of social classes and their antagonistic relations.

On the level of faith, where concerns for the poor and the mandate to contribute to their welfare are at the heart of the gospel ethic, we must be particularly sensitive to the fact that *Marxist ideology has powerfully contributed to the advancement of the working class*, and to giving it a sense of pride, precisely where it was the most unfortunate and the most despised and where the ruling classes were the least receptive to its demands. It is because it has this positive image that, in certain western countries, many workers vote for the communist party, when for all practical purposes they are totally ignorant of Marxist theory.

True, that theory has served—it too—as a mask and camouflage, in those places where it has come to power, as a screen for a new social inequality and an oppression of a new kind. The Soviet Union, for example, is hardly egalitarian in practice and the so-called dictatorship of the proletariat is really the dictatorship of a bureaucracy over the working class and the whole of society.

These failures, due to other reasons, cannot alter the positive aspects of the ideology, which on the contrary must profoundly challenge the Christian world. It is true that attitudes have changed over recent decades and that the lower classes have made real advances. But the time is not so long gone when, in "Christian" Europe, those who wished to rise in the social scale did not dare admit that they were the offspring of a peasant, a manual worker, or a small shopkeeper. And, in Christian communities, the severe warnings of St. James's Epistle against preferential treatment for the rich were obviously overlooked.

From the viewpoint of faith we must be equally careful to give full consideration to the results of socio-historical analysis, which reveal the *highly conflictual aspects of collective existence*, and especially to those that depend on interpretation made in terms of class struggle. It would be interesting to analyze the inhibitions that prevent persons from seeing and recognizing them. An examination of the dynamic of social conflicts in our industrial society of the advanced western variety reveals them, however, in clear outline. We must therefore be circumspect in regard to any talk of "collaboration" or "reconciliation" of classes.

Not that this is an undesirable goal! From the political point of view one must desire it to the degree that one desires some assured minimum of national unity. And, if we have understood the concrete demands of evangelical forgiveness, how could we not desire *reconciliation* between unreconciled individuals? This is at the very heart of the Christian ethic. Paul VI, in assigning the theme of reconciliation to the Holy Year, had no other goal than to make us rediscover it at a time when Christians are so reluctant to accept their differences. We would betray Christianity if we were to renounce it.

However, we would also betray the truth of the gospel by suggesting that reconciliation comes easily. The goal of reconciliation makes sense only if it is presented as the fruit of a demanding effort to promote social justice. Let us recognize that, by and large, Christians are not yet sufficiently conscious of this need and that some theological and pastoral utterances lack prophetic clarity and power. We will be effective in behalf of true reconciliation only if at the same time we fight energetically against social injustice.

In the same way, although analysis of the most profound reality of the church, which depends on the action of God and our free response to that action, cannot be confined to interpretation in terms of class struggle, it is necessary to show its impact on the behavior of different participants, the ideologies to which they relate, and the structures that they support. We will then see better what the social categories are that create the dominant mentality in that church. We will understand better why the working class is ill at ease there, at least in certain countries. We will become aware that the effort of evangelization that has been directed toward the most advanced elements of science and culture, as well as to political and union leaders, is on the whole clearly inadequate.

If it is well done, such an analysis will throw a good deal of light on pastoral activity and make it easier to distinguish the objective content of the faith from questionable ideologies. But it will do this only if it is sufficiently competent and carefully refrains from trying to explain everything.

It is crucial, in fact, to *take one's distance* from the Marxist theory of class struggle, which calls for serious criticism. It clearly extends the concept of "class" too far into history. This concept is fully applicable only within the framework of industrial society. For ancient times or other kinds of civilization, it would be more accurate, for example, to speak of "tribes," or "castes," or "orders."

Class conflicts are far from being always the major conflicts. As Raymond Aron notes, "It would be absurd, for example, to ignore the fact that in South Africa it is the opposition of *races* that determines the entire organization of society. In the same way, in the majority of countries in the Near East the distinctive criteria are more religious than truly social."[18]

It is equally absurd to try to reduce all other conflicts to class conflict: for example, the wars of religion in sixteenth-century Europe, racial conflicts in the United States, the two world wars. It is strange that Marxists still continue to write, as in a recent *Marxist Treatise on Political Economy*, that "the polarization of the social relations of the two fundamental classes manifests itself with more and more force,"[19] precisely at a time when the middle classes continue to grow in importance in all advanced industrial societies.

Father Chambre is correct in noting that "the problem of the middle classes is one of the crosses of Marxism," that "the fascist parties are the cohesive centers for the bourgeois of those middle classes that Marx expected one day to join up with the proletariat," and that "born of the anguish of persons who lose faith in indefinite progress . . . they are the expression of the triumph of extraeconomic factors over economic factors, in deciding the position of a whole group of persons in relation to economic questions."[20] François Perroux adds that "the cadres . . . form a large part of the intermediary categories that defy the Marxist dichotomy."[21]

As for identification of the revolutionary class, the observation of history supports the view of Frédéric Bon and Michel Burnier when they state that "there are no revolutionary classes by nature; only by accident."[22] Berdyaev is also right in observing that "Marx's very idea of a class is 'axiological,' " that "the distinction between 'proletariat' and 'bourgeoisie' unwittingly coincides with that between 'good' and 'evil.' "[23] And it is not without reason that he wrote that "Marx's 'proletariat' is not the empirical working class that we observe in actual life," that "Marx's proletarian myth resembles J. J. Rousseau's democratic myth, but its content is radically different."[24]

In my opinion, the most penetrating criticism, all told, of the Marxist theory of class struggle has been done by François Perroux in his book *Masse et classe.* Here is one of the key passages:

> The Marxist schema is misleading in the light of a number of historic changes: agrarian revolutions in agricultural and rural milieus that are led by small revolutionary groups; fascist revolutions by minorities who seize power and hold it by manipulating the masses; counterrevolutions or more gradual political movements organized by minorities who know how to benefit from majority votes by making methodical use of concession, negotiation, compromise, pseudodialogue, a mixture in varied doses of payoffs and kind words, and, if one may say so, the use of carrot and stick in regard to youth, the more turbulent intelligentsia, and labor. The manipulation of the masses by small energetic groups has no direct relation to class struggle, even if one considers it as a political conflict with a particular orientation and organization. Is there any doubt? To eliminate any doubt it is enough to observe the practice of the communist parties in the West.[25]

What strikes me as most important in these critical observations is *the concept of manipulation of the masses by small energetic groups.* I believe that it is *even more fundamental as an objective, in-depth interpretation of social reality than is the theory of class struggle.* Its significance seems universal, both in time and in space. We can verify it as well in industrial countries of the communist variety (with their dominant role of the party and state bureaucracy) as in industrial countries under capitalist domination (and in these as much in political parties of the right or center as in political parties of the left or the trade unions, as well as in private groups trying to influence economic life). One may verify it just as well among the underdeveloped peoples, and nowhere so well as in communist China.

We should therefore devote to it the serious study that it deserves. The exclusive concentration on class struggle has the serious disadvantage of concealing it. It remains nonetheless true that the antagonistic relationships of social classes remain an essential of social reality in industrial countries. It is therefore indispensable to pursue their study, but without neglecting to trace their interrelation with the fundamental and universal dialectic of the masses and small energetic groups. In that way we should be oriented toward the basic problems of *knowledge* and *power,* which are still more decisive than that of *property,* at least in advanced industrial society.

The *critique of faith* presupposes the rational critique that I have just sketched. The serious error of some Christians is to overlook this critique, accept as totally proven the Marxist theory of class struggle, and project onto it the gospel values, without realizing that they are *sanctifying a political theory and practice* and that they are confusing realities of different orders (for example, the Marxist "proletariat" with the gospel's "poor"). A worker-priest declared a few years ago, "The class struggle can become an impulse of vibrant love to blot out the sin of the world and to make of humanity a comradely and upright people."

I do not question the sincerity of such intentions, but it would be gratifying if this priest were to step back a bit and give evidence of a little more lucidity in regard to realities that are much less idyllic than he imagines. Language like his is typical of a kind of pseudo-evangelical ideology. If Jesus Christ had behaved like that, he would not have failed to adopt the politico-messianic ideology of the great majority of his compatriots instead of rejecting it categorically as a temptation. Many want the church to make a choice on the basis of class. How can they not realize that they would thereby put it at the service of Marxist ideology?

To be sure, certain negative reactions to this kind of choice are not without their own ambiguity. I would readily agree with some of the following statements of Giulio Girardi:

> The scandal that some see in the very idea of a choice of class on the part of the church is very revealing. It shows to what extent Christians can be blind to the fact that the church is presently committed to a political choice, that of the established order, even if it presents itself under the guise of neutrality. What we ask again of the church is therefore not to make a choice of class, but to make another choice, one that is humanly and evangelically more just and liberating.[26]

The attitude of the church should not be dictated by the Marxist theory of class struggle, even if it might well be challenged by it. The church must be open to all the poor, to help them in their immediate needs and in their fight for justice, but also to call them to evangelical conversion. As for the rich, it is not the church's function to contest them directly, but to call them also to evangelical conversion—conversion that would bring them eventually to a consciousness of those injustices for which they are responsible: the narrowness of their mentality, their egotism, their privileges, their failure to understand the popular classes.

Christians have to give political support to the struggle of the popular classes for justice, but they ought to be aware that their motivation and the concrete means implied by their commitment logically involve important differences with Marxism.

Berdyaev points out:

> If Christianity takes sides with the working class in the social struggle, it does not do so in the name of that class; it is in the name of humanity, of the dignity of workers, in the name of their human rights and of their souls, which capitalism so grievously grinds down. There is a great difference between this and materialistic socialism. . . . Christianity leads to individualization rather than to collectivization. . . . But Christianity does not require individualization only; it also calls for the conquest of individualism in behalf of the fellowship of all human beings.[27]

In a certain sense the *reformulation of the faith in terms of its concrete ethical demands* will start from a position similar to that of Marxism in industrial society. It will be the same as that formulated by Jean Girette in the context of his experience as a worker in a Paris suburb, when he noted that "the workers' world does not accept the present socio-economic system," that "it always has the feeling that it is being exploited," that "society seems to it to have been designed for the advantage and the well-being of a minority, to the detriment and by the subjugation of the majority."[28]

Marxist analysis of the class struggle will therefore be given due consideration, but not exclusively, and with the necessary degree of critical detachment. In this way we can develop an original theological reflection in the light of the gospel ethic.

Theology will then be much more attentive than in the past to the essential element of conflict in the social dynamic. It will try to discover its structural causes, while showing that they are not the only causes. It will propose a renewed theology of justice that will not be content to recommend a just wage, decent conditions of work, and other social advantages, but will challenge the authoritarian and bureaucratic structures of power, in economic life as well as in political life. It will also challenge the extreme social inequality that still characterizes advanced industrial society of the liberal variety. It will encourage those internal resolutions that stimulate persons to undertake the necessary changes of structure, even if they must challenge established privileges and easy solutions.

However, the vast experience of the Christian centuries—that also of the revolutions in our time—as well as the powerful light that revelation sheds on the depths of the human personality, will keep it from being trapped in an understanding that is focused exclusively on *structures*. They are what we make them to be. Their evil bias can pervert even the best. That is why, even in the domain of social justice, theology must always proclaim the call for evangelical conversion, which appeals to the deepest part of each human conscience to create that "new human being" who alone will be fully the "comradely human being" capable of promoting a fully humanized society.

The True Dimensions of Charity

The gospel ethic is clearly an ethic of charity. The problem is to know if we understand it correctly, and to ascertain whether it has been distorted by Christian theology and practice. It is no less clear that the Marxist ethic is an ethic of class struggle. The two approaches are radically different, which does not mean they are absolutely opposed on all points, as one might think at first sight and as Marx himself thought, with general agreement from the Marxist-Leninist tradition.

It is again in the *Circular against Kriege* that Marx best explained his ideas on love as the basis for a social ethic. True, his adversary had recourse to a sentimental language of the worst kind:

> Women, priestesses of *Love*. . . . Even in the attire of a queen you cannot deny your *femininity* . . . nor have you learned to speculate upon the tears of the unhappy; you are too softhearted to let a *mother's* poor child starve so that you may profit. . . . The *holy spirit* of community must evolve from the *heart of Love*, etc.

It is easy to understand why such language would irritate a mind as realistic and rigorous as that of Marx and why he would see in it a mortal danger for the young revolutionary movement. It was an attack on what he clung to most strongly. Therefore his reaction was violent in the extreme. In casting out all who had such sentimental notions, his weapon was the most satirical irony.

The first chapter of the circular is entitled "How Communism Became Lovesick." Marx stacks up quotations with a ferocious joy. He then concludes:

> In this *one* issue, then, we have love in some thirty-five shapes. It is exactly like the drivel that Kriege, in his *Antwort an Sollta*, and elsewhere, mouthes when he depicts communism as the mushy opposite of selfishness and reduces a revolutionary movement of world historical importance to a mere juggling with words: love-hate, communism-selfishness.[29]

Kriege's remarks are, from Marx's viewpoint, as he writes a little later, only "slobberings on the subject of love,"[30] the prattle of "a country pastor." The abstract language and religious simpering made him nauseous:

Kriege marches into battle, then, in order to take seriously the desires not of the real and the secular, but of the religious heart, not those of the heart made bitter by real need but those of the heart inflated by a phantasy of bliss. He forthwith offers proof of his "religious heart" by marching into battle as a priest, in the name of others—that is, in the name of "the poor"—and in such a manner as to make it absolutely plain that he does not need communism for himself. He would have it that he is marching into battle in a spirit of pure, generous, dedicated, effusive self-sacrifice for "the poor, the unhappy, and the rejected" who are in need of it—a feeling of elation that swells the heart of this worthy man in times of isolation and dejection, and outweighs all the troubles of this evil world.[31]

To a great extent Marx's reaction was healthy. The sentimentalism of the "Christian communists" of that period threatened to blunt all the bite in the young revolutionary movement and, by proposing a quick transfer of the gospel imperatives to the political domain without benefit of specific political analyses and decisions, it distorted its true characteristics. But Marx should not have limited himself to such a curt rejection. He might have distinguished between true love and its distortions.

On this point Marx made the same mistake in method as on the question of human rights. He was incapable of seeing that the necessary demythologizing should lead to a recognition of what is true and authentic. By that failure did he close off the only road that could lead to real liberation?

In similar fashion he repeatedly fired red-hot cannon balls against *fraternity*, or *fellowship*—for example, in his *Speech on the Question of Free Trade* of 1848:

We have shown what sort of fraternity Free Trade begets between the different classes of one and the same nation. The fraternity which free trade would establish between the nations of the earth would not be more real; to call cosmopolitan exploitation universal brotherhood is an idea that could only be engendered in the brain of the bourgeoisie.[32]

In *Class Struggles in France* he attacks the third term of what was becoming the famous republican slogan: "The phrase that corresponded to this imaginary abolition of class relations was *fraternité*, universal fraternization and fellowship. This pleasant dissociation from class antagonisms, this sentimental reconciliation of contradictory class interests, this visionary elevation above the class struggle, this *fraternité* was the real catchword of the February revolution. . . . The Paris proletariat reveled in this magnanimous intoxication of fraternity."[33]

In a letter of October 19, 1877, to F. A. Sorge he vigorously denounces again the whole ideology of fellowship:

The compromise with the Lassalleans has led to compromise with other halfway elements too; in Berlin . . . with Dühring and his "admirers," but also with a whole gang of half-mature students and super-wise doctors of philosophy who want to give socialism "a higher, ideal" turn— that is to say, to replace the materialist basis (which calls for serious, objective study by anyone wanting to make use of it) by modern mythology with its goddesses of Justice, Liberty, Equality, and Fraternity. Doctor Höchberg . . . is a representative of this tendency and has "bought his way" into the party—with the "noblest" intentions, I assume, but I do not give a damn for "intentions."[34]

The "League of the Just," predecessor of the Communist League, had taken as its motto the Christian axiom: "All men are brothers." This was sentimental mystification in the eyes of Marx. He saw to it that it was replaced by the revolutionary slogan: "Proletarians of all countries, unite!" Fellowship, love, charity—these were words he could not endure. He scorned them to the point that they could evoke in him nothing but irony: "They lack the bump of Christianity," he remarked in *Capital*[35] apropos of the pagan theoreticians of ancient slavery.

One can understand the reasons for his disgust: perfumed sentimentality and the ideological use of the ideals of fellowship serve only too often to maintain the status quo, if not exploitation and oppression. But, in rejecting love and comradeship so abruptly, without doing them the honor of a purifying critique, did he not risk the loss of something vital for a revolutionary movement that had the more need of devotion and spirit of sacrifice as it faced a long and difficult struggle and, worse still, felt compelled to justify in advance all its temptations to resort to inhuman behavior?

For him the question had been settled: Christian charity had shown itself to be totally ineffective for more than eighteen centuries. From his viewpoint, there was no need to question this judgment of history, there was no need to begin a new inquiry, there was no need to look for a more authentic interpretation of the gospel. He saw in it only flagrant failure, thus rejoining by a different route the position of Nietzsche: "If Christ really intended to redeem the world, may he not be said to have failed?"[36]

This theoretical intransigence of the father of Marxism could hardly be maintained in quite the same way by others, at least not by participants in the revolutionary enterprise who feel the need to perceive one another as comrades. *The Moral Code of the Builder of Communism*, an expression of the official ethical ideology of Soviet communism in the post-Stalin period, is interesting to examine on this subject. In many respects its language is no longer Marxian:

Love of one's own socialist country . . . ; collectivism and comradely mutual assistance: one for all, and all for one; humane relations

and mutual respect: one person is to another a friend, a comrade . . . ,
friendship and fellowship among all peoples of the USSR . . . ; comradely solidarity with the workers of all countries, with all peoples.[37]

Marx would have seen in these expressions—which for my part I regard as
excellent in themselves—only a dangerous idealism. Does this therefore represent a complete turnabout from the original Marxism? Not at all, for the
same *Code* advocates "intolerance of the enemies of communism, the enemies of peace, and those who oppose the freedom of the peoples."

In short, friendship and fellowship are limited to the friends of communism. For its enemies the toughest toughness is demanded. If one is familiar with the regular practice of the Soviet Union, even after the death of
Stalin, one knows that the threat is not to be taken lightly: the concentration
camp and the psychiatric hospital stand silhouetted against the sky. Besides,
is this not logical, when the political adversary is regarded as simply an enemy
and all human solidarity with him or her is rejected?

From such a perspective Christ's demand that we love our enemies can only
appear as nonsense: "The Soviets," writes V. I. Prokofiev, "reject that religious morality, for it has a clearly reactionary character. A true humanism, a
real love of humanity, presupposes hatred for the enemies of humanity."[38] (It
is true that many Christians are themselves no more inclined to accept the
gospel demand for love of enemies and that the official statements of noncommunist political authorities often call for intransigence toward enemies
of the state.)

Marx, by rejecting the appeal to love, in fact opened the door for hate, by
reason of his Manichaean conception of the class struggle, in which the adversary was only an exploiter and oppressor, whereas the proletariat was
endowed with all the virtues and regarded as the sole possessor of the "truth"
of history. How was it possible not to hate absolute evil?

The prescriptions of Mao Tse-tung represent perfectly the fundamental
dichotomy introduced by Marxism: "As for the so-called love of humanity,
there has been no such all-inclusive love since humanity was divided into
classes." In terms of dialectics, he adds, "We cannot love enemies, we cannot
love social evils; our aim is to destroy them." In his opinion, love can exist
only after the triumph of the socialist revolution, when social classes have
ceased to exist (at least in terms of conflict): "Classes have split society into
many antagonistic groupings; there will be love of all humanity when classes
are eliminated, but not now."[39]

In other words, there is a colossal parenthesis around love that covers all
recorded history. Evangelical Christianity does not deny the conflictual reality of history, but its wager is on the ability of love to act in history, in the
present, and by that action to contribute to its transformation in the direction
of a greater fellowship.

A new kind of language, however, is beginning to be heard in the Marxist
world from those who are sensitive to Christian values, even though their

general opinion is that such values represent a time that has passed in the history of humanity. They have begun to reintroduce love into a global perspective that was originally hostile to it. This reintroduction is a remarkable fact and carries with it a powerful challenge to Christians.

We should not, however, exaggerate its importance, for its protagonists tend to be intellectuals rather than political leaders, and their position is hedged with qualifications. This should not surprise us. The Marxist theory of class struggle, in its political and ethical articulation, as in its anthropological underpinnings, is based on an entirely different perspective.

The following proclamation of Maxim Gorky is well known: "With socialism, for the first time, the true love of humankind is organized as a creative force. . . ." This is great lyricism, but when one thinks that the lyrics envision the massive totalitarian transformation of Russia, with its concentration camps, its "Gulag Archipelago," how can one go on dreaming of such flattering visions from the pen of the great writer?

Solzhenitsyn tells of Gorky's one official visit to the Solovky Islands, which the Soviet state had just transformed into a sinister prison. Despite the efforts of the prison guards to conceal things, he could not help witnessing certain horrors. A fourteen-year-old boy—shot immediately after Gorky's departure—had the courage to reveal to him what was going on.

Gorky had nonetheless written in *The Golden Book*: "I am not in a state of mind to express my impressions in just a few words. I wouldn't want, yes, and I would likewise be ashamed, to permit myself banal praise of the remarkable energy of people who, while remaining vigilant and tireless sentinels of the Revolution, are able, at the same time, to be remarkably bold creators of culture."[40] (It is true that many Christians have also been hypocrites.)

Michel Verret, who assures his readers that "Marxists are not content simply to deny religion," that "they want to understand it,"[41] makes a great effort to analyze the Christian conception of love. As one might expect, he sees in it essentially abstraction, idealism, and ineffectiveness:

> They love everyone in God and by God, the latter being expected to distribute all the love for which he is made responsible. Inasmuch as they are unable concretely to love every single person, they love spiritually—through prayer—the general idea of the person. . . . An abstract love will always have a weakness for abstractions. Christian love, which wants to be incarnate and concrete, in the likeness of its own God, nevertheless founds contemplative orders, whose entire function is to pray. This is a lazy love, whose entire action exhausts itself in contemplation, verbiage, and effusion.[42]

The lack of understanding is remarkable. (Obviously, someone who does not believe in God can hardly understand the human richness of the contemplative orders.) Let us note, however, this author's conclusion: "What atheistic morality has against religious love is not that it loves. It is rather that it does not love enough; it is not knowing how to carry love to the level of practical truth."[43] Such a reproach cannot be based on the gospel idea of love; that is where Verret's failure to understand is situated. It is more on target, however, in what concerns the behavior of too many Christians. Not to recognize that would be blindness on our part.

In *St. Joan of the Stockyards* Bertolt Brecht contrasts authentic goodness with charity. He shows us how his heroine discovers the first, which, according to him, is quite a different thing from the second, for it consists not only in helping individuals in their misfortune, but it devotes itself to creating a world where each person would be a friend to everyone else. Without being aware of it, Brecht is talking about authentic gospel love under the label of "goodness." But Christians should realize that it is their own conception of charity, too often an individualistic one, that has led him into this error!

Erich Fromm, on the other hand, gives a central place to love. On the subject of the awareness of others he writes, "There is, however, another path to knowing man's secret; this path is not that of thought but that of *love*. Love is active penetration of the other person, in which the desire to know is stilled by union."[44] His perspective is still broader. He notes, in deploring it, that "modern man is lonely, frightened, and little capable of love" and that "psychology becomes a substitute for love, for intimacy, for union with others and oneself," that "it becomes the refuge for the lonely, alienated man, rather than a step toward the act of union."[45] More recently Fromm declared, "If the revolutionary movement is led by people who know only how to hate and not to love, then the victorious revolution will bring with it nothing but the same garbage that it wanted to eliminate."[46]

These are words that we can only greet with joy. Let us be sure to note that they are at the opposite pole from the language of the founders of Marxism and that they come to their author from a very different source: essentially, from the early influence on him of psychology, and especially the influence of Freudian psychoanalysis.

As much can be said—and even *a fortiori*—of Roger Garaudy, although his "faith" in love is explained by a very different influence. "Without love," he writes beautifully, "a human being or a society can function but not really exist. A socialist revolution will not mean the triumph of science but of love." If he has understood this clearly, he confesses, it is to Aragon that he owes the fact. Then he continues: "If the future belongs only to those who are capable of having faith in love, it is because the experience of love is experience of the absolute: the experience that teaches us to be conscious of our limits and of our power to surpass them. Like prayer, love is to be awake and as ready to give as to receive."[47]

We could quote many other passages of a similar nature from the famous and likable Marxist thinker. His distance from the founders of Marxism is even more striking than in the case of Erich Fromm. On this point, to speak in Teilhardian language (and that language is here the most appropriate), Garaudy belongs explicitly to the Christian phylum.

Would we therefore be justified in maintaining, with Girardi, that the eschatological society" (he seems to be speaking of the realization of the utopia of classless society) "will be a community of love" and that "the organic view of humanity outlined by Marx has some affinities with the Christian concept of the Mystical Body?"[48] That is exactly the kind of concordance that Marx rejected so violently in the case of Weitling, Kriege, and others. It leaves us in a field of total ambiguity. What is provocative, on the contrary, is the contrast between these two conceptions.

Love and Hatred

It is, in fact, *the crudity of the Marxist approach that hits us with the most force*, precisely because it proposes for the liberation of humanity a very different dynamic from that of evangelical love: the dynamic of the theory and practice of class struggle for the benefit of the popular classes, especially the industrial proletariat. A basic concern for efficiency motivated the founders of Marxism and their disciples. We cannot question their sincerity, for history has furnished them with an abundance of arguments. True, they did treat history in a cavalier fashion. They were unable to perceive that in spite of many failures Christians have given innumerable proofs of the efficiency of love. Nor did they take sufficient account of the historical obstacles that stood in the way of greater efficiency.

However, having expressed these important reservations, let us acknowledge that too many Christians have hardly been witnesses of love in their personal lives, and especially that very few political or economic leaders have been inspired by it in their collective action. They believed that its domain was completely foreign to politics and economics, on which point, in short, Marxism agreed with them. The only point on which I reject entirely the Marxist critique is the charge of inefficiency that it levels directly at evangelical charity. I reject it because it rests on a totally erroneous interpretation—namely, on its reduction of charity to almsgiving, individual commitment, and, at most, a very narrow conception of justice.

But here again the Marxists are far from bearing the prime responsibility for their error. They have, in fact, only picked up the erroneous interpretation held by the great majority of Christians of the nineteenth century, one that has not yet entirely disappeared, whose three characteristics I have just listed, making it but a caricature of authentic evangelical charity.

The fact that we acknowledge the power of its challenge cannot prevent us from faulting Marxism for rejecting the crucial role of the dynamic of love. It is true that certain contemporary Marxists have a more open attitude on this subject, and for this we are grateful. We hope that their reevaluation will lead them to a much more radical inquiry. Furthermore, I gladly acknowledge the commitment and sense of service that many militant communists demonstrate. It remains nonetheless true that the official theory, as it comes down to us from original Marxism, turns on the axis of conflict and not of love, that, by its Manichaeism, it leads logically to hate and that, by reason of its exclusive concentration on change of structures, it risks not only the toleration of the worst means to achieve its ends, but also the cynical sacrifice of whole masses of human beings, including sympathizers and even militant adherents. And the theory has a decided tendency to become transformed into a brutal practice that is insensitive to the sufferings that it engenders.

Berdyaev wrote:

> At the base of Christianity there is love of neighbor, love of humankind. At the base of Marxism there is negation of the love of God and neighbor. Marxism loves neither God nor humankind. It denies God and it is pitiless toward humankind as toward a means or an instrument; it loves only the socialism of the future, social collectivism. This love of society, this is what Nietzsche called, for another reason, the love of "the distant," as contrasted with the love of "the near." This distant, this future society, is the vampire that devours everything "near," every human personality, for it demands unlimited sacrifices. There is no cruelty that cannot be justified in its name. Christianity also aims toward a remote goal, toward "the distant," the kingdom of God, but it does not deny the love of "the near," the neighbor, the human personality. On the contrary, it demands it as a prerequisite for the realization of that kingdom. Only those will enter the kingdom of God who possess that love of neighbor.[49]

It is true that when Berdyaev wrote those lines he had Stalinism in mind and we should be careful not to identify Stalinism purely and simply with communism. The harshness of existing communist regimes, however, needs no proving. Machiavellian tactics, "reasons of state," and autocracy are current practice. It may be true that their origins lie somewhere else, but is it progress for humanity to perpetuate and intensify them? On the contrary, humanity needs the axial dynamic of love.

One can certainly object that love must still prove its efficiency and that social relationships still retain a strongly conflictual character. This accent on realism is indispensable. But only a dynamic of love, however difficult it may be to apply it to collective relationships, will keep the struggle for justice from sinking into inhumanity and the exercise of power from degenerating into oppression. Hate has always been the strong drink of barbarism, the poisoned spring from which flow the worst atrocities, ever since the sinister boastings that the book of Genesis (4:23–24) placed on the lips of Lamech ("I have slain a man for wounding me, a young man for striking me. If Cain is avenged sevenfold, truly Lamech seventy-sevenfold").

The Marxist theory and practice of class struggle, combined with the anthropology that we have discussed, does run a chronic risk of leading us into this kind of hatred, as Berdyaev again points out:

Christianity does not accept the sufficiency of class and its hatreds, the denial by one class of the image and likeness of God in the representatives of another class. We may violently repudiate the bourgeois spirit and principles, we may fight against a social system—but we may not hate the bourgeois as a human being with all his varied attributes. Moreover, there is a psychological law by virtue of which whoever hates comes to resemble the person hated.[50]

Once again, there is no question of denying either the reality of social classes and class conflicts or the necessity of the struggle for justice. All we ask is that this struggle remain human.

In reformulating the faith the important thing to remember is to *identify the essential characteristics of evangelical charity*, using a method of inquiry that will take full account of the contemporary situation but refrain from distorting the fundamental meaning of that charity.

In no way is that charity purely interior, though the commandment to love God is "the great and first commandment" (Matt. 22:38). Bergson has notably highlighted that characteristic of authentic Christian mysticism that emerges in passionate commitment to the service of humanity. The synoptic text is clear: the second commandment is like the first; it states, "You shall love your neighbor as yourself. On these two commandments depends all the law and the prophets" (Matt. 22:39-40).

For Jesus Christ the neighbor is not simply my parent, my friend, my next-door neighbor, my compatriot, my coreligionist, the one who shares the same ideology as I; the neighbor is every human being. Whatever their religion, their race, their country, their ideology, even if they live at the opposite pole and behave like my enemy, I must treat each of them as one who is close to me, as my brother or sister, for they are in fact my brothers and sisters, as sons and daughters of the same God who is in heaven. Even my class adversaries remain my neighbors, even when I must confront them in a vigorous struggle to put an end to exploitation for which they are responsible, or to obtain a greater measure of justice. Any interpretation of the gospel concept of "neighbor" that is not as universal as this distorts its meaning. And the two commandments blend with one another, throw light on one another. Both are inseparably joined in the evangelical concept of "charity" as are the two sides of a coin.

We can go so far as to speak of a *dialectic of the two commandments*. The commandment to love God calls for the love of neighbor and is fulfilled by it. In its turn love of neighbor is the most authentic sign of the authenticity of one's love for God and nourishes it with the milk of human kindness. This is exactly the thought of St. John, the fruit of profound Christian experience: "If anyone says, 'I love God' and hates his brother, he is a liar; one who does not love his brother whom he has seen, cannot love God whom he has not seen" (1 John 4:20).

By all the weight of the gospel, by all the directives that are given there, and especially by the example of him who "came not to be served but to serve, and to give his life as a ransom for many" (Matt. 20:28), charity therefore calls for a *consistent practice*, for the most complete and concrete commitment, for the pursuit of maximum *efficiency*, not in our personal interest, but for the effective service of neighbor.

The key word in the parable of the good Samaritan and in the scene of the last judgment in St. Matthew is the verb *poiein*: to do. It is a question of *doing* everything required to provide the effective service that one's neighbor needs. For this reason the more accurate formulation of the commandment of charity would be the following: *the commandment of the efficiency of charity.* And, as we recall that it should animate all human activity in all its dimensions (collective as well as interpersonal) and that, as St. Paul put it, it is "the fulfilling of the law" (Rom. 13:10), we could synthesize the formula further: *the commandment of evangelical practice (or praxis).*

In this way we can satisfy that demand for efficiency that is characteristic of all the ideologies of industrial society and that is expressed in Marxism by the primacy of praxis, but we strip it of all the implications of egotism and power that constantly threaten it. For here the rule of action is no longer personal or collective advantage but the unselfish service of the neighbor, and especially of the poorest neighbor.

Perhaps there will be objections that evangelical charity is limited to *interpersonal relationships*. For a long time, in fact, that has been the interpretation that has prevailed in the theory and practice of Christians who have held political office, and often even in theological works.[51] Such a restrictive interpretation can in no way be justified and has no other purpose than to open the road to license. It ignores completely the clear proof that the divine commandment strikes at the heart of conscience and the root of freedom and responsibility—which means that each of us is called to live the dialectic of charity in all the dimensions of our existence. It also ignores that other essential characteristic of the evangelical ethic—that it is an *ethic of responsibility.*[52]

Everyone who is called to pursue maximum efficiency in the service of the neighbor is by that very fact also called to employ those means that appear to be most likely to realize that service, means that could well be in the area of collective action and structural change. Charity can therefore lead to *political action* and to a new constitutional, administrative, judicial, economic, social, or cultural politics.

Pius XI saw clearly when he declared that "the field of politics . . . is the field of the widest charity, of political charity." Perhaps some will say that this is unrealistic and utopian, or pure mystification. The *Realpolitik* advocated by Marxism—and practiced everywhere without acknowledgment—at least has the merit of being frank and open, whereas a recourse to charity in politics could well lead only to hypocrisy. Such objections have a point, but are not decisive. History shows that friendship, fellowship, and forgiveness can be effective, even in politics. What is lacking is the conviction among political figures that it can be so. In certain cases politics inspired by charity might even be the only kind that is capable of resolving situations that are otherwise beyond solution. That is the bold and daring route, as compared with the timid, shortsighted way of *Realpolitik*.

Love and Justice

Another objection is possible and is often expressed. It is that, from the ethical point of view, what is fundamental in collective relationships is *justice* and if primacy is given to charity, we risk dragging in the worst mystifications to camouflage injustice, as did those employers of the nineteenth century who organized child-care centers while giving their workers miserable wages. The objection would be valid if evangelical charity were in reality only a horrible caricature.

Let us not forget that the teaching of Jesus Christ is founded on that of the prophets and that he always presupposes it. The vehemence of the prophetic cries for justice retains all its power to challenge and give direction in the very name of God. Not only does the New Testament in no way weaken this appeal; it gives it, on the contrary, a new force: that of the formidable appeal of the beatitudes and the commanding energy of the love lived and taught by Jesus Christ.

Was this not the most authentic love? No one can doubt it. But can love be authentic if it consorts with injustice or even if it only neglects to promote justice? Evangelical charity is by definition the *dialectic of love and justice*: always assuming the latter, accomplishing it, but suffusing it with that human warmth, that devotion of which justice alone is incapable. A world that is ruled by justice alone could turn out to be a cold and pitiless monstrosity where everyone would be occupied with calculating "what is owed and what is owned." Only a companionable world is a world where the human being can really blossom. Such a world obviously supposes justice, but it can be companionable only if human beings have learned to love one another.

It is true that authentic love encounters conflicts in collective life, and we know how formidable they can be, how likely to end in the mutual annihilation of adversaries, as with the threat of nuclear arms. Among these conflicts we have seen class conflicts clearly emerging in industrial society, even if not all conflicts necessarily begin there. Choices will be necessary, conflicts must be faced, a certain toughness will often be unavoidable. The problem of violence will often surface. A love that would overlook these hard realities would be unreal and a sham. It must, on the contrary, confront them with courage and a sense of responsibility.

The Christian primacy given to love will therefore lead neither to disengagement nor capitulation, precisely because evangelical charity is the dialectic of love and justice that we have described. It will not necessarily bring conflicts to an end, because they can be necessary for the promotion of justice. Eventually, it will instead provide the strength to engage in certain conflicts. But this will be because charity will be constantly at work, seeking to make its own the cause of justice and not that of injustice, even when there is a heavy price to pay. And, while struggling—if need be—against heavy odds, it will reject those barbarous means that degrade those who use them and it will not permit hatred to penetrate to the heart of its attitude.

"Class struggle does not coincide with class hatred," Girardi writes accurately.[53] But it is essential to note, first, that this is a very different interpretation from that of Marxist thought, which does *not* reject that hatred, and that the effort to keep free of it "requires great maturity, both personal and collective," as well as "a constant inquiry as to ends and means."[54] Once again, this is the language of a Christian and not of a Marxist who adheres to official theory and praxis. A Christian practice of class struggle will be Christian only if it recognizes the *primacy of love* and, by so doing, it will *no longer be Marxist*.

The love of enemies—so characteristic of evangelical charity that without it such charity cannot exist—will especially have a place in that practice. "What Christianity must make evident amid the violence of history is the peculiarly Christian power of the love of enemies. Only the love of enemies, practiced even in times of extreme tension, can heal, first in myself, that political neurosis that consists in fleeing our own death by projecting it onto the enemy."[55] It is that love alone that can, in certain circumstances, preserve us from barbarism.

The primacy of love in the midst of conflicts will be capable eventually of preventing the explosion of violence or at least of stemming its tide by preparing us internally for *dialogue*, according to the perceptive remarks of Jean Girette: "To the extent that we recognize before Christ that we are fallible and sinful, it is possible to examine with other eyes and another spirit our mutual antagonisms. Dialogues appear ever more necessary; they take on another tone; and they can end with a 'mutual recognition.' "[56]

By this process we become capable of examining ourselves and recognizing that we are not always completely right. Also we no longer regard the adversary as an absolute enemy or as a being of another species than our own. In the end we can recognize that we ourselves have need of conversion and we can believe that the adversary is also capable of conversion.

In this way, in the thick of conflict, the road to *reconciliation* opens up: not a road of mystification that conceals injustice, nor one of pacification imposed by force, but one of reconciliation in which, on all sides, the participants seek the promotion of justice and solidarity. Such reconciliation can only be reciprocal and it presupposes freedom. Only the primacy of love will have the strength and the creative capacity to take initiatives that will unlock difficult situations. As Olivier Clément wrote:

> The problem then does not confront us in terms of violence or non-violence; its solution, always partial, comes with the capacity to trans-

form as much as possible, in each historical situation, destructive violence into creative strength. The cross, which, to use the admirable expression of Berdyaev, makes the rose of earthly existence bloom again, is not here inscribed in resignation, but in service, not in weakness, but as the creative act.[57]

At first sight, the Marxist conception of merciless class struggle and of combat exclusively focused on justice is the more satifying, because more realistic. But it forgets that it risks glorifying the law of the jungle and of prolonging the struggle indefinitely.

Besides, how can we define justice in a way that would be indisputable? The promotion of justice is certainly necessary to peaceful coexistence between peoples. But it is not enough. True peaceful coexistence is possible only if the parties to it perceive each other as brothers and sisters. Such is the foundation, objective, and methodology of the Christian conception. It alone has a chance of reaching its goal because it takes account of all the aspects of human reality, because it is a dialectic of justice *and* charity. What is important, above all, is that Christians understand its true nature and that they put it into practice.

Marxist Morality and Christian Morality

Let us never forget it: Marx was a revolutionary who hungered for the radical transformation of the capitalist society of his time. All his scientific work had that one goal in mind. The paradox is that this man who fiercely rejected all transcendence made an *absolute* out of the revolution: "The categorial imperative to overthrow all conditions in which the human person is a debased, enslaved, neglected, contemptible being"[58] is the way he put it while still a young man. For him that was to be the task of the working class, once it had seized total power. Always, even in the full maturity of *Capital*, he was persuaded that its "coming into power" would "inevitably" occur.[59]

Let me underline the paradox: does not the conscious rejection of transcendence expose one to the danger of unconsciously investing transcendence in some human enterprise, and is not the gravest danger that of crushing human beings in the name of this worldly absolute? We can certainly applaud the Marxian objective: full human liberation. However, how could we possibly be in full agreement with the way Marx conceived it? Moreover, in making an absolute of it, did he not open the way to justifying any means whatsoever to accomplish it?

This last question is of decisive importance and it is there, finally, that we must locate *the basic value of the Marxist ethic*. Marx was a cold calculator. In his eyes the effective politics in a society of classes could only be a politics that did not raise questions about the morality of means; therefore, a *Realpolitik*. He was convinced that the revolutionary change that he envisioned would not be accomplished without terrible violence, even though he believed that it was inscribed in the book of historical necessity.

The violence of oppression that he wanted to stop seemed to justify fully the violence inherent in the revolutionary enterprise. "Communists," we read in *The Communist Manifesto*, "disdain to conceal their views and aims. They openly declare that their ends can be attained only by the forcible overthrow of all existing social conditions. Let the ruling classes tremble at a communistic revolution. The proletarians have nothing to lose but their chains. They have a world to win."[60]

A little earlier, in *The Poverty of Philosophy*, he had, still more brutally, envisioned the class struggle as a struggle to the death in which the revolutionary denouement could bring with it acts of extreme violence:

> Meanwhile the antagonism between proletariat and bourgeoisie is a struggle of class against class, a struggle that, carried to its highest expression, is a total revolution. Indeed, is it at all surprising that a society founded on the *opposition* of classes should culminate in brutal *contradiction*, the shock of body against body, as its final denouement? . . .
> It is only in an order of things in which there are no more classes and class antagonisms that *social evolutions* will cease to be *political revolutions*. Till then, on the eve of every general reshuffling of society, the last word of social science will always be: "Combat or death, bloody struggle or extinction. Thus the question is inexorably put" (George Sand).[61]

Realism was the thing he was invoking, the harsh realism of history, over against the "utopian" socialisms that he ferociously attacked. "Matters of this kind," he wrote in 1849, "cannot be accomplished without many a tender national blossom being forcibly broken. But in history nothing is achieved without violence and implacable ruthlessness, and if Alexander, Caesar, and Napoleon had been capable of being moved by the same sort of appeal . . . what would have become of history?"[62] At the same time he foresaw a revolutionary confrontation that would take on the aspect of a world war: "Every social reform remains a utopia until the proletarian revolution and the feudalistic counterrevolution measure swords in a *world war*."[63]

This was in conformity with his perspective, according to which the revolution fought by the proletariat within the framework of industrial society would necessarily have its repercussions throughout the entire world, because this type of society was, in his opinion, the extreme vanguard of human societies and effectively dominated all other types. Let me put it briefly: *the Marxian ethic is completely subordinated to the revolutionary goal*.

Can we even speak of a Marxian ethic? The Marxism of the founders presents itself as an *antiethic*. Besides, I have already mentioned their repugnance for appeals to "values" that are usually invoked from a humanist or Christian point of view: "justice," "liberty," "equality," "love," and the like. They do not hesitate to give frank opinions in support of this position. "Communists," we read in *The German Ideology*, "do not preach *morality* at all, as Stirner does so extensively. They do not put to people the moral demand: love one another, do not be egotists, and so forth. On the contrary, they are very well aware that egotism, just as much as selflessness, *is* in definite circumstances a necessary form of the self-assertion of individuals."[64]

Here we find a clear statement, all in one package, of their theoretical rejection of all transcendence, their concern to base their revolutionary practice and their political realism exclusively on a scientific footing. What they wanted, in effect, was to prove to the working class that its own interests should lead it to the revolutionary enterprise and that historical necessity, and not some theoretical or moral justification, guaranteed it success.

Did they want actually to reject every kind of ethic? Their personal behavior certainly proves the contrary. What they rejected was a transcendental ethic, or an ethic that would provide a cover for a mystification benefiting the ruling class. They wanted a revolutionary ethic. Their theoretical antiethic was untenable, even from an exclusively theoretical viewpoint. How could one in practice conceive of a revolutionary enterprise without recourse to some kind of ethic, some kind of morality, at least to a morality accommodated to the demands of efficiency? The founders of Marxism found themselves, fortunately, in a posture of plain contradiction on this subject.

Marx was perhaps not fully aware of it. Engels, however, was, at least at the time he was writing his *Anti-Dühring*, in which he brilliantly tackles the problem of a revolutionary ethic while trying not to contradict the theoretical antiethic of *The German Ideology* period. Like Pascal before him he states that "The conceptions of good and evil have varied so much from nation to nation and from age to age that they have often been in direct contradiction to each other." From this comes the ethical relativism that we can see in history. One can distinguish, he says, *three types of morality*: the *Christian feudal* morality; the *modern bourgeois* morality (that of capitalism); and the *proletarian* morality, which in his opinion is that of the *future*.

For him the only morality that is worth any consideration is the third. If he calls the first "feudal" it is obviously because he considers it backward and locked into a historical situation that is past and gone. We should note that he places under the same pejorative rubric the Protestant morality—though historically it arose after the feudal period—as well as the Catholic morality.

Each of these moralities, he says, is that of a social class at the time (past or future) of its domination: the first, that of the feudal aristocracy; the second, that of the bourgeoisie (then dominant); the third, that of the proletariat (whose success in the revolutionary enterprise will confirm its domination, which will bring with it, we know, the end of class society.

The reason for this is that for Engels, according to the interpretation of historical materialism, human beings, "consciously or unconsciously, derive their ethical ideas in the last resort from the practical relations on which their class position is based—from the economic relations in which they carry on production and exchange." Things will remain the same, he thinks, as long as a society of classes endures. In such a society, he assures us, it is pure illusion or pure mystification to pretend to have recourse to "an eternal, ultimate, and forever immutable ethical law on the pretext that the moral world, too, has its permanent principles, which stand above history and the differences between nations." It is only in a classless society that has been fully realized that one will be able to transcend the morality of class: A really human morality that stands above class antagonisms and above any recollection of them becomes possible only at a stage of society that has not only overcome class antagonisms but has even forgotten them in practical life."[65]

Let us salute in passing the proclamation of this "really human morality," even as we wonder if the classless society of the utopia will be as harmonious as the founders of Marxism believed. Meanwhile, as we await that day in the context of the class struggle, the morality advocated here will retain its cold, tough realism.

The problem of the revolutionary morality or ethic therefore remains intact, even though the founders of Marxism clearly stated—explicitly or implicity—the principal elements of their thought. They lacked an overarching theory that could be operative in a revolutionary movement, and therefore an action guide for militants as well as for leaders. The theoretical antiethic of early Marxism would not work. You do not mobilize the masses with that kind of language. What was needed was a revolutionary ethic that would lend itself to fervid exhortation.

Class Struggle vs. Transcendence

Lenin was the man who accomplished this—in a definitive fashion, in my opinion, as long as the communist movement remains faithful to the basic conceptions of its founders—and he did it with an impact that was the more effective because he knew how to express himself in language that was at once clear and simple. His most famous text on this subject—subsequently a classic—is that of his address of October 2, 1920, to the Third Congress of the Union of Russian Communist Youth. To the question, "Is there such a thing as communist morality?" his answer is categorical, "Of course there is." This was very clever on his part. From then on communist leaders could proclaim loudly that they do have a morality, in fact, one more demanding and more true than all the others. Thus they could galvanize the masses and inspire militants to acts of heroism.

Lenin explains further. What communism rejects are false moralities only. First, those that claim to be founded on transcendence, for the simple reason that communists do not believe in God. Besides, he remarks, this morality is only a mask: "We know perfectly well that the clergy, the landlords, and the bourgeoisie spoke in the name of God in pursuit of their own interests as exploiters." Communism also rejects every other morality of an idealistic variety, even without reference to God, because there again one is faced with a mask: "We say that it is a deception, a fraud, a befogging of the mind of the workers and peasants in the interests of the landlords and capitalists."

This is perfectly consistent with original Marxism: in a society of classes the dominant morality is always that of the dominant class, which uses it for its own profit and for the mystification of the classes dominated.

Then follow the famous iron-clad affirmations:

> We say that our morality is entirely subordinated to the interests of the class struggle of the proletariat. Our morality is derived from the interests of the class struggle of the proletariat. . . . What does this class struggle mean? It means overthrowing the czar, overthrowing the capitalists, abolishing the capitalist class. . . . The class struggle is continuing and it is our task to subordinate all interests to this struggle. And we subordinate our communist morality to this task. We say: morality is what serves to destroy the old exploiting society and to unite all the toilers around the proletariat, which is creating a new, communist society.[66]

There we have it then: the class struggle set in place as the *ultimate foundation of morality*. This is logical from the Marxist perspective, where human beings are identified by their social class, where the class struggle is regarded as the dynamic axis of history, and where all transcendence that might raise questions about human behavior is rejected. Revolutionary practice is completely free in its movements and actions. Once the revolution has been raised to the level of an absolute, there is logically only one rule that counts: that of efficiency. Who can question it, if all transcendence is rejected? What could one appeal to from the Marxist point of view? Respect for humanity? But if we are dealing with a class enemy, we cannot respect them, for we do not see humanity in them: we see only an adversary to be destroyed.

Lenin of course invokes lofty finalities: "Morality serves the purpose of helping human society to rise to a higher level and to get rid of the exploitation of labor."[67] But who will judge the modalities of this vision? Answer: the party, in its role as the connoisseur of the true interests of the revolutionary class. Now it has its own hands free. In any case we have arrived at the Great Question: does the end justify the means?

The question is all the more crucial because the positions of the great historical leaders and theoreticians of Marxism converge along the same line. Their common morality is that of revolutionaries sacrificing everything for revolutionary efficiency, as a Clausewitz—admired, incidentally, by many of them—sacrificed everything for victory in war, or a Machiavelli for the exaltation of the state. The problem for them is not one of morality but of efficiency. Shall we say then that their morality is one of efficiency? Is a morality that sacrifices everything to efficiency still a morality?

Let us look at Trotsky, for example, in his violent polemic with Kautsky. The latter had openly criticized the barbaric practices of the Bolsheviks in their struggle against the counterrevolutionary insurrection: the taking of hostages, massive executions, punitive expeditions. He invoked the principle of the sacred character of human life.

Trotsky's first response is one of irony on "the Kantian pedantry" of his adversary as well as on his "Quaker babbling about the sacred character of life." Then he proceeds to justify without qualification the behavior of the Soviet authorities and army:

> Revolution requires of the revolutionary class that it pursue its end with all the means at its disposal. . . . The problem of the form and signifi-cance of reprisals does not constitute in itself a question of principle. It is a question of opportunity. . . . Terror is powerless . . . when it is used by reactionary forces against a class that is historically in full de-velopment. But, utilized against a reactionary class that refuses to quit the scene, terror can be effective.[68]

As the Yugoslav Marxist Svetazar Stojanovic emphasizes—in this, fortu-nately, breaking with classic Marxist thought—this text "shows to what ex-tent a great revolutionary can be stripped of every moral consideration when it comes to the problems of the revolution."[69] One may say perhaps that Trotsky spoke in his own name. In fact, Lenin was no more tender. Solzhenit-syn is right to insist on this. Did not Lenin stipulate, in January 1918, in organizing mass support, that it was "to rid the Russian soil of all the noxious insects?"[70] (The insects were human beings.) But it is enough to read his speeches of that period.

About the same time Georg Lukacs wrote about Soviet practice. In his opinion, the problem of legality is a false problem, at least if one claims to invoke moral limits. It is a purely tactical question; therefore a question of opportunity and effectiveness. His language permits no equivocation:

> The question of legality or illegality reduces itself then for the Com-munist Party to *a mere question of tactics*, even to a question to be resolved on the spur of the moment, one for which it is scarcely possible to lay down general rules, as decisions have to be made on the basis of *immediate expediencies.*[71]

He concludes by asking the proletariat to learn to "slough off both the cretinism of legality and the romanticism of illegality."[72]

Earlier he had stated that his morality was a class morality and that the party was its interpreter and its guarantor:

> Class consciousness is the "ethic" of the proletariat, the unity of its theory and its practice, the point at which the economic necessity of its

struggle for liberation changes dialectically into freedom. By realizing that the party is the historical embodiment and the active incarnation of class consciousness, we see that it is also the incarnation of the ethics of the fighting proletariat.[73]

In a similar manner Rosa Luxemburg, in the course of her polemic against Bernstein, spoke ironically of "the principle of justice," "that old battle horse, which, for thousands of years, all the reformers of the entire world ride, for lack of more reliable historical means of progress," "that rundown Rosinante on which all the Don Quixotes of the world have galloped toward the grand reform of the world, to return dejected with a black eye."[74]

She also reproached him for making himself "the champion of idealism, of morality," but at the same time for taking a stand "against the only source of moral knowledge for the proletariat, the struggle of the revolutionary classes." Then she continued, "In so doing he comes to preach to the working class what is the quintessence of bourgeois morality, reconciliation with the established order and the transfer of hope into the hereafter of the moral universe."[75]

Antonio Gramsci for his part glorified "the proletariat come to power" for knowing "how to develop its own morality, which admits of no transactions with the agents of extortion, sluggards and thieves."[76]

As for Mao Tse-tung, no one knew better than he, as reflected in his statements and behavior, how to claim absolute status for revolutionary morality, not only to crush the revolution's enemies but also to remodel—and, it seems, with great ingenuity—the mental structures of a people.

One could also evoke the bloody appeals of Che Guevara for hatred and merciless struggle: "Hatred as an element of struggle, relentless hatred of the enemy that impels us over and beyond the natural limitations of man and transforms us into effective, violent, selective, and cold killing machines."[77]

Once again, this idea that "the end justifies the means" is in no way peculiar to Marxism. It was necessary, however, to demonstrate its presence there with clarity because, from the point of view of faith, it is not possible to confront this precise proposition with anything but a radical rejection.

Ethic and Antiethic

First of all, let us acknowledge the power of Marxist morality to challenge us. I have already noted it, but I must reemphasize it here: the theoretical antiethic of the founders of Marxism actually conceals a high ethical inspiration. I gladly acknowledge it, even though I am obliged, by reason of my human and religious convictions, firmly to question its absolutist pretentions. There is here a basic contradiction in original Marxism, but it is frankly preferable to the noncontradiction of an antiethic on all levels.

On the contrary, following the example of Berdyaev, it is important to throw the spotlight on that imperative ethical inspiration that attacks so furiously the injustices or the feeble performance of so many Christians. He writes:

> The whole ethical *pathos* of Marxism is linked with the exposure of exploitation as the basis of human society, the exploitation of labor. It is clear that Marx confuses the economic and ethical categories. The doctrine of added value, which is what brings to light the exploitation of workers by capitalists, Marx considered a scientific economic doctrine. But in fact it is primarily an ethical doctrine. Exploitation is not an economic phenomenon but primarily a phenomenon of the moral order, a morally evil relation of person to person. There is an astounding contradiction between the scientific amoralism of Marx, which cannot endure an ethical basis for socialism, and the extreme moralism of the Marxists in the appraisement of life in general. The whole doctrine of the class struggle bears an axiological character. The distinction between "bourgeois" and "proletariat" is a distinction between evil and good, unrighteousness and righteousness, between what is worthy of censure and what is worthy of approval. In the Marxist system there is a logically contradictory combination of materialist, scientifico-determinist and amoralist elements, with elements that are idealist, moral, religious, and myth-creating.[78]

This ethical inspiration that is fortunately characteristic of Marxism is the more impressive when we note that the directives of its historical leaders usually advocate the imperative need for personal sacrifice, devotion to the revolutionary cause, unselfishness, hard work, and integrity. "At no time and in no circumstances," Mao Tse-tung, for example, insists, "should communists place their personal interests first; they should subordinate them to the interests of the nation and the masses." He wanted communists who hold the positions of governmental responsibility to set an example of "absolute integrity, of freedom from favoritism in making appointments" and "of hard work for little remuneration."[79]

There is without doubt a great deal of hypocrisy and constraint in the moral behavior within communist regimes. This is important from the ethical point of view, for morality presupposes a situation of freedom and responsibility. However, observers are in agreement that the atmosphere there is austere, if not puritanical, and that moral laxity is not so evident as it is all too often in advanced industrial society of the liberal variety where liberty degenerates easily into license. It is a morality of effort and of struggle that they recommend, and not that easy morality we know only too well in our consumer society.

Stoic grandeur, one might say? Perhaps, but is it not a requirement of moral education that someone advocate effort and solidarity? Gramsci wrote in 1928: "I would not change my opinions, and indeed would be willing to give up my life for them, not only to go to jail."[80] We know how well he gave proof of his sincerity and courage.

Although it has recourse to force whenever it believes it to be useful and possible, Marxism does impress one with its seriousness. It is a fact that it takes the side of the oppressed and exploited, even if, by its dictatorial and totalitarian methods, it creates other forms of oppression and exploitation. That is what explains its extraordinary power of seduction for those who do not see its fearsome ambiguity or who, prompted by what they consider realism, believe that it is necessary to side with it. Let us appreciate also its concern for realism and the search for efficiency, even if we cannot accept the idea of turning it into an absolute.

Let us acknowledge further that the churches have too often advocated or accepted a morality that played up the interests of the ruling class, even though the Marxist accusation is much too general. As Maurice Duverger observes, the church in the Middle Ages served the ruling class, "but it also limited the power of the ruling class by imposing on it a morality that transcended its class interests and contained them."[81]

Christians are thus challenged to adopt a morality that is more evangelical, more lucid, and more sincere. They must especially rediscover the compelling demand of their faith to contribute effectively to liberation from all oppression and all alienation. Christians of advanced industrial society of the liberal variety must also, in particular, rediscover the sense of effort and sacrifice that is painfully lacking at the present time.

The critique of Marxist morality will center essentially on its raising the revolutionary goal to the level of an absolute by the fact that it accepts the principle that "the end justifies the means." And this critique will be, first, in the order of reason, that the acceptance of such a principle can only lead to barbarism, although the revolution is said to envision a higher degree of justice and morality. To pretend to liberate a people by beginning with blind killing or by imposing a totalitarian regime is the most radical moral contradiction that one can think of, and an absolute lie. A liberating revolution will be moral in its realization or it will not be liberating, particularly inasmuch as barbarism, once at work, tends to perpetuate itself indefinitely, for unjust violence is an endless and vicious circle. As Girardi says: "To believe in revolution is to believe in the possibility of achieving it without violence and without dictatorship."[82] "No revolution launched in the name of liberty is complete until it has established a regime of liberty."[83]

Albert Camus has posed the problem remarkably well in an unforgettable scene from *The Just Assassins*. Stepan, the intransigent revolutionary, suddenly cries out:

Children! There you go, always talking about children! Cannot you realize what is at stake? Just because Yanek couldn't bring himself to kill those two, thousands of Russian children will go on dying of starvation for years to come. Have you ever seen children dying of starvation? I have. And to be killed by a bomb is a pleasant death compared with that. But Yanek never saw children starving to death. He saw only the grand duke's pair of darling little lapdogs. Aren't you sentient human beings? Or are you living like animals for the moment only? In that case by all means indulge in charity and cure each petty suffering that meets your eyes; but don't meddle with the revolution, for its task is to cure all suffering present and to come.

Kaliayev rejects with horror such a view:

Those *I* love are the men who are alive today, and walk this same earth. It's they whom I hail, it is for them I am fighting, for them I am ready to lay down my life. But I shall not strike my brothers in the face for the sake of some far-off city, which, for all I know, may not exist. I refuse to add to the living injustice all around me for the sake of a dead justice. . . . Brothers, I want to speak to you quite frankly and to tell you something that even the simplest peasant in our backwoods would say if you asked him his opinion. Killing children is a crime against a man's honor. And if one day the revolution thinks fit to break with honor, well, I'm through with the revolution.

Annenkov also opposes categorically the intransigence of Stepan. A little earlier he had told him:

Stepan, all of us love you and respect you. But whatever private reasons you may have for feeling as you do, I can't allow you to say that everything's permissible. Thousands of our brothers have died to make it known that everything is *not* allowed.[84]

To reject with all one's strength that the end justifies the means is to defend humanity against its worst temptations, to contribute effectively to the promotion of justice and civilization.

I also rejoice that on the Marxist side as well voices have been raised in the same kind of protest. Thus Rosa Luxemburg distinguished carefully between "violence" and "terror," and she categorically rejected the latter. "Terror perverts morality," she remarked; it "degenerates inevitably into despotism."[85] She insisted that it was dangerous to confer power on "a handful of socialist dictators" while relegating democracy to a distant time when socialism would finally be realized.[86]

Horkheimer believes that "our dubious democracy is still preferable to dictatorship"[87] and he rebels vigorously against every society that is founded on terror: "Even supposing that the building of the new society has already been finished, the happiness of its members could not compensate for the misery of those who are crushed in contemporary society."[88]

Roger Garaudy offers a moral aphorism of unusual quality when he suggests the following principle: "An idea that sets the goal of making the worker the subject of all rights cannot use means and methods that contradict this end."[89]

These statements correct Marxism in regard to its original aberration in the field of ethics, one that up to the present moment has left in its wake such serious historical consequences.

The God of Liberation

The critique of faith reinforces the rational critique in two ways. First, because it opens us to respect for all human beings and teaches us to discover a brother or sister in them, even if they are our adversary, even if, for serious reasons, we are obliged to struggle against them. Consequently we can never see in them an absolute enemy and we can never feel justified to use barbaric measures against them. Secondly, because in helping us to discover the one God, the only Absolute, it keeps us from any inclination to turn into an absolute whatever human goal may obsess us, whether it be revolution, for example, or the class struggle. It thus becomes a powerful instrument of liberation from such obsessions.

Cardinal Ratzinger has illuminated this last point apropos the creed of Israel and the Christian creed. The creed of Israel is its daily profession of faith in the *Sch'ma*: "Hear, O Israel, the Lord our God is one Lord." He notes with insight:

> As a renunciation of the gods it also implies the renunciation both of the deification of political power and of the deification of the cosmic *Stirb und werde* ("die and become"—Goethe). If one can say that hunger, love and power are the forces that motivate humankind, then one can point out, as an extension of this observation, that the three main forms of polytheism are the worship of bread, the worship of love, and the idolization of power. All three paths are aberrations; they make absolutes out of what is not itself the absolute and thereby make slaves of us. . . . Israel's confession is . . . a declaration of war on this triple worship and thus an event of the greatest importance in the history of human liberation.

As for the Christian creed, it is the restatement and development, in relation to Jesus Christ, of Israel's creed:

> Whoever assented to this creed, renounced at the same time the laws of the world to which they belonged; they renounced the worship of the ruling political power, on which the late Roman Empire rested, they renounced the worship of pleasure, and the cult of fear and superstition which ruled the world. It was no coincidence that the struggle over Christianity flared up in this field and thereby defined and grew into a struggle over the whole shape of public life in the ancient world.[90]

When one looks at it from this angle of liberation it is difficult to understand the coherence of the positions taken by certain Christians with the creed that they profess. For example, when Father Cardonnel in a bewildering article gives us his new "gospel" of the *word that is incarnate in class struggle*: "In sticking to the end with the class struggle for the future of a humanity in jubilation, I find the meaning, the *logos*, the word, that unites with matter."[91]

Or when Michel Blaise claims that the class struggle "can alone constitute the norm of morality," that "the proletariat is . . . presently the norm of universal good," that "it is the depository" of that good.[92]

Or again when Giulio Girardi, faced with the question, "How far can a Christian go in commitment to revolutionary theory?" responds as follows: "We have only one answer to give: to the end. And this without knowing exactly where this fidelity will take one. We mean: to the end of the revolutionary demands and their scientific, philosophical, and theological implications."[93]

Or finally, when a document of *Action Catholique Ouvrière*, quoted by Jean Girette, states that "because we are Christians no limit can be fixed to a total commitment to class struggle." As Girette remarks, "The risk run by this adventure is to place the absolute of faith at the service of human choices."[94]

I am convinced—or at least I hope so—that the intentions of the authors I have quoted do not go so far as to accept practically the idea that any means are permissible in the class struggle. At least, it will—I hope—be acknowledged that such statements imply logically an absolutization and admission of the principle that the end justifies the means. These statements are indicative of an uncritical Marxist permeation and a serious lack of theological rigor. By sanctifying the class struggle they are responsible for the worst kind of absolutization. In such a struggle, as in other conflicts, one can act as a human being—and *a fortiori* as a Christian—only if one is capable of relativizing what needs to be. That is the indispensable guarantee for not falling into barbarism.

Karl Barth is right in saying that politics becomes possible only "from the moment when the dogmatic tone of theses and antitheses disappears and gives way to plans that are perhaps relatively moderate, perhaps relatively absolute, on the question of human possibilites."[95]

Reformulation of faith will require the effort to achieve a better understanding of God as the *God of liberation*, as the one who calls us to commit ourselves to the liberation and promotion of the solidarity of humanity. From that starting point we can proceed to the elaboration of a responsible ethic for our time that responds to these goals. This will be a realistic ethic, for it is essential to take into account the conflictual dimensions of existence. But it will constantly remind us, even in the midst of conflicts, that the gospel insists on the primacy of love, as well as on the potentialities of nonviolence and on concern for assistance to the poor.

The concrete elaboration of such an ethic will always be difficult and will probably not escape dispute on the part of other tendencies, even among Christians, because it will necessarily depend on the rational analyses that are chosen, which will introduce differences of opinion at the very start. A rigorous effort in analyses and in theological reasoning, as well as an ear for dialogue, should, however, permit some lines of convergence to emerge. What I hope is that Christians will understand more and more clearly that faith calls for an ethic and that ethics is, in its turn, fertile ground for the flowering of faith. *Christian ethics is the praxis of faith. It is the faith that is lived.*

I agree entirely with the following statement of Karl Barth: "Ethics so-called I regard as the doctrine of God's command and do not consider it right to treat it otherwise than as an integral part of dogmatics, or to produce a dogmatics that does not include it."[96]

This is an excellent expression of the dialectics of theory and practice at the theological level, the dialectics of dogmatic theology and moral theology in the unity of the same faith—thought out and lived.

NOTES

1. *Je cherche la justice* (Paris: Ed. France-Empire, 1972), p. 219.

2. In *Marx-Engels Reader*, p. 220.

3. In *Marx-Engels Reader*, p. 538. Another text of Marx is just as important, one found in his annotations on the book of his adversary Bakunin, *Statehood and Anarchy*. Bakunin posed the question, "If the proletariat is ruling, over whom will it rule?" To which he added: "This means that there will remain another proletariat, which will be subordinated to this new domination, this new state." This is where Marx inserts the following personal comment, to express his own view: "This means that so long as other classes continue to exist, the capitalist class in particular, the proletariat fights it (for with the coming of the proletariat to power, its enemies will not yet have disappeared, the old organization of society will not yet have disappeared), it must use measures of *force*, hence governmental measures; if it itself still remains a class and the economic conditions on which the class struggle and the existence of classes have not yet disappeared, they must be forcibly removed or transformed, and the process of this transformation must be forcibly accelerated" (original text in Marx-Engels, *Werke*, Vol. 18 [Berlin: Dietz, 1969], p. 630; English trans. in *Marx-Engels Reader*, pp. 542-43).

4. In *Marx-Engels Reader*, p. 490.

5. Cf. *State and Revolution* (1917) (New York: International Publishers, 1943), p. 30. It is public knowledge that the French Communist Party, at its 22nd Congress, following the lead of other western communist parties, renounced using the notion of the "dictatorship of the proletariat" to designate, according to Georges Marchais, "the political power to be exercised in the socialist France we are struggling for, . . . because it does not correspond to the reality of our politics, the reality of what we propose for this nation" (*La Croix*, February 5, 1976). This relinquishment is not unimportant and could mark the beginning of an irreversible process. However, it would be good to reflect on the following remarks of Jean Boissonat: "Communism is a 'totalitarian' system, in the sense of a system that gives an overall—and scientific—interpretation of society. It is totalitarian before it is dictatorial. Marx and

Lenin had explained that it had to be dictatorial for a time: the time to convince everyone of the scientific character of this totalitarian truth. . . . But the fact remains that the final goal remains the construction of a political and social system based on a doctrine that claims to be scientific. Is that not a real danger? . . . When temporal power is exercised in the name of a truth that claims to be scientific, then there is no way out. The labor camp and the asylum are rigorously justified, since it is a matter of bringing misguided spirits to a higher level of consciousness'' (''Les communistes ont-ils changé?'' in *La Croix*, February 8–9, 1976). We recall the similar remarks of Berdyaev. The debate around the 22nd Congress of the PCF revealed that the Soviet Union and the parties most dependent on it, including Red China, are still firmly committed to the concept of the dictatorship of the proletariat.'' Althusser and his school have been more than reticent about abandoning it. See Etienne Balibar, *Sur la dictature du prolétariat* (Paris: Maspero, 1976).

6. *Réponse à John Lewis* (Paris: Maspero, 1973), p. 26.

7. In *Marx-Engels Reader*, p. 473.

8. *Marx-Engels Reader*, p. 474.

9. Cf. *Anti-Dühring* (Moscow: Foreign Languages Publishing House, 1959), p. 41.

10. *History and Class Consciousness*, trans. Rodney Livingstone (Cambridge: M.I.T. Press, 1971).

11. *The 18 Brumaire of Louis Bonaparte*, in *Collected Works*, Vol. 11 (New York: International Publishers, 1979), pp. 99 ff. See Henri Weber, *Marxisme et conscience de classe* (Paris: Union générale d'éditions, 1975).

12. 1885 Preface to *The 18 Brumaire of Louis Bonaparte*, in Karl Marx, *Selected Works in Two Volumes*, Vol. 2 (New York: International Publishers, n.d.), pp. 314–15.

13. *The German Ideology*, p. 54.

14. *The Class Struggles in France (1848–1850)*, in *Collected Works*, Vol. 10 (New York: International Publishers, 1978), p. 122.

15. *A Contribution to the Critique of Political Economy*, ed. Maurice Dobb (New York: International Publishers, 1970), pp. 21–22.

16. *Philosophy of Right*, trans. T. M. Knox (Oxford: Clarendon, 1957), p. 10.

17. Cf. *Anti-Dühring*, p. 393.

18. *La lutte des classes* (Paris: Gallimard, 1964), p. 356.

19. *Traité marxiste d'économie politique*, Vol. 1 (Paris: Editions sociales, 1971), p. 199.

20. Cf. *From Karl Marx to Mao Tse-Tung*, trans. Robert Olsen (New York: Kenedy, 1963), pp. 127–28.

21. *Masse et classe* (Paris-Tournai: Casterman, 1972), p. 84. [Tr.'s note: ''Cadre'' is a word that is much more common in Europe, and in Marxist discourse, than in usual American parlance. As used, it means either a group of militant party members, or a member of such a group, depending on the context.]

22. *Classe ouvrière et révolution* (Paris: Seuil, 1971), p. 105.

23. *The Russian Revolution*, trans. Donald Atwater (London: Sheed and Ward, 1931), p. 68.

24. *The Russian Revolution*, p. 72.

25. *Masse et classe,* pp. 14–15.

26. *Christianisme, libération humaine, lutte des classes* (Paris: Cerf, 1972), p. 209.

27. Cf. *Christianity and Class War*, trans. Donald Atwater (New York: Sheed and Ward, 1933), pp. 116–17.

28. *Je cherche la justice*, pp. 19–20.

29. In Henri Descroche, *Socialismes et sociologie religieuse* (Paris: Cujas, 1965), p. 323; cf. English trans. in Marx-Engels, *Collected Works*, Vol. 6, p. 41.

30. *Socialismes*, p. 327; cf. English trans., p. 46.

31. *Socialismes*, p. 329; cf. English trans., p. 47.

32. In *Collected Works*, Vol. 6, p. 464.

33. Cf. *The Class Struggles in France*, pp. 57–58.

34. *Letters to Americans, 1848–1895* (New York: International Publishers, 1953), pp. 116–17.

35. *Capital*, p. 200.

36. *Human, All-Too-Human*, Part II (New York: Macmillan, 1911), p. 54.

37. Cf. *The Road to Communism. Documents of the 22nd Congress of the Communist Party of the Soviet Union, October 17–31, 1961* (Moscow: Foreign Languages Publishing House, 1961), pp. 619–20. Cited by Paul D. Dognin, *Initiation à Karl Marx* (Paris: Cerf, 1970), pp. 224–25.

38. "Le caractère anti-humaniste de la morale religieuse," in *Cahiers du communisme* (November, 1959), p. 1081. Quoted by Dognin, *Initiation à Karl Marx*, p. 210.

39. *Talks at the Yenan Forum on Literature and Art*, in *Selected Works of Mao Tse-Tung*, Vol. 3 (Peking: Foreign Language Press,1967), p. 91.

40. In *The Solovky Islands* (1929), p. 3, quoted by Alexander Solzhenitsyn, *The Gulag Archipelago*, trans. Thomas Whitney, Vol. 2 (New York: Harper, 1975), pp. 62–63.

41. *Les marxistes et la religion*, 3rd ed. (Paris: Editions sociales, 1965), p. 7.

42. *Les marxistes*, pp. 158–59.

43. *Les marxistes*, p. 159. In his *Appeal* of June 10, 1976, Georges Marchais claims for the Communist Party the strength to promote an authentic *fraternité*: "All our efforts are aimed at building up . . . a society where fraternity will no longer be simply a word engraved on the facades of public buildings."

44. *The Dogma of Christ and Other Essays on Religion, Psychology, and Culture* (Garden City, New York: Doubleday-Anchor, 1966), p. 201.

45. *The Dogma of Christ*, pp. 203–204.

46. Interview in *Panorama* (Italy), October 16, 1975.

47. *Parole d'homme*, p. 37. Another text of the same author: "On all levels we are brought back to this fundamental truth regarding life: What is most intimate and essential in myself is in fact the presence and love of others. The other, others, are my transcendence, they are what calls me beyond my individual limits, what makes me a human person. Humanity is not a solitary adventure. It is a victory of community. A communion. The only possible mediation with the totally other. On condition that others be loved one by one. Not as a collective abstraction" (*Parole d'homme*, p. 148).

48. *Marxism and Christianity*, trans. Kevin Traynor (New York: Macmillan, 1968), p. 52.

49. *Christianisme et réalité sociale* (Paris: "Je sers," 1932), pp. 51–52.

50. *Christianity and Class War*, p. 74.

51. See René Coste, *Evangile et politique* (Paris: Aubier, 1968), pp. 118–21.

52. See Coste, *Théologie de la liberté religieuse* (Gembloux: Duculot, 1969), pp. 237–43.

53. *Christianisme, libération humaine, lutte des classes*, p. 179.

54. *Christianisme*, p. 180.

55. Olivier Clément, *Questions sur l'homme* (Paris: Stock, 1972), p. 139.

56. *Je cherche la justice*, p. 96.

57. *Questions sur l'homme*, pp. 139–40.

58. *Contribution to the Critique of Hegel's "Philosophy of Right,"* in *Critique of Hegel's "Philosophy of Right,"* trans. Annette Jolin and Joseph O'Malley (New York: Cambridge Univ. Press, 1970), p. 137.

59. *Capital*, p. 240.

60. In *Marx-Engels Reader*, p. 500.

61. In *Collected Works*, Vol. 6, p. 212.

62. Cited by Jacques d'Hondt, *De Hegel à Marx* (Paris: PUF, 1972), pp. 78–79; English trans. in *Collected Works*, Vol. 8 (New York: International Publishers, 1977), pp. 370–71.

63. *Wage Labor and Capital* (1849), in *Collected Works*, Vol. 9 (New York: International Publishers, 1977), p. 198.

64. Cf. *Collected Works*, Vol. 5, p. 247.

65. All of the preceding quotations are from: *Anti-Dühring*, pp. 130–32.

66. V.I. Lenin, *Speech Delivered at the Third All-Russia Congress of the Russian Youth Communist League*, in *Selected Works in Two Volumes*, Vol. 2 (London: Lawrence and Wishart, 1947), pp. 667–69.

67. *Speech Delivered*, p. 670.

68. See *Terrorism and Communism*, with foreword by Max Schachtman (Ann Arbor: Univ. of Michigan Press, 1961).

69. *Critique et avenir du socialisme* (Paris: Seuil, 1971), p. 211.

70. Quoted by André Glucksmann, *La cuisinière et le mangeur d'hommes* (Paris: Seuil, 1975), p. 104.

71. *History and Class Consciousness*, p. 264.

72. *History and Class Consciousness*, p. 270.

73. *History and Class Consciousness*, p. 42.

74. In *Oeuvres*, Vol. 1 (Paris: Maspero, 1969), p. 66.

75. *Oeuvres*, p. 83.

76. *La costruzione del partito comunista (1923–1926)* (Turin: Einaudi, 1971), p. 315.

77. *Message to the Tricontinental*, in *Che: Selected Readings of Ernesto Guevara* (Cambridge: M.I.T. Press, 1969), p. 180.

78. Cf. *The Origin of Russian Communism*, trans. R. M. French (London: Bles, 1955), p. 100.

79. *Role of the Chinese Communist Party in the National War*, in *Selected Works of Mao Tse-tung* (Peking: Foreign Language Press, 1965), p. 198.

80. Letter of May 10, 1928, quoted in Giuseppe Fiori, *Antonio Gramsci: Life of a Revolutionary*, trans. T. Nairn (London: NLB, 1970), p. 290.

81. *Sociologie de la politique* (Paris: PUF, 1973), p. 401.

82. *Marxism and Christianity*, pp. 253–54.

83. *Marxism and Christianity*, pp. 257.

84. All the preceding quotations are from: Albert Camus, *The Just Assassins*, in

Caligula and Other Plays, trans. Stuart Gilbert (New York: Vintage, 1958), pp. 258, 260, 257.

85. *Die russische Revolution*, pp. 75–76, quoted by Gilbert Badia, *Rosa Luxemburg* (Paris: Editions sociales, 1975), pp. 303–304.

86. *Die russische Revolution*, p. 78; *Rosa Luxemburg*, p. 304.

87. *Théorie traditionelle et théorie critique* (Paris: Gallimard, 1974), p. 11.

88. *Théorie traditionelle*, p. 89.

89. *The Alternative Future*, trans. Leonard Mayhew (New York: Simon and Schuster, 1974), p. 175.

90. Cf. *Introduction to Christianity*, trans. J. R. Foster (New York: Seabury, 1979), pp. 73–74.

91. In *Frères du monde*, Nos. 72/73 (1971), p. 70.

92. "La lutte des classes comme fondement de la morale," *Frères du monde*, p. 80.

93. "Foi chrétienne et matérialisme historique," in *Parole et société* (1974), p. 297.

94. *Je cherche la justice*, pp. 139–40. The text quoted by Jean Girette is taken from a pamphlet of the *Action Catholique Ouvrière* entitled *Eléments de réflexion sur la lutte des classes* (1970). Out of context, it can in fact give rise to this author's criticism. It seems indispensable, however, to resituate it in its context: this is the only way to come to an accurate interpretation. Here, then, are the lines that follow immediately the text at issue: "It [class conflict] entails risk, to be sure: risk of giving in to hatred, risk of being unjust, because one is partial. One needs to be conscious of it, conscious that one could be seduced, but conscious also that, whatever one does or does not do, other risks are involved." This points out that the practice of class conflict advocated by these authors is intended to avoid hatred, injustice, partiality: i.e., limits are set on the choice of means for action, for higher reasons of human and Christian ethics. How is it then that they did not perceive that this view—altogether correct from the perspective of faith—precluded their calling for "a *total* engagement in class conflict?" Such a manner of speaking exposes one at least to serious ambiguities: most of all to that of absolutizing class conflict, which one really does not intend.

95. *L'Epître aux Romains* (Geneva: Labor et Fides, 1972), p. 461.

96. *Church Dogmatics*, Vol. 1/1., trans. G. W. Bromiley (New York: Scribner's, 1955), p. xiv.

Chapter 6

Rediscovery of the Revolutionary Character of Christianity

The course I have followed has repeatedly portrayed Marxism as *a formidable challenge* to Christianity: as a frontal attack, a radical critique, and even a death sentence, which could eventually lead to persecution wherever communism is in power. In any case it claims, on scientific grounds, to predict the progressive extinction of Christianity as a result of the combined advance of culture and the development of structural relations of the socialist type. In my opinion *it is the most formidable challenge in the entire history of the church.*

True, for three centuries Greco-Roman paganism was a formidable foe of emerging Christianity. It attacked frontally with all its socio-cultural weight: all the prestige of western reason and all the power of the empire. But the reason that it invoked did not have the impact of the science with which Marxism decks itself.

The ideology of liberalism, inherited from the philosophy of the Enlightenment, which characterizes so profoundly western advanced industrial society of the liberal type, is also at the opposite pole from Christianity in its pragmatic materialism and is perhaps the more dangerous because it insinuates itself slyly without our being aware of it. But it does not try to attack the Christian faith frontally. It does not declare itself either for or against God. It does not claim to be a fundamental conception of all reality. I have sufficiently highlighted the fact that it works very differently from Marxism. Which means that the Christian faith must do some rethinking in depth as it faces this radical challenge.

It is this very thing that has been—and remains—my main concern: a result contrary to the predictions of original Marxism, which was convinced that it had already won the victory. The indictment has become for me a challenge: a pressing and fully accepted invitation to a new and profound discovery of the founding event of our faith and to impassioned effort to rethink it in terms of contemporary problems. Under the impact of this challenge and as a consequence of the new kind of inquiry that it provoked, that founding event now appears as *the revolution of God*.

Here again Berdyaev will be our guide:

Christianity is revolutionary in its most profound essence, much more revolutionary than all the other revolutionary efforts in the world. This revolutionary character of Christianity clearly results from the opposition of the kingdom of God to all the kingdoms of this world, from the confrontation of the eternal and the temporal, of the whole and its parts. The deification (sacralization) of all that is finite, all that is partial, all that is temporally limited, is the temptation *par excellence*. The revolutionary character of Christianity is determined eschatologically and is necessarily oriented toward the final cataclysm. By contrast, the false eschatology of the revolutions of this world habitually gives to a future limited in time the character of an eternal future.[1]

We must clearly understand this. The revolution of God is in no way a substitute for social or political revolutions. It is not of the same order. Nor can it be invoked to justify conservatism. Quite the contrary! It is on the basis of the founding event, as the source of light and energy, as permanent challenge, that *the Christian identity* can be established with precision.

A Formidable Challenge

We know this formidable challenge in its broad outline. It was the original Marxism, with its enormous power and gift for radical questioning, that formulated it. Marxism-Leninism has consistently maintained it, simplistically on the theoretical plane, but on the practical plane placing at its service the entire panoply of means that a modern totalitarian state can command.

It is true that the challenge has clearly been toned down—although it has not disappeared—in the current positions taken by the communist parties of Western Europe and in those of theoretical neo-Marxism of the "revisionist" variety. A fair number of Christians are very sensitive to this evolution (which, for my part, I also note with satisfaction). But they generally tend to exaggerate it because they do not see that the advertised refusal to resort to force against the church after the eventual takeover and the recognition of some historical value to Christianity do not necessarily change the fundamental challenge. Even neo-Marxism, when it wants to recapture all the authenticity of Marxist thought, is quite as radical and virulent as the original Marxism.

Althusser is, we know, perfectly representative of this tendency. And his great intellectual prestige gives his positions a considerable impact on the French intelligentsia, even though he is beginning to be questioned from the left. I regard as particularly significant the viewpoint he expressed in a letter of May 2, 1969, addressed to the editors of the review *Lumière et vie*.[2]

He explains that his goal—and he makes it clear that he is applying to everything he is going to say his "convictions as a Marxist and communist"— is to "understand the great shocks that are shaking and will more and more shake the Catholic Church." It is therefore the present crisis of the church that he wants to analyze with the instruments of Marxist analysis. We are immediately warned that in his opinion this crisis can only worsen—as also that of capitalism, I might add, according to the basic economic analysis of Marxism.

How does he justify his diagnosis? First, by a historical analysis according to which "the church has been the major cog of a mode of production that has now disappeared from our Western countries: the feudal mode of production. . . . It was the instrument *par excellence* for the reproduction of feudal relations of production." This is the classic Marxist thesis regarding the nature of the church. It is taken for granted that the church remains what it was at that historical period and that it is therefore destined to disappear from the stage of history, just as that ancient mode of production disappeared, even if, by reason of the special effectiveness of the superstructures, it has continued to survive for a long time.

Pursuing his broad-stroked historical analysis, Althusser estimates that by the end of the nineteenth century "the capitalist school had practically replaced the church in its role of reproducing, ideologically, the relationships of production." The "social doctrine" of the church, based on the notion of "the common good," appears to him backward and reactionary. In his view, "despite its recent amendments,' " it "remains profoundly conservative," which explains "the atheism of the workers" and why, "in the mass," they "ignore the church, at least in France." He says he is convinced that "in this domain the game is over" for the church.

From there he enlarges his horizon to the whole world, and especially Latin America. There, still according to the classical Marxist analysis since Lenin, the church finds itself up against that "other terrible reality: imperialism." For him it is especially tied to "the most reactionary forces of the still feudal landowners," but he states that a reaction of protest is developing in certain religious circles, that "a part of the clergy is rebelling against the role that the hierarchy has forced upon them," and even that some members of the hierarchy are "associating themselves openly with that protest."

If critics object that he is ignoring the *aggiornamento* of Vatican II, he responds that it can only be a failure, for a religious institution "cannot resolve a problem that is not in principle a religious problem, but a problem of class struggle." This is the more true, he says, because the reality of this problem "can in no way be known with the theoretical instruments available to the theological tradition and can even less be resolved with those measures that, on the one hand belong to another age and on the other were designed, when they were forged, not for the defense of the exploited classes but for the service of the ruling classes."

The diagnosis is clear: theology has no value for rational explanation; Christianity can be explained only by historical materialism and class struggle; the church's ideology is at the service of the ruling classes. The church is therefore condemned by the advance of history and by that of the revolutionary movement. "It seems to me," Althusser concluded, "that the crisis in the church can only get worse." Does the revolutionary movement therefore have nothing to hope from it? Such is not the conclusion of the famous philosopher. For there to be hope, however, there is in his opinion one indispensable condition: "the disappearance of the myth of 'the community of Christians' that prevents the recognition of the class society and class struggle."

Is this condition even thinkable? The political evolution of a certain number of Christians gives him reason to hope so. "For the cause of the proletarian class struggle," he believes, "the crisis of the church can produce this result: to rally to the cause of that struggle a portion of the Christians, those whose class position and sensitivity to the suffering of 'the humble ones,' those whose understanding of the causes of that suffering, will rescue them from the myth of 'the community' of believers."

There we have then the church "justified" by its reduction to the (provisional) role of a support force for the revolution—on condition that it deny that which constitutes its essence. We might ask ourselves if, despite their clearly more favorable appreciation of Christianity, that is not, in the end, the thought of most of the neo-Marxists of the "revisionist" variety, even among those who are most open.

Some Christians believe, however, that they can apply historical materialism and class struggle unreservedly to the analysis of the church and deliberately introduce into the church a revolutionary practice of class struggle in the name of the proletariat (or the exploited classes), *and* remain Christians themselves throughout. They insist that it is the demands of both science and their faith itself that move them to take this position and that this is even the indispensable condition for discovering and putting into practice authentic Christianity, which has been deformed over the centuries by its transformation into an ideology of the ruling classes.

The work that appears to me the most representative of this state of mind and in which, furthermore, others who share this tendency have largely recognized themselves, is that of Jean Guichard, *Eglise, luttes de classes et stratégies politiques.*[3] His basic point of departure, he explains in substance at the start, is the political viewpoint, more precisely that of Marxism, which is in his view much more than an instrument of political analysis—namely, a (the) science of the human person, an (the) anthropology. This leads him to downgrade the social teaching of the church, which does not accept that viewpoint, and to give an affirmative response to the question: "Is not concurrence with Marxist thought today a condition for the renewal of the faith and its future?" (p. 93).

What he wants is a political church that is revolutionary, therefore committed to the class struggle and anticapitalist. Whether it wants it or not, he explains, in fact the church is obligated to a political role: "It is the political domain that today conditions the expression and development of the faith; there is a political determination of the faith" (p. 52).

He proposes a typically Marxist interpretation of the work of Vatican II:

"The council has represented the transfer to the interior of the world episco-pacy of all the contradictions at the base of the church; those contradictions were themselves the consequence of the totality of class struggle" (p. 68). He believes that contemporary theology is a means of integration into capitalist society. Theological currents that put the accent on interpersonal relations, subjectivity, interior dialogue of the human being with God are, for him, "the response and adaptation of the tendency of bourgeois society to privatize the faith" (p. 70).

The teachings of the magisterium are a failure, according to Guichard, because of their misunderstanding of objective social structures, their nega-tion of the real dialectic of social classes, their rejection of the inevitability of conflict between these classes, their lack of a scientific grasp of reality—of which their rejection of Marxism is *the sign*—and their idealistic system of religious belief.

Politically, in his analysis, the church presently situates itself "in a strategi-cally centrist position that runs from an enlightened conservatism to a moderate reformism" (p. 116). A good relationship with the United States is necessary to it. Its rejection of communism in western countries is fundamen-tally tied to its conservative reformist option. It adapts itself now, after a long delay, to the mold of bourgeois democracy.

Christians and Revolution

What remains then for revolutionary Christians to do? Leave the church or withdraw to the periphery of its life? No, says Jean Guichard. On the con-trary, they should boldly take on the task of transforming it from within so that it will adopt a revolutionary strategy, all the while, however, respecting its special character and refraining from any attempt to make of it simply "an ideological powertrain between the party and the masses" (p. 168)!

Let me acknowledge that this book deals with some genuine problems and contains points of view that deserve consideration. The importance of class affiliation on the part of those who exercise pastoral functions (bishops and priests) or theological functions (professional theologians) calls for empha-sis. The risk of identification with the ruling classes exists, and it is true that the church has yielded to it during certain periods of its history and in certain places. One can understand how its present directives on political, economic, and social questions appear to be centrist to those who look at them from either a conservative or revolutionary viewpoint, although this conclusion does not do them justice and ignores the significant reflection in the light of the faith that they contain. It is entirely legitimate that Christians who have made a revolutionary option should want to be as active as possible within the church. The only question is that concerning their means and ends.

By the same token it is fruitful to use political analysis to reflect on the life of the church—that is, provided we do not suggest that this is the *fundamen-tal analysis*, because the church in its essence is not a political reality, even if politics has repercussions on its life and if, in its turn, the church has an impact on politics.

This is precisely the objection I would raise with Jean Guichard—namely, that he makes his *political* analysis of the church the fundamental analysis, which clearly takes precedence over any *theological* analysis. He also makes exclusive reference to Marxism, as if it were beyond discussion, as if it were perfectly scientific and undeniable, as if it did not involve a conception of the world that raises fundamental objections from the viewpoint of the faith. He criticizes the church in his book, but we do not see him criticizing Marxism. Consequently Marxism—not the gospel or Jesus Christ—becomes the supreme reference point. From the objective viewpoint (I refrain from making any judgment on the subjective state of mind of those who share this view) can they not see that this is a radical apostasy, inasmuch as the very heart of the Christian faith consists in making Jesus Christ the supreme reference point?

Over against these Marxist views of the church—whether they be that of an Althusser who, sharing entirely the Marxist worldview, situates himself outside it, or that of a Guichard who, as a Christian, situates himself inside it—over against all views that want to take an essentially political approach to the subject, I strongly insist on *the special character of church analysis*. By this concept I mean to emphasize the necessary originality of any analysis that wants to account for *the ontological reality of the church* as a community of faith founded by Jesus Christ, as a community of faith made up of those who believe in him with the fullness of faith found in the New Testament: faith in the risen one, in the one sent by God, in the Son of God, in the savior of humanity, in the judge of history.

By reason of the realities that it must learn to understand and the fact that these are in the end only known by the revelation of God in Jesus Christ, its essence is *theological analysis*. Although it must take into account the entire gamut of rational analyses (and Marxist analysis among them) and must concern itself with the concrete problems and needs of human persons in all the dimensions of their existence, this approach does not see either human persons or groups from the same point of view. Its fundamental and characteristic point of view will be that of Jesus Christ—that is, one that sees realities in their relationship to the salvation that he offers us. As a result of this fact, *ecclesiastical practice* (pastoral practice, theological practice, the practice of Christian communities) will be a very different thing from political practice, even if it eventually has a political impact. It will be of the same order as the action of Jesus Christ and the Apostles. Its goal will be the bringing together of all persons in a renewal of faith, prayer, and the sacraments, which is the characteristic mark of the church in the New Testament.

It is only by situating itself on this axis that it can, for example, develop correctly from the viewpoint of faith *its own practice as regards the class struggle*. This will have a double aspect according as it is seen from outside or from inside the church. In the first case the mission of the church is one of urgency, to help in making social injustices and their structural causes known to those who are unaware of them or do not want to see them, but also to question uncritical adhesion to Marxist theory and practice. It is also that of an urgent mobilization of energy, to stimulate Christians to assume their responsibilities in the fight for justice.

In what concerns the inner life of the church, members would strive to identify the impact of the class struggle within it, but, because of the nature of the church as Jesus Christ intended it, *it is not possible to accept that the practices of the class struggle should be deliberately introduced within it,* because these are dependent on politics for their goals and their means. If there is a "struggle" to take up within the church, its goal is clearly to make sure that the popular classes are not dominated therein, but also to ensure that all social classes are welcome there so that all may hear the call to evangelical conversion. And this "struggle" must be carried on by specific means (biblical renewal, examination of conscience, amendment of life in the light of faith and mutual respect, practice of the sacrament of reconciliation, etc.) and not by those of a political praxis.

To take an example from fairly recent events, the greeting given by the Italian worker-priests gathered at Serramazzoni from January 3 to 6, 1976, to the bishop delegated by the Italian Bishops' Conference (a salute with raised fists while singing the *Internationale*),[4] is contrary to responsible church practice, however legitimate may have been the grievances that the priests had to address, even vigorously, to their bishops.

If there is one place where everyone should be able to confront others in peaceful dialogue, because they have all gone to school at the same gospel and all perceive themselves as sinners and not as sinless "pharisees," the church, by virtue of its nature and its mission, ought to be that place. True, its unity is continually in the process of being rebuilt and it must not be monolithic or at the service exclusively of the ruling classes, but it would be contrary to faith in Jesus Christ to invoke the class struggle or any other social difference for the purpose of dividing the faithful. The Epistle to the Galatians bears witness to this fundamental principle in the theology and practice of the New Testament church: "For as many of you as were baptized into Christ have put on Christ. There is neither Jew nor Greek, there is neither slave nor free, there is neither male nor female; for you are all one in Jesus Christ" (3:27–28).

St. Paul did not mean to deny differences or conflicts, but, in accord with the thought and practice of Jesus Christ, he believed that such differences should not prevent Christians from coming together in the same community of faith. I state unequivocally: if we want to be faithful to the demands of God's word, it will not be by promoting a new class church and rejecting another class church, but by promoting *one church where all classes and social categories can agree to meet together,* because they know by their faith that in spite of their differences and their conflicts they are all called together in conversion in the gospel.

In view of the formidable challenge of Marxism it is important to *explain the concept of church practice*, starting from a conviction that is based on both science and faith that the Marxist explanation of the genesis of Christianity by historical materialism and class struggle does not even deal with the essence of Christianity. It must therefore be rejected, even if it does throw some light on certain historical elements, which I readily acknowledge.

Christians believe that the only final explanation is that of their faith: the intervention of God in history as witnessed by the New Testament. How can we be Christians without such a conviction? And, if we are Christians, how can we think of the church and its practice in any other way than Jesus Christ thought of them and desired them to be? That also we know only by the New Testament. The Marxist challenge leads then to a new articulation and a new energizing of church practice.

The mission of the church is that of a community of faith. Its reference point is the word of God in Jesus Christ. In the face of politics and all the other problems of collective existence, as Karl Barth has said so well, the church is called to seek out "its *own* way."[5] I have already underscored this. It is called to develop independently its own analyses and its own practices. These will take account of the whole constellation of circumstances. In certain cases it will be better to speak out and in others to remain silent. Both its speech and its silence can be, for the church, a true imperative. The same faith and consciousness of its one and only mission will dictate on each occasion the church's attitude, but on the basis of the diversity of circumstances revealed by its analyses.

I quote again the forceful, accurate observation of Karl Barth:

Ten years ago we said that the church is, and remains, the church, and must not therefore keep an un-Christian silence. Today we say that the church is, and remains, the church, and must not therefore speak an un-Christian word. We have reason to say precisely that today and for the same reasons as ten years ago.[6]

For those reasons, faced with political systems and collective conflicts, the church cannot take positions that would make it purely and simply the ally of one camp against the other. Even if, on certain points, it agrees with one of the adversaries, it will be because of its own motivations (of the order of faith) and in all independence. This means that it will retain all its capacity for criticism, that it must be impossible to co-opt it, and that it must remain free to dialogue with all parties.

Again I agree with Karl Barth: "That is the first element in our Christian political attitude: our refusal to fight one way or the other in this conflict."[7] I have expressed radical objections in regard to Marxism and historical communism, while recognizing elements of truth in them. Speaking as a theologian, this in no way means that I am trying to launch a crusade against them. My sole intention is to encourage the critical discernment of Christians in their regard, while maintaining the same freedom of critical evaluation as regards the practical materialism and other deficiencies of western industrial society of the liberal variety.

As Karl Barth puts it: "Not a crusade but the word of the cross is what the church in the West owes to the godless East, but above all to the West itself, the word through which the church itself must allow itself to be rebuilt completely afresh."[8] At the time when that sentence was written (1949), it was the mentality of the anticommunist crusade that especially transfixed Christians. Today it still does with some, while others face the opposite temptation as a commitment to Marxism that ignores its significant deficiencies. The "word of the Cross" challenges both the one and the other.

Moltmann describes the church as "the people of God on the march," "the exodus community." He asks it to contribute to the promotion of "a historic transformation of life." He explains:

> Not to be conformed to this world does not mean merely to be transformed in oneself, [but] to transform in opposition and creative expectation the face of the world in the midst of which one believes, hopes, and loves. The hope of the gospel has a polemic and liberating relation not only to the religions and ideologies of humankind, but still more to the factual, practical life of persons and to the relationships in which this life is lived.[9]

I agree with these statements, but in order to avoid the politicization of the church to which those theologies that are polarized on the biblical theme of the exodus succumb at the present time, I should prefer to give priority to his definition of the church as *the community of the resurrection*, while still retaining the concept of "the exodus community." That is to say, I prefer the idea of a community of those who adhere to Jesus Christ and meet together in the community of faith that he founded, having broken away from the politico-religious complex of the ancient *polis*.

Church practice is therefore situated at the heart of the most profound reality of the church and distinguished clearly from the practices (political, economic, etc.) that are assumed by Christians in the context of their personal responsibilities in the midst of collective existence, practices that can lead to profound disagreements among them. It is only on the basis of such a judgment as to the church's essence that we can tell what is most important in its practice and therefore avoid evaluations that are based primarily on its political effectiveness:

> Those who really believe do not attribute too much importance to the struggle for the reform of ecclesiastical ritual. They live on what the church always is; and if one wants to know what the church really is one must go to them. For the church is most present not where organizing, reforming, and governing are going on, but in those who simply believe and receive from it the gift of faith that is life to them. Only those who

have experienced how, regardless of changes in its ministers and forms, the church raises persons up, gives them a home and a hope, a home that is hope—the path to eternal life—only they who have experienced this know what the church is, both in days gone by and now.[10]

I address this fraternal message in my turn to all those Christians who have doubts about the church because of institutional deficiencies or who might be tempted to demand of it first and foremost a kind of political practice and effectiveness. True, it must be concerned with politics, with political questions that are often of exceptional importance, as, for example, in the confrontation between capitalism and Marxism. "The church must seek an answer to the problem. And this answer must be an honest and authentic answer."[11]

But this answer is not directly political, just as the gospel is not directly political. It is based on the word of God in Jesus Christ. It addresses itself to the human conscience in the light of faith. This means that it is developed as much by prayer as by responsible reflection. It is word, but it is also action. It is, in the end, a "confession" of the gospel, as the fundamental reference point of thought, word, and action:

> In fact, if it has the gospel to confess, it is not the philosophy and morality of the West, not a religious disguise in the place of real life, not an injunction to escape into the inner life of the spirit or into heaven, no imaginary god, but the living God and his kingdom, the crucified and risen Jesus Christ as the Lord and Savior of the whole person.[12]

The church's position must be one of humility, for it knows that it can be wrong in taking practical positions and that "it has to reckon with God for its speaking."[13] It is this conviction that will lead it to the maximum of openness and dialogue, to a listening to the word of God that is continually deepened and renewed, and to respect for legitimate differences within Christian communities in the name of Christian freedom, which will make it more capable of correcting itself.

Actually, I am already speaking of the theological task of the church. *Theology* is the heart of its reflection on a word of God that has been listened to: the place where it reflects on its own nature in the light of its faith as well as on its responsibility and that of Christians in whatever concerns the witness of Jesus Christ and the evangelization of the world. Theology is the place where the church strives to think about God with all its resources of intelligence enlightened by adherence to revelation, even if one can only stammer before the mystery.

Giulio Girardi rightly insists on its necessary *creativity*. Speaking of the meeting of "Christians for Socialism" that was held at Santiago, Chile, in 1972, he declared, "At Santiago we were able to live an experience of Christian creativity that made it possible for us to understand what it could mean for the church to transform itself by participating in the transformation of the world." For him "the creative place *par excellence* for the church today, the locus of its new youth, is precisely where a faith lived to the full encounters a revolutionary commitment lived to the full."[14] The theme is repeated in the final document of the meeting: "Revolutionary praxis provides the milieu that can generate a new theological creativity."[15]

One of the problems, as the same document notes correctly, is "to identify and unmask ideological rationalizations that pretend to be Christian," to avoid "making the faith an instrument in the service of new political objectives, but on the contrary to restore to it its original gospel dimension."[16] It is also necessary, still according to this document, that "theological thought be transformed . . . into critical reflection within and on revolutionary action, in permanent confrontation with evangelical demands."[17]

It is not the principle of a revolutionary option that in itself poses the difficulty. Quite the contrary, it is confrontation with situations of injustice and oppression. It is rather the final ends and concrete means. That is where the questions arise. Is the option based on rational analyses that are sufficiently rigorous? Are the foundations of the theological analysis sufficiently consistent with the revelation of Jesus Christ? Is the theological analysis itself developed with competence, in relation both to the faith and to rational analysis? Has it avoided the pitfall of becoming an ideological instrument of the revolutionary enterprise? Does it practice a sufficiently critical discernment?

Although it is an indispensable task for theology to think about how coherent with the faith is the commitment of the church and Christians in the life of the world, it is also a difficult task and one that is exposed to the dangers of being used for ideological purposes. It requires dialogue and confrontation among theologians, which supposes the broadest theological pluralism, on the sole condition that it be consistent with the fundamental gift of revelation in Jesus Christ. As it must be open to the human sciences, so too must it know how to trace its own path in full independence. As it must be free, so too must it have the sense of the church. In short, it must fulfill its own task.

I am firmly convinced that we cannot reach the clarifications, especially in the broad field of politics, that are necessary today and to which the church today might have a word to say . . . without having first reached those comprehensive clarifications in theology itself. . . . Because it is expected of the church, and of theology . . . it should stick doggedly and particularly to the rhythm of its own relevant concerns—that is, consider carefully what the real needs of the day are, by which it has to direct its program. Because I have found by experience that ultimately "others" . . . then and only then take account of us, when, quite untroubled by what "others" expect of us, we do what is actually laid upon us. . . . For these reasons I hold myself forbidden to let myself be discouraged by such thoughts.[18]

These affirmations of Karl Barth are just as relevant today as in 1932. Then his special concern was to confront Nazism. Today in industrial society theology must confront the colossal phenomena that are neo-capitalism and Marxism. It is first necessary that it know them exactly. That is the first condition of its success, the other being the autonomy of its own inquiry. As concerns Marxism, there is no doubt: it is "an antitheology that can help us to rethink theology."[19]

East and West

Is this not an impossible task for the church, to witness to Jesus Christ in the face of systems of thought and action that are in themselves at opposite poles from the gospel: neo-capitalism with the practical materialism of a consumer society, Marxism with its materialism that is both theoretical and practical?

I can respond by repeating the substance of several splendid pages of Jacques Ellul in his book *Betrayal of the West*.[20] According to him, the decisive moment in the history of the West was the night when St. Paul had a dream in which God gave him the order to pass over the strait and enter Greece (Acts 16:6–10). "It was the moment when God took radical action in the political and intellectual spheres" (pp. 73-74). History would have been radically different if Christianity had turned toward the East rather than toward the West:

> Paul's dream is typical of God's action: Paul is summoned by a vision to preach the gospel; he is asked for help by a man who seeks salvation. It is thus a decision that refers only to *preaching* and to the proclamation of *salvation* that will determine the course of history far more than all the struggles between the political parties of the day, far more than the great leaders and the modes of production. God changed the course of history and politics and society and civilization by means of a vision that had nothing to do with history or politics or society or civilization [p. 74].

Let no one claim that divine providence led Rome to the conquest of the world for the spread of the gospel and that it was significantly helped by the Roman unification of the known world. Such an explanation does not take "into account the very great extent to which Greco-Roman civilization, which at every point was diametrically opposed to the gospel, was an obstacle to its spread" (p. 74).

The logical course, on the contrary, would have been a diffusion of Christianity toward the East. There the announcement of salvation by the death of God would have found a spontaneous and favorable response. If the Apostles had presented themselves to the Parthians, those ferocious enemies of Rome, and explained that the founder of Christianity had been put to death by the Romans, would they not have been welcomed with open arms? Have not the Asiatic peoples revealed in Buddhism their aptitude for the spiritual? There is no point in looking for elements in the West that were favorable to Christianity, as has so often been tried, even in the earliest Christian times. It is the opposite approach that is more fruitful: "Our only chance of understanding what happened is to accept that there was an irreducible contradiction between Christianity, on the one hand, and the sociocultural situation in the empire and in the civilization that succeeded it" (p. 76).

Thus we can sketch the following fresco of the theology of history:

> The greatness of the West, then, consists in this, that it is the place where God has issued his final and most radical challenge to humankind, because it is the only place where humankind has attained its own greatest stature. We are confronted by the challenge God issued in response to the human challenge. Christianity is the testimony to an Other Love and was proclaimed when humankind had renounced love for the sake of power. Nor did God fight humankind with human weapons; he did not come clad in the power of the one who had caused the confusion at Babel or who had unleashed the deluge. Instead, he attempted to penetrate to the center, the heart, the root, of the whole conflict; he attempted to go back and make the whole human adventure start all over again, so that its course might be entirely different. Once God had thus chosen the place and direction, the conflict was engaged. The West became the site of the most radical kind of spiritual combat. All the works and creations, all the political, intellectual, economic, and technical advances of the West had been the result of this tension and conflict, this constant head-on collision between humankind that wants to be itself and God who also wants humankind to be itself. The difficulty is that "itself" does not mean the same thing in both cases; in fact, the one meaning contradicts the other [pp. 76-77].

It goes without saying that this interpretation of God's action in history is open to question. It seems to me, however, that it throws a great deal of light on the present as well as on the past.

Marxism is a product of the West just as much as is neo-capitalism. Advanced industrial society in its totality defies the gospel and, at least in practical terms, claims that it can get along without Christianity. Would that be a reason for the church and for Christians to be afraid of it? The apostolic church did not recoil before the defiance of its time. What would be serious would be either to shut oneself up in a ghetto or to permit oneself to be contaminated by the current ideologies (liberalism, Marxism, nationalism, fascism, etc.), and therefore become incapable of criticizing them with clarity.

It is legitimate to look for elements that are favorable to evangelization— for example, in the devotion of so many militant workers to the promotion of their social class—and to show them that Christianity responds to the most profound aspirations in the heart of humanity. But it remains nonetheless essential today, as always, to understand that commitment to Jesus Christ presupposes for all of us a radical and continually renewed conversion.

God's Revolution

And so we are brought back to the founding event of Christianity, and how could it be otherwise for a church that claims to be the church of Jesus Christ? It is for us to discover its extraordinary originality, so extraordinary and so rich that it reveals itself only by degrees and one can never finish cataloguing its wonders, so that the more we become conscious of it, the more it impregnates our minds and gives proof of its own creativity, the more its newness burgeons yet again.

To a considerable extent it was the opposition that the early church very soon encountered that quickened its conscience and its consciousness—opposition from the Jewish world and from Greco-Roman paganism. The same thing may be happening to the church today as it faces Marxism, precisely because Marxism sees itself not only as the antithesis of capitalism and liberal ideology, but also as the radical negation of Christianity, which it charges with dangerous illusion and connivance with capitalist oppression.

Christianity and the West had become so used to one another that many no longer saw very clearly the power of the former to challenge and question. It was necessary for them to rediscover it in its original force behind and beyond all the historical accommodations. They had to convince themselves that these were not inevitable, that they were due to human weakness, that it was not through them that the gospel should be interpreted, but rather, to the contrary, it was the gospel that must judge them with all its power of truth. It was necessary to rediscover the shock that the gospel represented for centuries, until the conversion of Constantine. It was necessary to perceive clearly that it did not concern merely the private life of Christians and the life of the church, but also the collective existence of humanity. It was necessary to strip away every trace of fatalism in regard to the deficiencies of society and, first of all, look at them intently.

Historically, Marxism has made a powerful contribution to this development, both by its negations and by its revolutionary dynamism. It seems to me that God's intervention in history through Jesus Christ—more than ever now because we live in a historical context that is global and in which it is possible to change the structures themselves—is a formidable power for the transformation of hearts and the transformation of the world, a revolution in the strongest sense of the term, *the* revolution. Is this an abuse of words? In truth, there is great risk of the worst kind of confusions, as we see in certain "theologies of revolution." It is essential to avoid them. But the concept of *God's revolution* is fruitful. Berdyaev was without doubt the first theologian to think so and to sketch the theory of it. He could do this because of his profound knowledge of Marxism and Soviet communism.

God's revolution is not a political revolution. The gospel contains neither political analysis nor political practice, which does not mean that, once accepted by a responsible faith, it cannot and should not throw light on our analyses and our practices of this kind. Though we draw inspiration from it, we cannot directly draw any specific political programs therefrom.

The notion of "gospel politics" is ambiguous. It is demanded of Christians only that they develop, at their own responsibility and at the risk of error, political analyses and practices in the light of the gospel. A political program was not the goal of Jesus Christ, who deliberately placed himself on a very different plane, although he did want his disciples to draw inspiration from their faith in all the dimensions of their existence. It is there, in fact, that we must look for the articulation of the relations between gospel and politics.

The vision of the gospel is *transpolitical.* But, in giving to those who commit themselves to it a definitive sense of history and personal existence and helping them to see human nature in a certain way, it helps them to interpret human reality in all its dimensions and to orient their human practices (on all levels) in a powerfully original fashion.

Between the Marxist enterprise and the enterprise of Jesus Christ there is a radical difference in worldview (two different universes), but also in approach and goal. Marxism is a revolutionary enterprise for the transformation of social structures. (It could have been, of course, the product of Christian inspiration, but then it would have been a profoundly different reality from the one we know.) Christianity, as the personal enterprise of Jesus Christ and the mission entrusted to the community of faith that he founded (the church), is situated, as I said, *on the transpolitical plane of salvation.* It is, however, essential to understand, better than in the past, that persons animated by his "conception of the world" and the New Testament ethic can—and eventually must—strive to cooperate, in his spirit, for the transformation of structures.

Jesus Christ stood on the transpolitical plane because only he could bring to humanity salvation, which he knew was the supreme reality without which their existence would be a definite failure, even though they could by their own effort improve their historical condition, providing themselves with better political, economic, and social structures. It was not simply that this responsibility was left them by Jesus Christ. It was reinforced by all the urgency of evangelical charity, which insists that we place ourselves at the unselfish service of our fellow human beings.

That is the exact point on which *Marxism challenges Christians at the very heart of their faith* by reproaching them for the ineffectiveness of their charity, because they have not been promoters of justice or have even shown themselves to be authors of injustice. I will not here dispute the charge that the indictment is unjust in general, but I will say straight-out that it puts its finger on a sore spot that too often feels irritation. In any case, we would not be Christians if we did not feel ourselves deeply hurt by such an accusation and if we did not see in it a radical challenge to our historical weaknesses.

Berdyaev notes with his customary sharpness:

Revolutions in Christian history have always been a judgment upon historical Christianity, upon Christians, upon their betrayal of the Christian covenant, upon their distortion of Christianity. For Christians especially, revolution has a meaning, and they, above all, must understand it. It is a challenge to Christians and a reminder that they have not made justice a fact of experience. To accept history is to accept revolution also, to accept its meaning as a catastrophic interruption in the destinies of a sinful world. To deny any meaning to revolution must bring with it the rejection of history also. But revolution is horrible, grim; it is ugly and violent, as the birth of a child is ugly and violent, as the pains of the mother who bears it are ugly and violent.[21]

No doubt Berdyaev, in expressing himself thus, was reacting as a Russian, with the dramatic mentality of his compatriots at the end of the nineteenth century and in the light of the terrible revolutionary experiences of his country. That does not change the fact that the Soviet revolution and the Chinese revolution concern Christians of the entire world. Is it true to say, as some have often done, that "Marxism would never have seen the light of day if Christians had been faithful to the spirit of the gospel"? The hypothesis is simplistic, for the socialist challenge could appear only at a certain stage of history. In any case, we would then not have known those serious incidents of oppression and exploitation for which Christians who were unfaithful to the spirit of the gospel have been responsible.

Berdyaev's thought is even more daring, in that it does not stop short of stating that the revolutionary challenge of Marxism leads us to discover that, in the same words we quoted in the introduction to this chapter, "Christianity is revolutionary in its most profound being." In *The Origin of Russian Communism* he explicitly uses the concept of God's revolution:

This is a fundamental paradox of Christian thought. Christianity is historical; it is the revelation of God in history and not in nature; it recognizes a meaning in history. But at the same time, Christianity could never find room for itself in history; it always passes judgment upon the injustices of history; it does not allow optimistic views about history. For that reason history must come to an end, must be judged by God, because in history the justice of Christ is not made a fact.[22]

Christianity is "God's revolution," the most radical revolution because it touches persons at the deepest part of themselves and moves them to question themselves profoundly and to transform themselves radically in the spirit of the gospel. It is the gospel that helps them see the profound significance of sin in history and that protects them from adopting perspectives that are too naively optimistic: from thinking, for example, that a change of structures can suffice to establish harmonious relations among persons. It is also the gospel that gives them the most profound sense of their responsibility, because by faith they know that they will have to give an account of all their deeds, of all their thoughts, of all their feelings, before the sovereign judge of history, from whom nothing can be hidden and who will judge us especially by what we have done or not done for our neighbor (Matt. 25:31–46). We must rediscover the extraordinary power of the gospel to challenge all our egotism, all our hardness of mind or heart, all our resignation and passivity in the face of injustice, all our self-righteousness and acceptance of the status quo.

We could say, with Berdyaev:

> True Christians are "perpetual revolutionaries" because no order of life can ever satisfy them. They seek the kingdom of God and his truth, demanding the most radical transformation of individuals, society, and the world. Christians differ from other revolutionaries not because their ideas are less radical but because they demand that means and aims should correspond; they reject hatred and violence as a means for attaining perfect life.[23]

How many Christians have really understood this?

Liberation vs. Salvation?

In the concept of "God's revolution" we encounter the fundamental New Testament concept of *salvation*. It is interesting to note that the Marxist concept of *liberation* is not without analogies to it—even more, that it is deliberately a sort of Promethean rewrite. Marxism, in fact, dreams of the liberation of the entire person and of all humanity, of the human personality in all its psychic depths, which it wants to deliver from all its illusions, especially its religious illusions. It dreams of the liberation of the whole of human society.

We know that the revolution it announces and prepares is not simply a political revolution like the others: it is a *social* revolution, in the plenary sense of the term, for it wants to transform radically the most basic structures of society, and it is the *ultimate* revolution because it will be finished only when it has encompassed all of humanity. It will be the work of humanity itself—more exactly, of the revolutionary class dragging along its allies (representing therefore the great majority of the population) in its colossal enterprise.

All transcendence is firmly rejected, for it would necessarily constitute an alienation. The *myth of Prometheus*, so dear to Karl Marx, is basic in Marxism, as it is also in the capitalist dynamism of industrial society of the liberal variety. Let me add that this total liberation is stubbornly limited to the earthly horizon, by reason of the materialism of the underlying worldview.

Is it necessary to take a stance contrary to the Marxist concept of *liberation* in order to develop the Christian concept of *salvation?* Such a simplistic solution would lead us into a trap. It is undeniable that Christian salvation is essentially defined as the work of God, but it is no less certain that it requires human cooperation and that it fully respects human freedom. It is also certain that it is accomplished first in the depth of the human person and that in its essence it is a new kind of relationship with God, including not only faith in God, but also the gift of God's life, as in a new birth. It is no less necessary to understand that through the free action of those who want to live the dynamic of faith, hope, and charity, salvation is meant to have an impact on all the dimensions of existence. It is not therefore a simple inner reality. It logically has social and historical dimensions.

"Salvation *(soteria)*," Moltmann writes accurately, "must also be understood as *shalom* in the Old Testament. This does not mean merely salvation of the soul, individual rescue from the evil world, comfort for the troubled conscience, but also the realization of the eschatological *hope of justice*, the *humanizing* of the human person, the *socializing* of humanity, *peace* for all creation."[24] We can and we must, with him, speak of the transformation of the world: "Not to be conformed to this world does not mean merely to be transformed in oneself, but to transform in opposition and creative expectation the face of the world in which one believes, hopes, and loves."[25]

From the Christian point of view then, far from there being a contradiction between salvation and liberation, the former demands the latter. Are we then led to accept Marxist liberation? Yes, in a certain sense, because Christianity sees itself as liberator on the plane of history. No, because Marxism stubbornly rejects salvation by rejecting God and pinning itself to the earthly horizon, whereas Christian salvation can be finally accomplished only beyond history, thus providing the dynamic horizon for the unfolding of all history. Christian salvation in all its truth is therefore at the same time the liberation accomplished by God in the innermost depth of the individual with its consequences for eternal life and the demand for historical liberation entrusted to the free choice of humanity.

Christians have still not sufficiently understood the importance and the urgency of historical liberation (still unachieved). The pitfall that lies in wait for many at the present time is to forget that the peculiar characteristic of Christian salvation is the liberation accomplished by God in the very depth of the individual with its consequences for eternal life. *This* is the horizon against which Christianity must be judged and not merely on the effectiveness of its contributions to historical liberations, for, once again, the latter are the work of human beings primarily. To insist too much on liberation as against salvation is to undermine the fundamental characteristic of Christianity and its irreplaceable contribution to human history.

Church of the Exodus, Church of the Resurrection

Such is the dangerous pit into which those Christians fall who give priority to *exodus theology* and who sometimes go so far as to give it exclusive status, with an almost total neglect of the theology of the cross, the resurrection, and the beatitudes, which are often interpreted in politico-revolutionary terms.

Certainly, as I have just said, New Testament salvation calls upon us to support historical liberations, and exodus theology has nurtured the entire Old Testament (I speak of the period after Moses), and it does have impact on the paschal mystery. In showing God at work in the political liberation of a people it teaches us that God wants liberty, not exploitation and oppression, and therefore that all those responsible for exploitation and oppression are in serious violation of the divine commandment. It protects us from all purely interior or interpersonal interpretations of the gospel commandment of charity.

But it is essential to understand that *the paschal mystery is of an entirely different essence from the exodus.* It signifies and embodies an entirely different intervention of God in history. It is no longer one people alone that is liberated, and essentially on the historical plane. (It is true that this liberation was a condition of the liberty of its faith in the context of the religious civilization of antiquity, and one of the founding events of its faith.) It is all of humanity that is liberated, and not on the plane of an essentially political liberation, but on that of the salvation I described a few moments ago. As I noted, according to the New Testament perspective, it is left to us to take up the cause of our own political liberation and to help those who are still oppressed and exploited, freely and on the basis of our own responsibility.

The essential and ultimate goal of the gospel revolution is the gathering together of all peoples in Jesus Christ—that is, in that God who was willing to be involved personally in the very core of our history. It is not the political organization of this world's society. But it is precisely because its essential and ultimate finality is what I have defined (a transpolitical, transhistorical finality) that it provides us with the maximum power for the transformation of human society, and that the gospel, once freely accepted, protects us from the formidable temptations of power.

At first sight, evangelical Christianity is singularly weak in comparison with Marxism when it comes to involvement in collective realities, inasmuch as it does not claim to provide us with either political analysis, economic analysis, sociological analysis, or a scientific interpretation of history. On all these levels it refers us to our own reason. But does not this apparent poverty constitute its real wealth even in relation to such involvement? For these reasons it refers us to our own responsibility and therefore to our initiative and our creativity; it communicates to us a definite meaning and orientation that are more capable than any other to engender solidarity; it provides us with the formidable dynamic of faith, hope, and charity.

All systems run the risk of petrification. Their validity is limited to a certain time span, even if, in exceptional cases, it extends over several millennia. Christianity, by the characteristic openness of its essence, remains always available, always creative. I speak obviously of *evangelical* Christianity, to which unfortunately *historical* Christianity is far from always corresponding. It remains the living source of the risen Christ, who challenges the latter and is capable of renewing it.

Those Christians who are tempted to search in Marxism for a kind of super-Christianity—one that would be politically effective compared to that which existed in history, judged to be utopian and ineffective because of historical circumstances—show that they understand nothing of the gospel. They are encouraged in this, it is true, by some neo-Marxists of the "revisionist" school who would like to recover for Marxism the intuitions of Christianity. What is excusable, and even worthy of our grateful acknowledgment, on the part of Marxists is much less so on the part of Christians, especially when they claim thereby to restore the authenticity of Christianity, whereas they are, in fact, radically distorting it.

The full recovery of the meaning of the New Testament concept of *salvation* calls for a similar recovery of the meaning of *conversion*, which is, we know, at the heart of evangelization according to the famous words of Jesus Christ in St. Mark: "The time is fulfilled, and the kingdom of God is at hand; repent, and believe in the gospel" (1:15). Exegetical studies rightly insist on the depth of the interior transformation to which those who hear the gospel are called.

As Rudolph Schnackenburg explains, Jesus wanted to awaken persons "from lethargy and trivial day-to-day preoccupations, and spur them to a passionate religious search and attachment to God. His desire was to urge them to free themselves from sin and passions, from greed and lust for power, and to strive toward a more unselfish love of God and their neighbor." He "deliberately weans his contemporaries from a worldly and egotistic, a political and nationalistic, way of thinking so that they may recognize that guilt, hatred, hardness, lust for power, and blindness are the real wretchedness and sickness of humankind."[26]

The point of departure has to be the *inner transformation* that is at the heart of evangelical conversion. Otherwise we miss the essential message of the gospel and fall into the pit of "pharisaism." But it is just as necessary to show that this inner transformation, which is the heart of evangelical conversion, is never finished once and for all, but must be renewed every day and every moment, and also that it will logically have impact on all our activities, personal and collective. The conversion of a number of Christians in an unjust society will never be convincing so long as they have not demonstrated an undeniable effort to change its structures. Here precisely is where the difference with Marxism surfaces.

No doubt the Marxist movement advocates a new way of thinking and behaving. No doubt it wants to develop a "new human type," on a higher level of humanness. But it expects this transformation to come from the transformation of structures. In its view it is the establishment of socialist structures (collective ownership of the means of production, etc.) that will progressively give birth to the new human person of solidarity and fellowship. From the Christian point of view we will not deny the importance of structural change, but we will emphasize that it is not such change that makes a person generous and open to others, and that there will always remain the necessity of inner conversion.

Such is the *originality of the gospel*: to call persons, first, to question themselves, instead of taking the easy way of accusing others, and to invite them to transform themselves in the direction of a love that is as total as possible toward God and toward others. Systems *can* change. Revolutions *can* be necessary. But it will *always* be necessary that there be persons striving to live a life of evangelical conversion, helping their brothers and sisters to create a companionable society, particularly in the bureaucratic and impersonal universe that is spawned by the advanced industrial society of the present day.

This explanation of the concept of God's revolution would be incomplete if I did not return to the question of *God*. Whether we be believers or not, this question is primary in the history of humanity, today at least as much as yesterday. This holds true if we see in God someone who is concerned only with our personal life or one who has interest only in the hereafter. In this latter hypothesis we would see in God at best only a tyrant or a pale abstraction. (If we loved God, we would perceive God differently, but is not the tyrannical and abstract deity, alas, the God of too many Christians?) The same holds if we see in God the nationalist deity, in the ideological framework of the religious city of antiquity or that of nationalist Christianity, still common in the twentieth century.

Let us not forget the war of 1914! Each belligerent believed that God was on their side and each camp developed a strong pietistic ideology. German soldiers carried on their belts the words: *Gott mit uns* (God with us). As for the French, they sang: "Save France in the name of the Sacred Heart." And in the churches the Sacred Heart was embroidered on the national flag. After the war, monuments to the dead invaded religious buildings. Let us recall also the Spanish civil war, with its powerful religious ideology and atmosphere of crusade on the nationalist side!

Possibly we reject God. Such rejection can be "merely" practical, as in the practical materialism of the West, where God is in fact absent, even if we theoretically admit God's existence. (We can hardly call this faith, because faith is not only an intellectual conviction but also the commitment of our entire being.) Or the rejection can be both theoretical and practical, as in various bourgeois philosophies and in Marxism. In contrast, one can believe in the God of Jesus Christ, in the God who loves human beings, who wants them to be free brothers and sisters, and therefore champions of liberation and fellowship.

For Christian faith this is the only God, the true God, of whom all other conceptions are only caricatures. I have already sketched God's principal characteristics and pointed out that it was not God that Marxism rejected, because the conception it had of God (the tyrant God) was entirely different. Let me add that faith in the true God, the only absolute, is a guarantee against all other absolutisms (state, class or revolution, money, sex, nation or race, etc.). Without that faith we run the risk of falling under their sway, and history teaches us that they lead only to barbarism.

Jacques Ellul is right in stating, ". . . the moment there is absolute belief, then massacres, exploitation, oppression, torture, and concentration camps follow immediately.''[27] He is equally right in insisting that Christian hope founded on faith in the divine promise can move us to a profound commitment to the service of humanity while protecting us from inhumanity: "It is that, and only that, which relativizes, yet at the same time also brings about a zealous involvement in this relative, which one never absolutizes.''[28]

For Hegel, we know, the choice is between God and the world: "Reading the morning paper," he thought, "is a kind of realistic morning prayer. One directs one's behavior toward God against the world, or else toward that which constitutes the world.''[29] It was, above all, Hegel's fundamental philosophical approach that led him to express himself in this way, but he could have been led into error by the behavior of so many Christians of his time, who did not know how to integrate their faith with openness to the world. As if for authentic Christian faith there was of necessity a choice to make, and not, quite to the contrary, the necessity to reject such a choice.

Christians do not have to choose between God and the world. They adhere at the same time to God, creator of the world, and to the world, God's creation and the field that God has given humankind for the unfolding of its liberty and its action. Christians do not have to choose between prayer and reading the newspaper. In the course of their day they will find time for both prayer and reading the newspaper. I have said and I repeat: faith in God properly understood will lead Christians to a profound and unselfish involvement in the service of their fellow human beings. If it were not so, it would be proof that their faith is not authentic.

Christian Identity

We cannot deny that the combination of faith in God and openness to the world does not come easily in the concrete life of Christians, even though they believe that God is present and at work in the world, a world that God created and saved, and came to live in as a human being. The combination does not come easily, because, if the world is "good" insofar as it is the work of the creator and, to some extent, the responsibility of human beings who are worthy of their humanity, of that "image of God" that they carry engraved on the deepest part of their souls, and who want to be in solidarity with others, it is also "bad" insofar as it is profoundly marked by sin, as the writings of St. John and the Epistle to the Romans bring out so clearly.

From the viewpoint of faith, powerfully articulated in the fourth gospel, not only has the world not recognized the Word, who is God (1:9–11), but it crucified God. It is easier to believe in God when one lives turned in upon oneself in a Christian milieu that is also turned in upon itself. But then faith is not authentically Christian, for it lacks the necessary dimension of openness to the world. Moreover, and most fortunately, such ghettos exist less and less, because the world is penetrating everywhere as the result of the increase in travel and the fantastic network of communications built up by the mass media. Everyone is now assaulted by a mass of information, a wild and contradictory maelstrom in the midst of which they no longer know how to make out their own identity if they live in the midst of an advanced industrial society of the liberal type, or a unique and onrushing current, carrying everything in its path, drowning out every other voice, suppressing, if possible, all contrary information, opinions, and thoughts if they live in a totalitarian state. In either case the world invades and manipulates them from within. Will they still be free and responsible persons?

Can faith in God still spread, or at least survive? Should we not expect that it will not even come to life or that it will deteriorate very quickly? In such a context Christians must squarely face the problem of their *identity*. Either they will see themselves as very different from others, in which case this difference will weigh upon them and perhaps lead them to wonder if they are still normal persons; or else they will feel so much like others in their conception of the world, in their way of life, in their political options, that they will begin to wonder if they are still Christians. The question may be traumatic for them.

Are they in contact with Marxists? No doubt they will be welcomed in friendly fashion if they share the same revolutionary struggle or, at least, if they appear to be useful allies. If they want, they could probably join a communist party. (Would they be entrusted with important responsibilities in such a party? That is a very different matter.) They will perhaps feel at ease in the camaraderie and joint action. Let us suppose, however, that their comrades are Marxist in the full sense of the word—that is to say, adhering not only to the political analysis of Marxism, but also to its materialist and atheist conception of the world—and that logically they attach some importance to their beliefs. Let us suppose further that they themselves are profoundly Christian by reason of their faith in the God of Jesus Christ. In this case I cannot see how the result would be anything but a feeling of mutual distance, even if both were absorbed in joint action.

Between the Christian and the Marxist there exists no true reciprocity and therefore no possibility of genuine dialogue in what concerns the faith. If the Christian acknowledges an important element of truth in Marxism—perhaps too much—the Marxist will see in the Christian faith an ideology only in the pejorative sense of the term—that is, ultimately an illusion.

An Althusser, for example, will not even take the trouble to conceal this, though he acknowledges the current renewal of Christianity. "Ideology changes," he will answer, ". . . but imperceptibly, conserving its ideological form; it moves, but with an immobile motion that maintains it *where it is*, in its place and its ideological role. It is the immobile motion that, as Hegel said of philosophy itself, reflects and expresses what happens in history without ever running ahead of its own time, because it is merely that time *caught* in the trap of a mirror reflection, precisely so that persons will be *caught* in it too."[30]

Leaders of western communist parties and, even more, neo-Marxists of the "revisionist" school, will be less than blunt, because they recognize in certain currents of Christianity a real dynamism and ethical values that they think worth recovering. But when you read or listen to them carefully you find that their basic judgment about the Christian faith is in the end identical with that of Althusser and the traditional Marxists. Christians are therefore challenged at the core of their identity. To their challengers it is only a false identity. They will acknowledge their sincerity, but they will think that in what concerns their conception of the world Christians remain bound to an obsolete stage of culture.

Let me note, however, that many besides Marxists share the same negative view of the Christian faith: materialism and atheism are conceptions that are widespread even among those who profess the liberal ideology. Irony is not the least formidable weapon. It is fairly common for Christians to hear remarks like this: "One must naturally keep one's distance from those believers whose religious conviction retains enough strength to handle everything."[31]

Under this flood of negative reactions to their faith, Christians will encounter *contradiction* at the very center of their life. (In a secularized society of either the Marxist or liberal type such a phenomenon is common.) Either they fail to grasp their own identity, or they become locked in a private interpretation of the word of God, not being able to understand that it must have impact on every dimension of existence. (This too is a common phenomenon, especially since the nineteenth century. You see it among Christians attracted by Marxism as well as among those who cling to the liberal ideology of capitalism. The latter tendency has long been favored by important theological currents.)

Or Christians may turn to a direct politicization of the Word of God, with the result that they lose sight of its true essence—namely, the personal intervention of God in human history, addressing the intelligence and free responsibility of human beings. One thing that will provoke uneasiness will be the discovery of *new values* having their own logic, accompanied by the realization that these are lived equally by non-Christians, perhaps even before Christians and better than they—for example, in the eighteenth and nineteenth centuries, the values of liberty, democracy, social justice, or socialism in the sense of a vision of equitable sharing of power and resources among all citizens. If these secular values can be justified without Christianity, they ask themselves, what purpose does it serve? (They do not see that the perspective of Christianity is located at a deeper level.) If, following the example of Marxism or certain technocratic ideologies of the liberal type, one can build a world without God, is it not tempting to turn God into an abstract question?

Many Christians make a revolutionary option. Many others, not Christian, have made it before them or are making it with them. Christian faith is therefore not necessary for one who wants to take this position. Dialogue and cooperation with Marxists reveal to certain Christians that it is possible to develop and complete with them a joint historical undertaking. Perhaps the attitude of these Christians in regard to Marxism is insufficiently critical. I leave that question aside for the moment. What counts here is their subjective attitude. From this arises for them the development of the historical venture.

It may also be that life becomes so polarized by secular values that one no longer feels a concrete need for anything else. In this case it is no longer Christian identity that is the problem, because it seems to have lost all significance. Some might think it possible to escape this impasse by replying that this identity is situated elsewhere, or in any case not at the level of political involvement. Do we not then run the risk of creating a true split in the conscience of the Christian: between secular involvement on the one hand and religious involvement on the other?

Let me summarize the question that so many Christians ask themselves: Is there a specifically Christian identity when it comes to problems of collective existence? My response is a categorical *yes*.

A negative response would lead to the distortion of the gospel. It would reduce it to interiority or the sacristy, and deny that it is a dynamic for transforming humanity and human society, for giving birth to "the new human person" and "the new creation"—and this in spite of the fact that, as I have noted, it *directly* involves neither *specific* political analysis nor practice. A negative response would again entrap one in the "privatization" of the word of God, which ignores the fact that the divine commandment in Jesus Christ touches humanity at its deepest core and therefore in all the dimensions of its existence.

An affirmative response does not mean that Christians are persons apart, that they cannot, or ought not, join with others in a common project or action on the political or economic plane. On the contrary, they ought to be much more present to others than if they did not have the faith. However, like Jesus Christ, they may be led by that faith to situations of confrontation and even rupture with political partners. This is why, if they are consistent with their faith, even while profoundly involved in the political party of their choice, they will never be unconditionally committed to it, as André Philip has explained in his own case:

> I have always had good relations . . . with all my comrades in the party, but at the same time they have always felt that I did not really belong to them, that they could not have complete confidence in me, that come the day of an essential decision I would not betray my ideas out of fidelity to the group, but on the contrary would stand against the group in fidelity to what I believe. This is something that is felt and my comrades have always had, in their relations with me, a feeling of uncertainty. The true militant, on the other hand, is certain. If the group decides to employ torture, that will distress him or her, perhaps even give them a bad conscience, but from the moment that the party has decided, they will go along with it.[32]

A political party does not appreciate this kind of independent spirit. The communist conception of the party is radically opposed to it. Is this stance not, however, the only guarantee of a truly liberating political party?

A problem that is at once theoretical and practical is that of the *articulation of the faith in harmony with rational analysis*. At the beginning of this book I sketched a theory of political analysis. I must add here a few specifics.

All serious *political analysis* that is rational is both scientific and meta-scientific. *Scientific*: faithful to the procedures of political science, combined with economics and other human sciences. *Metascientific*: that is, oriented toward basic options of civilization (I assume a positive perspective here, leaving aside the barbarism of certain options, such as Nazism)—for example, liberty, as in liberal ideology, or equality and solidarity, as in ideologies of a socialist type. Inasmuch as ethical values are involved here, the encounter between two approaches will take place within the conscience of each one who attempts such an analysis. Like everyone else, Christians must undertake their own rational political analyses and appeal to ethical values to guide their own options as to what constitutes a civilized society.

This is where their faith intervenes, because, by its own dynamic, it informs the entire ethical approach of the Christian. How, for example, could faith in the brotherhood and sisterhood of all persons under God, in the dignity of each one, created in the image of God, in the call addressed to all humanity to face the absolute future of the kingdom of God, as well as any serious consideration of evangelical charity—how could this kind of faith *not* lead to political and economic actions that have for their essential objectives social justice, peace, and solidarity among all peoples? The place for this encounter between faith and rational analysis will be conscience. That is why I use the concept of *the political conscience of the Christian*, in the sense of a political conscience that is illuminated by the example and teaching of Jesus Christ and especially by his commandment of charity that is at once universal and practical.

Christians who want to act in fidelity to their faith in the political or economic domain often telescope rational analysis and have recourse to a fideistic attitude that leads them into unrealism or into involvements that are as passionate as they are debatable—involvements that they have a tendencey to "sanctify" and to impose on all their fellow believers. They forget that they are human beings and that faith will never replace political or economic competence; that is not its role.

On the other hand, one will be Christian in the political and economic arena only if rational analysis is accompanied by a profound reflection—which cannot be improvised—in the light of faith. This will help us to understand human problems in four ways:

—By indicating the final meaning of history, the absolute future of the kingdom of God.

—By revealing to us the most profound source of our dignity, that of "the image of God," that of someone who is called to be an adopted child of God.

—By revealing to us the basic ethical values of a just and fraternal society, the components of evangelical charity, which is founded on universal brotherhood and sisterhood under God.

—By communicating to us the supreme energy of the Holy Spirit.

Some nonbelievers—especially Marxists—will be inclined to think this is an ideology without any connection with reality. But what counts is, on the one hand, the reasoned conviction of Christians themselves and, on the other, the reality of the dynamism that their faith has given them. Political activity lived in the sight of faith will become an *opportunity to deepen the faith.* As St. Paul, the Epistle of St. James, and the writings of St. John many times repeat, faith is genuine only to the degree that it is lived and therefore practiced. Political involvement has become important to our time as a place to serve humanity. If it is practiced in the context of faith, it can reveal a remarkable potential.

Let me add that Christian identity in the political context can lead to raising *ultimate questions of faith.* I mean that the behavior of Christians in this realm, if they are faithful to the gospel, can, at least in certain exceptional circumstances, lead them to martyrdom or at least to a "confession of faith"—that is, to confront serious personal difficulties, even persecution, for reasons that pertain to the fundamentals of faith. The martyrdom of the Christians of the first centuries was motivated, from their point of view, by a fundamental reason of faith: the confession of Jesus Christ as the only Lord *(Kyrios),* which disputed the claim of Rome's Caesar. On the other hand, from the viewpoint of Roman political power and the society in connivance with it, persecution was motivated by a political reason that appeared to them no less fundamental: the Christians, by rejecting the divinization (that is, absolutization) of the Roman imperial ideology, seemed to them radical traitors in respect to their collective solidarity.

At no period of history, it seems, has martyrdom been completely absent from the life of the church. It remains a current reality and fundamentally with the same significance as in the first three centuries. Many Christians were savagely persecuted in the time of Stalin and earlier in that of Lenin. In more subtle ways Christians still know all kinds of harrassment in the Soviet Union and in the "popular democracies" that are its satellites.[33] To the present moment all communist regimes have demonstrated great harshness toward Christians who refuse to play along with the official ideology (as they do, it is true, with all other opponents). As to the future, the declarations of even the most open leaders and theoreticians are not without ambiguity.

In Nazi Germany many Christians were sent to concentration camps. Christians determined to be faithful to the gospel in the political, economic, or social sphere have been just as severely persecuted in other dictatorships of a Fascist variety. Even in democracies of the liberal type, opposition to the privileges of money or to the prevailing mentality of egotism, eroticism, and practical materialism involve their opponents in real difficulties. To live one's faith is never easy in interpersonal relations, and still less so in politics. Christians know it from their own experience. That ought not to be a reason for them to be discouraged or to capitulate, but to understand and to live the *theology of the cross,* which is in no way a glorification of suffering, but a powerful dynamic of hope through difficulty and pain.

As André Philip tells us:

In the final analysis, I recenter everything on Christ, who is the only meaning, the only thing that provides meaning. By his crucifixion he changed relations between human beings. The role of Christians is to know that they must give witness and that their witness will be rejected. It is even more probable, it is the norm, that the way of the Christian will be the sacrifice of the cross. It is the continuation of the acceptance of the cross as the dynamic of life, which endlessly poses a question to persons, which endlessly compels them to face themselves, so that with patience they will continue their efforts.[34]

The problems confronted by Christians, when it comes to concern for consistency with their faith in their political involvement, are clearly numerous, of great diversity, and sometimes of extreme gravity, as I have noted. What would be more serious would be unawareness of them.

To take only two examples, from outside the specific problems of communism, how many Christians have fallen, in all good conscience, for an ultranationalist ideology or have supported a politics that is ultraconservative from the economic and social point of view, without sensitivity to the most legitimate problems and aspirations of the popular classes? I could say the same for a sizeable number at the present time.

In the same way, how many Christians are sufficiently clear on the true motivations of their anticommunism? They believe themselves Christians and yet they are, in reality, profoundly marked by a popular mentality that is radically opposed to Christianity—for example, by the practical materialism of advanced industrial society of the liberal type concretized in a self-serving polarization on comfort, consumerism, and sex.

Because I am concerned with the specific problems of Marxism, I shall limit myself to them. I shall consider only two: that of membership in a communist party and that of Christian Marxists.

Membership in the Communist Party

The problem of membership by a Christian in a communist political party has been clearly formulated by Berdyaev: "Can one be a communist, a member of the party, and at the same time a believing Christian? Can one take part in the social program of communism without sharing the communist world outlook, without being a dialectical materialist and one of the godless? This is a fundamental question."[35] Let us not forget that to the present day the communist parties have always professed an official materialist and atheist ideology and that, as noted, there are serious objections regarding the principal elements of Marxist theory and practice: historical materialism, interpretations of Christianity, conceptions of human nature, class struggle, morality, and so forth.

This is a problem that goes back nearly to the origins of the establishment of a truly communist party. Because it was a particularly acute problem in Russia, Lenin tackled it head-on in an article of 1909: *The Attitude of the*

Workers' Party to Religion.[36] After taking shelter under the authority of Engels, he begins with a strong statement of the unyielding opposition of Marxism to religion:

> Marxism is materialism. As such it is as relentlessly hostile to religion as was the materialism of the eighteenth-century Encyclopedists or the materialism of Feuerbach. This is beyond doubt. But the dialectical materialism of Marx and Engels goes further than the Encyclopedists and Feuerbach, for it applies the materialist philosophy to the domain of history, to the domain of the social sciences. We must combat religion—that is the ABC of *all* materialism, and consequently of Marxism. But Marxism is not a materialism that has stopped with ABC. Marxism goes further. We must *know how* to combat religion, and in order to do so we must explain the source of faith and religion among the masses *in a materialist way.*[37]

Note the clarity of this synthesis of the application of historical and dialectical materialism to religion. This does not mean that the struggle against religion will be carried on without discernment, for "No educational book can eradicate religion from the minds of the masses who are crushed by capitalist hard labor and who are at the mercy of the blind destructive forces of capitalism, until those masses themselves learn to fight this *root* of religion, fight *the rule of capital* in all its forms, in a united, organized, planned, and conscious way."[38] As we know, this is the classic thesis on the primacy of the revolutionary struggle against "oppressive" relations of production, because it would be these that explain the genesis of religion.

Lenin can then address the problem of the membership of Christians to the communist party, better still, the membership of priests. In their case, he envisions two hypotheses.

The first:

> If a priest comes to us to take part in our common political work and conscientiously performs party duties, without opposing the program of the party, he may be allowed to join the ranks of the Social Democrats;[39] for the contradiction between the spirit and principles of our program and the religious convictions of the priest would in such circumstances be something that concerned him alone, his own private contradiction.

The second hypothesis:

> If . . . a priest joined the Social Democratic Party and made it his chief and almost sole work actively to propagate religious views in the party, it would unquestionably have to expel him from its ranks.

This leads him to offer general guidelines concerning Christians:

We must not only admit workers who preserve their belief in God into the Social Democratic Party, but deliberately set out to recruit them; we are absolutely opposed to giving the slightest offense to their religious convictions, but we recruit them in order to educate them in the spirit of our program, and not in order to permit an active struggle against it. We allow freedom of opinon *within* the party, but to certain limits, determined by freedom of grouping.[40]

Let me summarize these directives: not only a welcome for Christians to the party, but an effort to attract them by avoiding a direct attack on their religious convictions, on condition that they accept completely the program and discipline of the party. The author does not conceal his basic motivation: the "education" of which they will be the target will make them lose their faith. And he does not fail to remind us that "freedom of opinion" within the party is enclosed within narrow limits.

It was necessary to quote these directives because they have inspired—and still inspire—the policy of communist parties to this day. We should note, however, that their later interpretation in Soviet doctrine has been particularly restrictive. Yaroslavsky, for example, a leading specialist in antireligious propaganda, reacted violently against the thesis of the Swedish communist Hedlund that a communist could also be a practicing Christian.[41]

Has the situation not been changed by *the evolution of certain western communist parties*? In the case of France, for example, that is the opinion of a certain number of Christians, and even priests, who have joined the Community Party and insist that they are at ease there and do not hide their Christian convictions.

To give an example, this is how a worker-priest explains why he joined the Communist Party: because Marxism is for him "a scientific analysis" that "gives us at the same time the means to struggle to change the economic and political system based on the exploitation of persons by the power of money," and because, in his opinion, this party is "the only one . . . that, for the past fifty years, has defended from day to day the interests of the working class." He insists on the human qualities of many communist militants: "Among them the word 'comrade' has taken on a meaning and a depth that has no equivalent but the word 'brother' in the gospels."

His preoccupation is missionary in character: "The only chance that we have of one day seeing Jesus Christ break into their lives is to accept for ourselves the necessity of fighting by their side without proselytism and without any complex of being believers." He recognizes, however, that this is not a comfortable situation: "We are questioned as much by our Christian brothers who doubt the authenticity of our faith as by the Party comrades who believe us to be in process of a detoxification cure from religion!"[42]

On the communist side the recent declarations of Georges Marchais, secretary general of the French Communist Party, have tried to reassure Christians who would like to join the Communist Party. He insists that "they are members of the party on the same basis as all the others, without any difference," that they "contribute not only to the development of our political policy but also of our theory on the same basis as all other communists" because "we do not make adherence to materialism a condition of entry into the French Communisty Party." He repudiates all dogmatism: "Marxism is not a dogma; it is a guide for action." He concludes: "Why would you want the Christian members of the Communist Party to be 'mutilated'? We hope, on the contrary, and this is what is happening, that they retain their position, their full position."[43]

Does this mean that no decisive objection any longer exists to the membership of a Christian in a communist party similar to the present French Communist Party? I respect the decisions and subjective motivations of my brothers and sisters in the faith. But I must in conscience raise several questions. Is Marxist analysis as indisputable as they think? Is it certain that the "liberation" of the working class pursued in practice by the Communist Party is the best and that it does not involve serious risks?

Even if the French Communist Party means to dissociate itself from totalitarian communist parties, should we not take note of their policies and especially of those of communist regimes? Besides, has it dissociated itself in fact as much as it claims? Does not its official ideology remain materialism and atheism? Does not membership of a Christian in this party put the faith in danger and put the Christian in a situation of serious ambiguity? Is it not possible to have friendly contacts with communists and to bear witness to Jesus Christ before them without joining their party? And is not such membership threatened by serious compromises?

These questions are not designed to condemn but to stimulate greater clarity. They are in the spirit of the noteworthy response of Henri Le Buan, then secretary general of *Action Catholique Ouvrière* (Catholic Worker Action), to a letter of fifteen members of that movement who had joined the French Communist Party and who were asking if one could be at the same time a Christian and an active member of a communist party.[44] His objections go to the heart of the problem.

Concerning the Marxist conception of the world: "The Communist Party, in the name of materialist philosophy, rejects Jesus Christ as savior. This is not only a rejection in principle, but this philosophy impregnates its action and its program, and not only impregnates them but is primary and determining."

Concerning the faith: "Communist comrades tell us, 'Inside the party you can keep your faith.' But what then is the faith? Is it a purely personal affair, something that has nothing to do with life, with action, or should it not, on the contrary, be translated into all our being, into every manner of living and acting? We all know how difficult that is."

Concerning the liberation of the working class: "We do not believe that humanity can be saved merely by the transformation of society. We know that it needs Jesus Christ in order to be saved from its sin and, in this way only, to be totally liberated.''

He concludes in fraternal fashion: ''That does not mean that we reject comrades who have taken or would take the gamble of continuing to live their faith as militants within the Communist Party; the church is a community of salvation for all, and the Catholic Worker Action has no mission to give authorizations or formulate interdicts.''

Taking full account of the directives of the Holy See,[45] this is also, as we have seen, my position. I will add this: a communist party will become fundamentally credible only if it gives indisputable proof, theoretically and practically, that it has abandoned the dictatorial and totalitarian conceptions that are traditional in the communist movement and if it becomes an authentically lay or secular party—that is, when it abandons its official materialist and atheist policy, inasmuch as a lay party has no business imposing a philosophy on its members.

"Christian Marxists"

The problem of Christian Marxists is different, at least for two reasons. First, because these Christians are not all members of a communist party and some are even radically opposed to the present communist parties, which they readily fault for having betrayed Marxism (this is probably the feeling of the majority). Secondly, because Christians enrolled in a communist party may not go so far as to describe themselves as Christian Marxists (see below).

In my introduction I have already said that this was not an entirely new phenomenon (what is new is the effort to develop a theory and the group's increased size) and that one should not condemn these persons without a hearing. It is only right to avoid hasty conclusions and to abstain from abusive simplification of problems:

> The church can no longer remain in a position where it is always presupposed from the start, allowing for more nuanced views that surface occasionally here or there, that a Christian Marxist is either a pseudo-Christian or else a pseudo-Marxist. To continue to operate today from such a starting point inevitably condemns one to misunderstand the new way in which the question now arises.[46]

Let us note, however, that the expression ''Christian Marxist'' (or ''Marxist Christian'') has something surprising about it, especially for those who have any concern to call things by their correct name without introducing apparent contradictions. Let us try to understand why many persons feel threatened by such a label. ''It is remarkable that none of the Christians encountered in the countries of the East who have been won to the socialist cause describe themselves as Marxists,'' Father Valadier remarks. ''The mere combination of the words Marxist and Christian provokes wonderment, as if one were marrying water and fire.''[47]

Marxist Christians claim to be both Christians and Marxists. When speaking to Christians, they insist that Marxist analysis and Marxist revolutionary practice are not necessarily contrary to the faith, that, properly understood, they can, on the contrary, contribute to clarifying, purifying, and energizing it. They want to break the bond between Christianity and conservatism, which they are quick to describe as permanent since the time of Constantine. When speaking to Marxists, they argue that Marxist analysis, properly pursued, does not necessarily lead to a totally reductive interpretation of the faith and that the latter is not necessarily counterrevolutionary, that, on the contrary, once purified by Marxist analysis, it can become the source of an authentically revolutionary dynamic.

Despite apparent contradictions and the tensions that they feel in themselves, they maintain that their position is tenable, and this is proven by their own movement, they say in substance. They add that it is affecting a genuine and beneficial renewal both for Marxism and for Christianity.

Let us then consider this "movement" as it is, noting immediately that it is not possible to reduce it to a single phenomenon. It constitutes rather a "tendency" in which many positions are far from convergent. I have, however, two questions to ask the Christian Marxists. Does their renewed Marxism remain consistent with the essence of Marxism? Does their renewed faith remain consistent with the essence of the Christian faith? Obviously we do not think of either Marxism or the faith as utterly fixed, nonhistorical realities. But do they not have essential characteristics that must remain through all historical changes? If not, we would be talking about *continually new* realities that ought to carry with them *continually new* designations.

The problem therefore is, first, that of defining the *essence of Marxism*, which comes down to a problem of interpretation. I have maintained that the following elements are part of the essence of Marxism:

—A materialistic and atheistic conception of the world.

—Historical materialism as the ultimate explanation of all human reality via economic life.

—The essence of the human person defined by the totality of social relationships.

—Class struggle as the ultimate foundation of morality justifying recourse to all effective means.

On all these points I do not see any possible agreement with faith in Jesus Christ. Christian Marxists who want to respect the essence of the faith are aware of this. That is why they either deny that these elements really represent the essence of Marxism, though they may pertain to its historical development; or else they offer an interpretation of them that substantially modifies their meaning.

From my viewpoint, Marxism is essentially a historical phenomenon and not one that is above or beyond history. I believe that one must recognize as essential characteristics the same ones that its founders and historical leaders, as well as its chief theoreticians, have considered—or consider—to be essential. Such is clearly the case for the four characteristics that I have listed (not as an all-inclusive list, but one including the elements that pose the most problems for the Christian faith). If one renounces one or the other of them, one can remain a socialist or revolutionary, but one will no longer be a real Marxist and one will no longer have the right to claim the name without qualifications.

The same conclusion follows if, claiming to retain the Marxist theses, one substantially modifies their meaning: if, for example, one believes in Jesus Christ as God and Savior of humanity, and yet claims to believe in historical materialism. Such a one forgets that historical materialism does not consist simply in placing a heavy emphasis on the undeniable influence of economics (forces and relationships of production) on human life, but that it sees itself as the ultimate explanation, and therefore essential and final.

Let me follow the same procedure as regards the second aspect of the problem: *the essence of the faith and its interpretation.* The objective content of the faith of certain Christian Marxists does not seem to be fundamentally disputable, inasmuch as it touches on God, Jesus Christ, or the church as a community of faith. But then it is a question of the consistency of that authentic faith with the essential theses of Marxism. That is the problem.

For other Christian Marxists the situation is reversed. Their commitment to Marxism is so deep and so marks their faith that it drives them to a reinterpretation that suppresses its objectively essential characteristics. This is the case, for example, with the view of Jesus Christ and the church in *A Materialist Reading of the Gospel of Mark* by Fernando Belo. But then can these persons still call themselves Christians? The faith has an objective content. Can one adhere to Jesus Christ in the same way if one sees God in him or merely a man?

The usual flaw of Christian Marxists is to emphasize the scientific character of Marxist analysis (in fidelity, it is true, to its claims) and to have an insufficiently critical attitude toward it, as if it were on all points beyond dispute. The result is that they are tempted to give it primacy in relation to the faith, in such a way that it is Marxist analysis that tends to become for them, at least on certain points, the final criterion, with the considerable risks that such an attitude entails in terms of the authenticity of their Christian faith. Thus we are brought back again, though in a new way, to the question of the primacy of the political.

Therefore I submit that the expression "Christian Marxist" is at least very ambiguous, because the rationalization behind it distorts either Marxism or the Christian faith, or both at the same time. From my point of view, as I have shown throughout this book, Christians can accept many important elements of Marxist analysis, but, if they wish to be consistent with their faith, they will be compelled to reject some essential characteristics.

Between true Marxism and authentic faith in Jesus Christ there is clearly a radical contradiction.

It is essential to be clear-eyed and not to create confusions. Although I do not in any way want to put Nazism and Marxism on the same footing, Christian Marxists should not forget the *Deutsche Christen*, the "German Christians," who claimed that they had reconciled Nazism and Christianity. Some did it out of self-interest, others in good faith. Karl Barth had the clear vision and the courage to unmask this imposture, in the same way as, a little later, the encyclical of Pius XI against Nazism, *Mit brennender Sorge*. Because Marxism is, in certain of its essential theses, in radical opposition to the Christian faith, it is indispensable to that faith that we learn to distinguish the wheat from the weeds.

Should our attitude toward the Christian Marxists therefore be entirely negative? What I have just written shows where my principal objections lie. My critical attitude does not mean that I take lightly their challenges, notably their invitation to use Marxist analysis to study contemporary reality, as well as some of the questions they pose to the church and theology:

—An "ideologizing" interpretation of the gospel in a conservative sense.

—Acceptance of the ideology of the ruling classes.

—Insufficient knowledge of social reality, with the result that, for example, we have not perceived the evils of capitalism.

—Authoritarian church structures.

I do not mean to say that their criticism—too often inspired by Marxist analysis—is always justified. It contains, however, real elements of truth that must give us food for thought. "Do we bar the door" to the Marxist current in the church, asks the editorial board of the review *Lumière et vie*, "because it would inevitably produce a church that would deny its own tradition *or* because it would contribute to the invention of another way of being the church, which, though no less the church of Christ, would imply a radical transformation of the present structures of power?"[48]

Personally, I believe that Marxist analysis must be taken seriously, on condition that we are sufficiently clear and critical in its regard, but that *the renewal of the church will come essentially from a return to its gospel sources.*

As Jean-Marie Domenach states:

Christians can integrate Marxism, and they should, as atheists once integrated Cartesianism. One can no longer think seriously without Marx. But he did not think of everything. There are so many things on earth and in heaven of which he did not speak, so many things that are important for our life and that must enter into our politics. . . . Marxism, like all dogmas, has become an obstacle to living, to understanding, to acting. Now that we Catholics have achieved some detachment from our own dogma, are we to replace it with this other one? In the name of revolution, in the name of liberations yet to be attained, let us begin by liberating ourselves from these anachronistic venerations.[49]

NOTES

1. *Christianisme, Marxisme* (Paris: Centurion, 1975), pp. 32-33.
2. In *Lumière et vie*, No. 93 (May-June 1969), pp. 22-29.
3. Paris: Cerf, 1972.
4. See *Le Monde* (January 13, 1976). One should not conclude, however, that this meeting had no positive results. On this, see the well-documented assessment of S. Corti, "Impressioni sul convegno dei preti operai," in *Studi Sociali* (1976), pp. 143-45.
5. *The Church between East and West*, in Karl Barth, *Against the Stream* (London: SCM, 1954), p. 132.
6. *The Church*, p. 137.
7. *The Church*, p. 136.
8. *The Church*, p. 142.
9. *Theology of Hope*, trans. James W. Leitch (New York: Harper, 1967), p. 330.
10. Joseph Ratzinger, *Introduction to Christianity* (New York: Seabury, 1979), p. 266.
11. Karl Barth, *The Church between East and West*, p. 127.
12. *The Church*, p. 141.
13. Karl Barth, *Church Dogmatics*, Vol. 1/1, trans. G. W. Bromiley (New York: Scribner's, 1955), p. 1.
14. *Informations catholiques internationales*, No. 409 (June 1, 1972), pp. 15-16.
15. *Informations*, p. 22.
16. *Informations*, p. 20.
17. *Informations*, p. 22.
18. Karl Barth, *Church Dogmatics*, Vol. 1/1, p. xiii.
19. Henri Bartoli, *La doctrine économique et sociale de Karl Marx* (Paris: Seuil, 1950), p. 403.
20. Cf. Matthew J. O'Connell, trans. (New York: Seabury, 1978), pp. 73-77.
21. *The Origin of Russian Communism*, trans. R. M. French (London: Bles, 1948), p. 132.
22. *The Origin*, p. 131.
23. Cf. *Christianity and Human Activity*, trans. Countess Bennigsen, in *The Bourgeois Mind and Other Essays* (New York: Sheed and Ward, 1934), p. 70. See the interesting dissertation of J. Greimel, *Die "Revolution Gottes" und die Revolution dieser Welt* (Bonn: Rheinische Friedrich-Wilhelms-Universität, 1976).
24. *Theology of Hope*, p. 329. See *Idéologies de libération et message du salut* (Fourth Colloquium of CERDIC [Strasbourg, May 10-12, 1973]), published by René Metz and Jean Schlick (Strasbourg: CERDIC-Publications, 1973); Jacques Rollet, *Libération des hommes et salut en Jésus-Christ* (Reflections offered by the French Bishops' Permanent Committee following the Pastoral Session of 1974); Yves Congar, *Un people messianique, salut et libération* (Paris: Cerf, 1975).
25. Cf. *Theology of Hope*, p. 330.

26. Cf. *God's Rule and Kingdom,* trans. John Murray (New York: Herder and Herder, 1963), pp. 199-200.

27. *Hope in Time of Abandonment,* trans. C. Edward Hopkin (New York: Seabury, 1973), p. 244.

28. *Hope,* p. 247.

29. Quoted by Karl Löwith, *Von Hegel zu Nietzsche. Der revolutionäre Bruch im Denken des neunzehnten Jahrhunderts* (Stuttgart, 1950), p. 60.

30. Cf. *Reading Capital,* trans. Ben Brewster (London: NLB, 1970), p. 142.

31. René de Lacharrière, *La divagation de la pensée politique* (Paris: PUF, 1972), pp. 313-14.

32. *André Philip par lui-même ou les voies de la liberté* (Paris: Aubier-Montaigne, n. d.), p. 263.

33. Nikita Struve, *Christians in Contemporary Russia* (London: Harvill Press, 1967); Trevor Beeson, *Discretion and Valour* (London: Collins, 1974).

34. *André Philip par lui-même,* p. 269.

35. *Origin of Russian Communism,* p. 164.

36. In *Collected Works,* Vol. 15 (London: Lawrence and Wishart, 1963), pp. 402-13. See another article of Lenin from the same period: *Classes and Parties in their Attitude to Religion and the Church,* ibid., pp. 414-23.

37. Cf. *The Attitude of the Workers' Party to Religion,* p. 405.

38. Cf. *The Attitude,* p. 406.

39. Officially, the future Bolshevik Party still considered itself a Soviet-Democratic Party. Later, in communist vocabulary, the latter expression took on a pejorative meaning: the Social Democratic parties came to be accused of collusion with capitalism.

40. *The Attitude of the Workers' Party to Religion,* pp. 408-9.

41. Nicholas Berdyaev, *Origin of Russian Communism,* p. 166.

42. *Peut-on être communiste et chrétien?* (statement of J. Galisson, priest-worker at Le Havre and militant in the Communist Party), in *Hebdo-TC* (July 18, 1974).

43. *TC rencontre Georges Marchais,* in *Hebdo-TC* (August 28, 1975). At the 22nd Congress of the French Communist Party, Bernard Friot, a militant Christian in the Communist Party at Meurthe-et-Moselle, declared: "I was never happy in my Christian faith until I became a member of the Communist Party." This enthusiasm stunned even the communist leaders themselves. One of them kept repeating: "It strikes me funny. . . . It strikes me funny." Another confessed: "For me, it's incomprehensible." Bernard Friot himself went on to say: "It is essential, not for opportunistic reasons, but very fundamental ones, not to emphasize philosophical differences." The journalist who reported this noted how open to question it is: "To consider man as the result of social relationships or as a son of God is not purely a matter of theoretical argument. This has consequences on the level of daily living and on that of building up society" (N. Copin, "Chrétiens et communistes," in *La Croix* [February 14, 1976]).

44. In *La documentation catholique* 68 (1971), p. 529.

45. Pius XI, encyclical *Divini Redemptoris* (March 19, 1937): English trans. in *The Church and the Reconstruction of the Modern World,* ed. Terence McLaughlin (Garden City, N.Y.: Doubleday-Image, 1957); Decree of the Holy Office (July 1, 1949): English trans. in *Canon Law Digest,* ed. T. Lincoln Bouscaren (Milwaukee:

Bruce, 1954), pp. 658–59; John XXIII, *Pacem in terris*, Nos. 157–60: English trans. in *Renewing the Earth*, ed. David O'Brien and Thomas Shannon (Garden City, N.Y.: Doubleday-Image, 1977); Paul VI, *Ecclesiam suam* (August 6, 1964), Nos. 105–6: English trans. in *The Pope Speaks* 10 (1965) 253–92; Apostolic letter *Octogesima adveniens* (May 14, 1971), Nos. 25–36: English trans. in *Renewing the Earth*. See Coste, *Eglise et vie économique* (Paris: Editions Ouvrières, 1970), pp. 106–23.

46. Alain Durand, in *Lumière et vie*, Nos. 117/118 (1974), p. 5.

47. "Marxisme et chrétiens. Un essai de typologie," in *Etudes* 343 (October, 1975), pp. 337–38.

48. Nos. 117/118 (1974), p. 201.

49. "L'histoire n'est pas un absolu," *Etudes*, p. 155.

Conclusion

. . . Will He Find Faith on the Earth?

I have set forth my objections in regard to the approach of the "Christian Marxists," based on the objective content of the Christian faith and Marxism itself. I have in hand a striking document in which some worker-priests proclaim their passionate attachment to Jesus Christ, as well as their desire to live their faith, their priestly ministry, and their membership in the church in the context of a commitment to Marxism that they insist is unstinted. It is, they explain, their very roots, their habitual solidarities, that have led them "unmistakably" to take their stand with Marxism. They see two ways of doing this: either by "taking into account the originality of Marxists *and* Christians, of Marxism *and* the faith," through appreciation of their mutual enrichment; or by learning "to live the faith while being Marxists to the very end."

They reject the first approach, which seems to them an "attitude of competition." "It is necessary," they insist, "to cut off the wings of the expression, 'Christians and Marxists.' " Their experience, they say—which for some of them is that of faithful membership in the communist party for many years—leads them to a joint set of resolutions: "To be Christian with a materialist philosophy; to live in relation to the Father within a materialist mentality; to renew their unity with the Father through a materialist practice; and that central expression that summarizes the rest: to live Jesus Christ while being Marxist."

They face up to questions that pertain to the dynamics of the faith and the responsibility of evangelization: "Within the party how does one live authentically and give expression to the faith, the ministry, and one's commitment to the church? More and more believers are joining the Communist Party; how do they carry out within the party their responsibility for the collective life of faith?" They respond that they are engaged in an adventure, for they have changed "ideological countries." They see risks:

It is . . . the test of the demystification of the faith: risk or opportunity. The Marxist critique of religious alienation leads to fear or, on the contrary, to joy—the joy of rediscovering Jesus Christ as the historical root and support of the faith. It is also a matter of relocating the question of God. Marx maintains that the idea of God will be displaced by a social act. To accept that challenge is to live and seek the presence of God within a materialist practice.

It is a real gamble that they want to take "in the name of the church": "To prove that the faith endures, a phenomenon that is beginning to challenge our Marxist comrades. The faith endures—that is, . . . not only do we keep the faith, but it grows and can be witnessed and announced. Not only a faith that is lived individually, but faith that is lived in the church."

In no way do these Christians want to be loners doing their own thing. To charge this would be an accusation that would provoke their protests. They want to persuade their readers: "Even if we must struggle against the risks of marginalization, it is truly a concern for the church that moves and inspires us when we say: To live Jesus Christ as Marxists!"[1]

This kind of approach will provoke, according to each one's viewpoint, enthusiasm, strong opposition, or puzzlement. From my perspective I see no reason to question the quality and objective content of their faith, especially inasmuch as they emphasize its ecclesial character, as well as the imperative that it have impact on all the dimensions of collective life. It is even remarkable inasmuch as it presents itself as that *post-Marxist faith* whose advent I called for—that is, a faith that has confronted head-on the powerful challenge of the Marxist critique and, instead of dissolving before this formidable test, has boldly renewed itself in an original way, in the context of a new situation.

Have they, however, gone as far as they might in this confrontation? The very fervor of their commitment to Marxism leaves room for doubt. Have they really understood that the Marxist critique of religious alienation wants not only to question the weaknesses of the church but radically to destroy any idea of the supernatural origin of Christianity, or that Marxist materialism involves the absolute rejection of God? How can they not see that "to live in relation to the Father" while claiming to adhere to "a materialist philosophy" is to situate oneself in the midst of a total contradiction? Otherwise, words have lost all their meaning.

Perhaps they are referring to historical materialism—which is really, in the end, a philosophical extrapolation—but have we not noted that this theory claims to be the ultimate explanation of all history in terms of economics and therefore, once again, the total denial of the supernatural origin of Christianity? In order for it to have a minimum of consistency with their faith, their "materialism" would have to be rethought as a radically different conception from Marxist materialism, as well as all the other materialisms registered in the history of philosophy. It is therefore the very reality of their "Marxism" that is in question.

We can be sure that they do profess some elements of Marxism (analysis in terms of class struggle, a radical critique of capitalism, the socialist plan for the future, etc.), but is this enough to justify their calling themselves "Marxists to the very end''? Because of the authenticity of their faith, their "Marxism" can be neither the original Marxism, nor Marxism-Leninism, nor even the neo-Marxism of the revisionist school. This should have been made clear. Otherwise, they are falling into total ambiguity, an ambiguity that also applies to their relations with the Marxists themselves if the latter are consistent on their side and if they personally share the materialist and atheist worldview that remains the official ideology of communist regimes and parties.

The statement of philosophical differences by Georges Marchais seems to be more honest. It is only respect for those before whom one wants to witness to Jesus Christ that demands that one should not gloss over any differences when they exist. What good is it to use the same words if they do not have the same content? Is it not to expose oneself and others to mutual deception? Or else, when the persons addressed are intelligent, does this not make them look with contempt on the incoherence of our thought? As Jean Lacroix remarks, "the kind of confusion that is spreading these days, even more among Christians than among Marxists, is as contemptuous toward Marxism as it is toward Christianity."[2]

It is the desire to avoid this that leads him to make the following severe judgment about "Christian Marxists":

> To be worth something, an idea must be coherent: one can be Marxist, one can be Christian, one cannot be at the same time fully Marxist and authentically Christian. The Christian Marxists or Marxist Christians distort both Christianity and Marxism; they are incoherent.[3]

I have sufficiently explained my own thought a few pages earlier on the subject of these Christians and their viewpoint. I wanted to clarify it here only in regard to an unquestionable witness in the spirit of deep faith and missionary zeal, but where I see at least a serious danger of ambiguity. For does not authentic evangelization presuppose a constant critical discernment as well as a fraternal presence?

Critical Discernment

My readers must have noticed that this striving for *critical discernment* has been one of my primary preoccupations. It imposes itself as much by a conviction of reason as by that of faith. It crops up constantly in the New Testament. Jesus Christ practiced it diligently in regard to the ideologies of his time. The apostolic church followed his example, using as its criteria both his example and his teaching. The invitation to distinguish the "good grain" from "the weeds" constitutes one of his essential directives to future communities. "I know," St. Paul declares to the elders of Ephesus, "that after my departure fierce wolves will come in among you, not sparing the flock; and from among your own selves will arise some speaking perverse things, to draw away the disciples after them. Therefore be alert . . ." (Acts 20:29–31).

From the point of view of their own conceptions the founders of Marxism had exactly the same concern, which has always been shared by the leading theoreticians who followed them. There can be no true dialogue in a context of ambiguity. One can disagree even with a friend. What is important in dialogue is the search for truth.

The specific characteristics of this inquiry will be apparent, I hope, in all the clarity and complexity of their interaction, according to the dialectic that I have followed from the start: *welcome/challenge—critical confrontation—reformulation of the faith.* My "steps" were themselves complex. In relation to Marxism I situated myself in the complexity of its history. I took it—and I take it—very seriously, even if, for decisive reasons of rationality and of faith, I can accept only certain elements of its analysis and its historical practice. It has contributed a great deal, even if its contribution has led in my case, as in others, to the opposite of its intention: to an energizing of the faith that it wanted to destroy.

In relation to other Christians, themselves deeply involved in relation to Marxism, I situated myself on a continuum that includes all the nuances, from visceral rejection of Marxism to passionate commitment, any one of which can coexist with a bewildering ignorance of its true nature. Some fearfully shut themselves up in a ghetto, but others readily take their dreams for reality and show nothing but hostility toward those who try to awaken them from their sleepwalking. Through all of them I have traced my own path. The confrontation with many of them, to which the search for truth has compelled me, in no way signifies any contempt or rejection of dialogue.

I will be just as candid in confessing that *confrontation has taken place within my innermost self.* This solidarity with the working class, this critique of capitalism, this rejection of social inequalities, this desire for collective liberation and progress, this dream of a companionable society, this conviction of the necessity of planning, this concern for rationality and effectiveness, this myth of Prometheus, this temptation to give a priority to violence, even this critique of a church that does not seem to have shown sufficient interest in liberation, perhaps even this temptation to philosophical materialism: all that, in its positive and negative complexity, I bear within myself. There is some "Marxist" in me as there is some "capitalist," to recall the dialectic of "pagan" and "Jew" that the Epistle to the Romans inspired in Father Fessard.[4]

If the Christian that I am and want to become more and more perceives himself—and wants to be—different from the Marxist, it is in solidarity, a solidarity that will lead, according to circumstances, to dialogue and cooperation or to confrontation. In a certain way I see myself *at once as outside and inside Marxism.* An uncomfortable situation, you may say. Perhaps. But what if that is the dynamic of history itself, of a history compounded of grace and sin, where each one retains only partial truths, where each one has to sacrifice something in order to coexist with others? I have wanted to avoid a climate of passion, as well as the anathemas and infatuations that inevitably result from it.

You may have noticed that my steps have often followed after those of Berdyaev, not out of obsequiousness, but because my own reflection led me to similar conclusions. Before closing this book, I should like to make one last commentary on one of his most penetrating pages on the relations between Marxist analysis and Christian faith.[5] "Socialism," he writes, "can in no way claim for itself an absolute and eternal meaning; it is immersed in relativity and temporality." The absolutizing pretensions of Marxism, we have seen, have been constant throughout its history. I have underlined their terrible consequences. I have shown how faith in the only absolute—God— which relativizes all our human actions, is liberating. "However, it is in it [socialism] that we must find the Christian truth on the subject of human relations, in the same way that there resides at the base of nationalism the countertruth that is proper to paganism, the pitiless animal struggle" (Berdyaev).

This is what I have called the "socialist utopia," which is at the source of the inspiration of Marxism, as of other forms of socialism, and which it claims wrongly to have monopolized: that human aspiration to equality and fellowship, to the equitable sharing of resources and power, which the Christian must salute with enthusiasm because it springs from the heart of the gospel. Christians would be less than honest if they did not acknowledge that the followers of Jesus Christ have not contributed enough to its realization throughout history. They are themselves forcefully referred back to the sources of their faith.

Berdyaev continues:

> The realization of socialism in our time will not be the beginning of perfect life. Socialism too, like everything else that has found its way into the history of the world, will be disfigured by human sin. But what will be true in it is—as was the case not so long ago on the occasion of the suppression of slavery and serfdom—the further liberation of humankind from its condition of servitude.

There is no reason to dream of an idyllic humanity. The mistake of the Marxist ideologues—as it was of the founders before them—has been to promise too easily a dreamlike future to which history has even more cruelly given the lie. On the Marxist side it seems that the neo-Marxists of the revisionist school have alone really faced the reality: that it is foolish to blame all the failures on "the cult of personality." An analysis in the light of faith highlights the role of sin and provides a sense of the relative. The totalitarian character that has marked the entire history of communism to date, everywhere that it has come to power, cannot be seriously questioned. Totalitarianism is never liberative. But that history, already long, is rich with lessons. Does it not help us to see more clearly the realistic conditions of an authentic human liberation? Cannot socialism be realized in some other way, with another conception of the world and other policies than those of Marxism, while still benefiting from its history?

Again Berdyaev: "The methods of combat can be atrocious, as were almost all the methods of combat employed in the course of history, and must therefore be condemned by the Christian conscience." I have just referred to the crimes of that history. The Christian conscience would be untrue to itself if it simply accepted them as an accomplished fact. Its protest and its refusal serve the cause of humanity. But we may not see only those crimes and forget others, as well as the serious deficiencies that punctuate the history of the western nations in the same period.

"However, the Christian understanding must see in socialism a grandeur of global dimensions, the judgment pronounced on a lying humanity that has betrayed Christianity, the judgment pronounced on a human civilization founded on a mystification" (Berdyaev). This "judgment" I have frequently mentioned in the course of my inquiry, in seeing Marxism as a challenge, as a justified indictment of so many historic deficiencies of the church and of Christians. "This is the demonstration, in all its complexity, of the relationship of Christianity to Marxism and its conception of history. Marxism unmasks the idols, and it unmasks a Christianity that has not lived its truth. That is where its religious and prophetic vision lies" (Berdyaev). Yes, I say again, to take Marxism seriously—but lucidly and critically—can lead to a remarkable renewal of the Christian faith for our time.

Throughout my inquiry I have indicated *my agreements with Marxism*:

—The goal of liberation, equality, and fellowship.

—Promotion of the working class.

—The major importance of economic factors in the origins and unfolding of history.

—The social dimensions of the human being.

—The conflictual character of social relationships, notably in terms of class struggle.

—The critique of capitalist society and of the historical deficiencies of Christianity.

And *my disagreements*:

—Metaphysical materialism and atheism.

—The ultimate explanation of history in terms of economics.

—Reduction of the human essence to social relationships.

—The class struggle as the ultimate foundation of morality.

—The dictatorial and totalitarian policies of communist regimes and their official ideologies.

I would add only a few remarks. One would have for its objective to underline once more—this time with Cornelius Castoriadis—my disagreement with Marxism on *economic motivation as the fundamental motivation of human beings*:

The theory that makes of "the development of productive forces" the motor of history presupposes implicitly an unchanging model of basic human motivation, roughly the economic motivation: from all time human societies must have pursued (consciously or unconsciously, it matters little) first and foremost the increase of their production and consumption. But this idea is not merely false materially; it forgets that the different kinds of motivation (and the corresponding values that polarize and orient the lives of a people) are social creations, that each culture develops values that are peculiar to it and trains its members in relation to those values.[6]

He continues by noting that it is capitalism that has introduced into history the predominance of economic motivation and that by making it the law of history the Marxists are establishing as a characteristic of human nature a particularity that is limited in time:

> If there is an ethnological curiosity in this affair, it is precisely those "revolutionaries" who have erected the capitalist mentality as an eternal constant of human nature that is everywhere the same and who, while babbling endlessly about the colonial question and undeveloped countries, forget in their ruminations two-thirds of the population of the world.[7]

It should be recalled, as I have insisted: Marxism remains strangely dependent on capitalist ideology, which it claims to be fighting vigorously. Obviously we cannot deny the primary importance of national economies, but, on the plane of reason and faith, I submit that it is high time that we promote a kind of society where the economic is not the supreme value, but is harnessed to the service of what is most essential in human beings and in their relations with others: the full flowering of the human personality and human fellowship. That is clearly what the founders of Marxism wanted for the classless society of their utopia. The misfortune is that their conception of history and political practice was not in harmony with such a goal—a contradiction that, to this day, has weighed heavily on the entire unfolding of the revolutionary movement that they inaugurated.

My second addendum deals with the *relations between ideals and political practice*. In February 1961, Walter Ulbricht, president of the state council of East Germany, declared at a meeting of church leaders:

> It appears to me that capitalism and basic Christianity are really irreconcilably opposed to each other. Socialism, on the other hand, despite all the imperfections it may still have, will bring about the implementation of the Christian humanist and socialist ideals. . . . There is naturally a contradiction between our philosophy of historical materialism and the philosophical idealism in which Christianity, like all religions, is rooted. But these philosophical differences, which we do not wish to underestimate, cannot hide the fact that there is such a wide area of agreement between the humanist and social aims of basic Christianity and the humanist and social aims of socialism that cooperation becomes imperative.[8]

The "socialism" of which Ulbricht speaks is obviously socialism of the Marxist variety—even Marxist-Leninist—which is the only kind he recognizes. We should note the frank admission of the radical differences in worldview between Christianity and Marxism. As for his appeal for cooperation on the plane of achieving "common social and humanist goals," we could in principle respond favorably to it. The problem is "whether," as Trevor Beeson notes, "the policies of the ruling party in that country really do reflect the humanist values that Christianity and socialism share."⁹

No doubt the problem of relationships between ideals and practice is present in all political systems, to the extent that they proclaim lofty human values. This does not lessen the need to emphasize it in the case of Marxism. Christians will do well to be particularly attentive to the actual practice of regimes that claim allegiance to that creed. *It is their actions that will measure the truth of their intentions.*

My last complementary remark bears on *the role of the church in a communist regime*. Trevor Beeson says, apropos of East Germany:

> The government is ready to accept the church's cooperation and to welcome its declarations of solidarity with the socialist state, but it cannot agree that the church has a critical role vis-à-vis society or that Christian faith has anything to offer that has not already been provided by the insights of Marxism.¹⁰

All serious analyses agree that it is the same in the other regimes under Soviet tutelage. This fact cannot fail to give Christians serious cause for reflection. Some perhaps will object that these regimes have betrayed Marxism. We could argue that point for a long time. Everything we have seen of the ideas that the founders of Marxism had on the subject of Christianity bears witness that, on this point, there is no deviation. Even neo-Marxists of the revisionist school show hardly more agreement with Christians on a critical role for the church that would not echo the theory and objectives of Marxism.

Creative Faith

An extraordinary "word" of Jesus Christ comes to mind at this point: "When the Son of man comes, will he find faith on earth?" (Luke 18:8). It is a question that I ask myself frequently, clearly, objectively, without anguish. We cannot fail to ask it in regard to historical Marxism, which not only claims to predict the progressive disappearance of the faith under the impact of the historical process of socialization and cultural progress, but which wants also to speed it up with some of its own revolutionary measures.

We must ask it as well in regard to the practical materialism of advanced industrial society of the liberal type and those philosophical currents that advocate metaphysical materialism and atheism. Is this the fault of Christians, of the churches? To an important degree it is, no doubt. We have seen enough to confirm that. The Christian conception of history permits us to look at it with some detachment.

Henri Marrou has written:

> Failure, at least a relative failure, is the law of all history, the theater of so many defeats in which even victories won at great cost are always precarious and partial. We must be capable of facing this truth. If our Christian faith is to avoid becoming completely insipid, it needs to be tempered by the experience of facing up to this sinister picture, of feeling the fearful wing of despair brush by. . . . Sin also has dynamic energy of its own, which works to expand the frontiers of destructive action . . . as though there were a dark and sinister fecundity in evil.[11]

These deep, somber reflections throw light on the unfolding of history. Will it end then with that final nothingness projected by all materialist conceptions of the world when we push them to their final conclusions? Faith in God, in the resurrection of Jesus Christ, in the absolute future of the kingdom promised to humanity—this makes possible a turnaround. A faith that has confronted the radical critique of Marxism, a faith that is a "post-Marx faith," is a faith that responds in the affirmative, for this period of history that is ours, to the question of "the Son of man."

It is a *faith that looks for charity and strives for coherence*, obedient to the directives of Jesus Christ himself. As Eduard Schweizer put it, paraphrasing several gospel texts:

> The disciples of Jesus must reflect coldly and seriously about what they are about to do; they must understand clearly what they are setting in motion and what they want to accomplish. Those who make war must compare exactly the strength of their forces and those of their enemies, and they who want to construct a tower must calculate with precision their materials so that they will not leave it half-finished and thus become the laughingstock of the neighborhood.[12]

This is the design that has guided all my inquiry and that explains the rigorous critical confrontation that I have undertaken. My final criterion was the word of God in Jesus Christ. Christian faith in no way jeopardizes the lucidity of rational analyses. It demands them, on the contrary, and supports them, when it is itself thought through with the best conceptual tools.

It also calls for *inventiveness and creativity*, for it must be a responsible faith and it benefits from the inexhaustible dynamism that comes from the presence of Jesus Christ risen in the very midst of history. Roger Garaudy calls revolutionary "any politics that is founded on a wager on the creative possibilities of each and every human being."[13] Christian faith that is authentically evangelical will agree with such a perspective and, although having a broader vision, will support it with its own critical discernment and with the dynamic of its own hope in the absolute future of humanity.

Marxism, I have noted several times, sees itself as a liberator and messenger of hope. Christian faith salutes such a perspective. What it questions is the part that appears to be pseudoliberation and truncated hope.

Marxism is now part of the history of humanity, with historical consequences, some positive, others negative. That history continues. The present generation is responsible for it for the time in which we live. What is certain, from the viewpoint of faith in Jesus Christ, is that we can be Christian only if we strive to be promoters of liberation and messengers of hope, with all the fullness of meaning that those words assume in the founding message of the gospel.

NOTES

1. *Lettre aux communautés* (of the *Mission de France*), No. 53 (September-October 1975), pp. 8–9.

2. "Marxisme et christianisme," in *A l'écoute du monde* (Chronique sociale de France), (January 1976), p. 18.

3. "Marxisme et christianisme," p. 18.

4. See especially his major work, *De l'actualité historique*, 2 vols. (Paris-Bruges: DDB, 1960). See Nguyen-Hong-Giao, *Le Verbe dans l'histoire. La philosophie de l'Historicité du P. Gaston Fessard* (Paris: Beauchesne, 1974).

5. *Christianisme, Marxisme* (Paris: Centurion, 1975), pp. 36–38.

6. *L'institution imaginaire de la société* (Paris: Seuil, 1975), pp. 34–35.

7. *L'institution*, p. 36.

8. Quoted by Trevor Beeson, *Discretion and Valour* (London: Collins, 1974), pp. 177–78.

9. *Discretion*, p. 178.

10. *Discretion*, p. 186.

11. *Time and Timeliness*, trans. Violet Nevile (New York: Sheed and Ward, 1969), pp. 49–50.

12. *La Foi en Jésus-Christ. Perspectives et languages du Nouveau Testament* (Paris: Seuil, 1975), p. 46.

13. *Parole d'homme* (Paris: Robert Laffont, 1975), p. 201.

Index

Compiled by William E. Jerman